PRAISE FOR
CHANGE YOUR STORY, CHANGE YOUR LIFE

"...a rich guide to shedding old limiting stories and dream a new world into being."
— *ALBERTO VILLOLDO*, author of *Shaman, Healer, Sage*

"Carl Greer has written a wonderful and compassionate guide for seekers of psychological and spiritual growth. He introduces the reader to basic shamanic and Jungian concepts to link timeless ritual methods with modern active imaginal techniques. His clear explanations provide perspective, and his suggested exercises support personal exploration. A lovely book."
— *SYLVIA BRINTON PERERA*, LP, Jungian Psychoanalyst and author of *Descent to the Goddess: A Way of Initiation for Women*

"We live our own story, and, if we change it, we can change our lives. When we rewrite our story, we also rewire our brain to live by a new manuscript. Researchers call this the Neuroplasticity of the brain. In his compelling book, Jungian Analyst and Shaman Dr. Carl Greer invites us to be a storyteller in our own narrative: one who has the Imaginatio, or creative vision, to create a new story to live our true destiny—our teleos. He offers a brilliant synthesis of Jung's Analytical psychology and the ancient Shamanic practices and rituals, such as Journeying into and Dialoguing with our multiple worlds to go beyond personal life experiences to the source, the Unus Mundus, to rework our story. Hands-on exercises and case examples make this treasure trove accessible to the reader in practical ways to implement in their life story. The purpose of this personal transformation is to live a life that honors our true skills, potentials and spiritual purpose, and in turn deploy these in service to our family, our community, and our world—revitalizing them for generations to come. This is a timely book for individuals who wish to live an informed life based on the timeless wisdom of the past, and to deal with contemporary challenges in order to claim a purposeful future."
— *ASHOK BEDI, M.D.* Psychiatrist and Jungian Analyst, author of *Path to the Soul* and *Crossing the Healing Zone*

CHANGE YOUR STORY, CHANGE YOUR LIFE

~

USING SHAMANIC AND JUNGIAN TOOLS TO ACHIEVE PERSONAL TRANSFORMATION

CARL GREER, PhD, PsyD

FINDHORN PRESS

Published in 2014 by Findhorn Press, Scotland

ISBN 978-1-84409-464-6

A CIP record for this title is available from the British Library.

Edited by Nicky Leach
Cover and Interior design by Damian Keenan
Printed in the USA

Published by
Findhorn Press
117-121 High Street,
Forres IV36 1AB,
Scotland, UK

t +44 (0)1309 690582
f +44 (0)131 777 2711
e info@findhornpress.com
www.findhornpress.com

CONTENTS

Disclaimer

Acknowledgments

Some years ago, when I was asked to teach classes about shamanism, I decided to teach how shamanic practices can be used to deal with everyday life issues. This book is an outgrowth of my shamanic teaching, as well as my Jungian training, experiences, and perspective.

I am indebted to many people for helping make this book possible. My shamanic mentors and friends have given me gifts of friendship and companionship as we have joined each other in using shamanic practices. Alberto Villoldo started me on my shamanic path and has been a mentor, teacher, and friend. We have explored some fascinating and mysterious frontiers together. Theo Paredes has taught me much about Andean shamanism and shared his wisdom and many adventures with me. Marv and Shanon Harwood have shared their Blackfoot traditions with me, and our experiences together have been spiritual, provocative, and fun.

Many Q'ero shamans, and shaman Don Martin, have initiated me into their traditions, for which I am grateful. I thank the shamans in Australia, Mongolia, and Ethiopia with whom I have spent time and worked.

Those who attended my workshops and those for whom I have been a shamanic practitioner or Jungian analyst have taught me much, and I am grateful for those who shared their experiences for inclusion in this book. Your generosity will help others better understand how to use various practices and techniques to change their own stories.

I acknowledge my Jungian colleagues, with whom I have shared friendship and exploration of the transpersonal realms. Special thanks to Murray Stein, Lee Roloff, Mary Doherty, James Wylie, and Judy Shaw, who were important parts of my Jungian journey.

Charlotte Kelchner has given me invaluable editorial assistance and helped me organize a large amount of often seemingly disjointed material. Nancy Peske's insights and editorial guidance were very useful in helping me to get the book ready for publishing and in navigating the world of book publishing. Gladys Burow, my administrative assistant for 46 years, has helped me with numerous drafts of this book. Devra Jacobs, my agent, has been diligent in finding me a publisher.

I want to acknowledge my children, Caryn, Michael, and Janet, and my stepchildren, Michael, Susie, and Jeannie, as well as their significant others, Rudy, Jenny, Joe, Leslie, and Mike, who have all been part of my journey.

I want to acknowledge Pat—my love, my wife, and my partner in exploring the symbolic and the literal realms of our lives. She has supported my shamanic journey and my devoting time to writing this book. Her careful reading of the drafts and her comments helped make the book better.

Finally, I am thankful for being part of life's plan and having the opportunity to write this book.

Dedication

To all the spiritual seekers who use the wisdom they gain
from their experiences to choose a new story.

Foreword

When I first began to study the wisdom teachings of the ancient shamans of the Andes, I struggled to understand what my mentors were trying to explain to me. It wasn't a language barrier that stood between them and me so much as a barrier of perception. I had plenty of academic knowledge, but a Western way of thinking and perceiving kept me frustrated until I learned to turn on my intuitive mind and quiet my analytical mind. Only then could I access wisdom and energies hidden from my awareness and use them to create a new path for myself.

Years later, when I was asked by my mentors to bring their teachings to the West, I was humbled and, frankly, intimidated by the challenge. I remembered how long it had taken me to let go of my need to have validated all that I'd learned in years of school and hard work at a prestigious university. How was I going to explain to others the process of tuning in to the wisdom of the collective unconscious we all share? How could I help them travel to realms of consciousness where past, present, and future all flow together, and tap into the archetypal energies that allow us to dream a new world into being? I wasn't excited about facing rooms full of people who would be as skeptical as I had been years before and urging them to leave behind what they had been taught and embrace a new way of looking at their lives, each other, and the world we inhabit. But my mentors warned me, "If your people do not change their ways, our people will no longer be able to survive." With their prodding, I decided to do the best I could to teach other Westerners the wisdom ways that honor Earth and all her inhabitants.

Many years after embarking on this new venture and starting The Four Winds Society, I met Carl Greer. He was a Jungian analyst and businessman who had achieved much success according to the values of the West. Unlike many who are just looking to learn some new ways to manage stress, understand themselves a little better, and get a clearer sense of what they want to do next, Carl was willing to answer a deeper calling and achieve what Buddhists call "beginner's mind." Very quickly, he immersed himself in the indigenous wisdom ways. He learned to dance with archetypal energies and transpersonal realms and employ them to become a healer. After completing Light Body School training, he became a Four Winds Society teacher and a friend. Over the years, I've enjoyed our shamanic work, sharing experiences that were strangely powerful and exotic.

Since we first met, Carl has gone on to study with shamans around the world and committed to sharing their wisdom with others. He became the first Westerner to have the Q'ero elders of the Andean mountains bestow upon him the Munay-ki rites: blessings passed from person to person to person that initiate them into a new way of walking softly on the planet and harmoniously with each other. Through his own healing practice, Carl has generously shared the Munay-ki rites with people of all walks of life.

As both a Jungian analyst and shaman, he has been leading trainings on how to access the ancient wisdom through the portal of the unconscious. These trainings help participants understand how to change their ways of thinking and perceiving so that they can write a new and better story for themselves. And Carl's work with numerous community-based organizations that strive to enact change, person by person, family by family, is a reminder that the wisdom we gain through our journeys is not meant simply to inform a new and more satisfying personal story; our wisdom can also guide us in co-creating a more sustainable world. His book is not just a primer for casual seekers but a rich guide to shedding old, limiting stories and dreaming a new world into being.

—*ALBERTO VILLOLDO, PHD*

Preface

As a clinical psychologist, Jungian analyst, and shamanic practitioner, I have listened to many stories. Some are sad, some are humorous, some are heroic, and some are bleak. Some stories have themes of wanting to make a difference in the world but not knowing how. To transform our lives, we need to change our stories.

Each of us is living a life about which a story can be told. The story has chapters about our body and health; our relationships; our psychology, including our emotions and ways of thinking; our jobs; our relationship to a higher power; and our ways of being of service in the world. Every chapter is an important part of the larger whole, yet we can be blind to the patterns in the story and the themes that are interwoven throughout, tying together seemingly disparate events. We find it difficult to see a unified tale when we are reacting to the details of life and are caught up in our experiences. But if we step back from time to time and reassess our stories, we can make conscious choices about how we might change them and tell a new and better story in the future.

Sometimes we become so identified with our stories, so certain that we can't live according to a different one, that it seems as if the story is dictating itself to us. The truth is that none of us is our story, and each of us has the power to be the storyteller. We don't have to be stuck in a narrative we didn't actively choose. We don't have to live with the same themes that have been a part of our story to this point. We can retell the tale of our past and present, and thereby change how the story will unfold in the future.

Everyone has challenges; everyone has disappointments, weaknesses, and failings they would rather not acknowledge. Some people don't have mastery of important life skills, such as setting healthy boundaries in relationships or communicating effectively with others. Too many individuals are living without financial security—an illness, divorce, or car accident can derail their lives and reinforce their feelings of helplessness and hopelessness. The greater our struggles, the easier it is to start believing we can't influence our stories very much . . . but we can.

The exercises and practices in this book are not a panacea. They do, however, provide opportunities for you to engage your story in a variety of ways, to see your problems from a larger perspective, and to enlist spiritual help in telling a better story, starting now. The practices—derived from shamanic and Jungian traditions and, in some cases, a blend of both—can help you activate your innate motivation to surmount your problems, even your seemingly insurmountable ones. You can come to see a wider range of possibilities for yourself. First, however, you need to detach from your current story and recognize your power of agency. Then, you can begin to make conscious decisions about how you would like your life to unfold, writing a new story for yourself in the process. Using the techniques in this book, you can bring new energy and information into your everyday life to help you manifest your new story.

You don't have the power to determine all the details of your story; no one does. Your personal story, like everyone's, is part of a collective story told by your family, friends, and community. And for all of us, Source serves as a co-storyteller. We are all part of Source, which is the divine, creative, wise force that permeates everything around us and from which all energies derive. Source is also called God, Goddess, the Tao, the Ein Sof, and the Quiet—there are many names for this conscious force.

Although Source influences your story, you have more power than you might think to change the way you live, and to change the collective story shared by you, your family, your community, and the world.

My Shamanic Path

Shamans talk about each of us having many potential roles in one lifetime. In my own life, I have changed my roles and my story several times. After graduating from college with a degree in metallurgical engineering, I went to graduate school and received my PhD in finance and management from Columbia University. I taught for several years at Columbia's Graduate School of Business before moving to Chicago, where I have been involved in a number of businesses.

When I was in my forties, I began acting on my interest in psychology, and eventually, I received my doctorate in clinical psychology. I became a practicing clinical psychologist and Jungian analyst. I had been drawn to the idea of shamanism for a long time, so I started my formal shamanic training at Dr. Alberto Villoldo's Healing the Light Body School and subsequently taught classes there. I have since continued on my shamanic path by working with shamans in South America, the United States, Canada, Australia, Ethiopia, and Outer Mongolia. I now teach seminars and workshops that incorporate shamanic techniques. My work as a clinical psychologist and Jungian analyst is informed in part by shamanism. In addition, I am engaged in some business and philanthropic activities.

For me, shamanism is a spiritual practice that gets me closer to Source and helps me to live a better life. My shamanic experiences have allowed me to see into other realms and dimensions and to perceive the everyday world with new eyes. As a result, I have a greater appreciation for its complexity, a deeper compassion for my fellow beings, and a profound sense of gratitude for being able to participate in the mystery of life. My shamanic journey has been one of personal exploration. Perhaps my journey can shed light on your own.

Many years ago, I had a dream that taught me a valuable lesson about being connected to all the parts of myself and to Source:

> The organizers of a judo tournament received a load of frozen, decapitated bodies. These bodies were to be the competitors, and they were to compete while having heads that were not their own. After the competition, each head was to be returned to its original body and sewn on. I received one of the bodies and, not knowing what the procedure was to prepare it for a new head, I cut it around the neck with a sharp knife. When I realized I had made a mistake, I wanted to get the person's body and his head to a surgeon to sew up the wound. After various difficulties, including my being wounded by gunfire, I got the body and severed head to a hospital. Skin was grafted onto the body, and the head was reattached, making a complete man. I had my own wounds tended. The man and I were both told that we would be good as new, although he would have scar tissue, and I knew my wounds would ache when the weather changed. The man and I talked; then, we embraced and became one. I said we would never be separate again. As I woke from the dream, I wept, realizing I had been the split-off man.

In this dream, I encountered myself as frozen and split off from the neck down, and with a dismembered body that I needed to make whole again. Similarly, my shamanic path has been one of "re-membering" and coming back to a unity that has always been there but that I had forgotten. I have come to realize that when we forget our power as storytellers, we become cut off from parts of ourselves—our logical minds, our emotions, our bodies, and our souls. When we reclaim our power as storytellers, we stop being confused about the events in our lives, and we start to access the wisdom that became lost to us when we disassociated from uncomfortable memories, insights, and feelings.

Our minds create an illusion of separateness from Source and from aspects of ourselves. Putting the pieces back together to experience unity with all our facets, thereby reclaiming what we have lost or denied, can be painful; however, the process leads to greater power over our lives and, ultimately, to greater happiness.

How to Use This Book

This book draws from the traditions of Jungian psychology and shamanism. Jungian psychology is based on the teachings of Dr. Carl Jung. He believed that if we can learn to identify and consciously work with the forces that are currently influencing us at an unconscious level, we can be less affected by them and experience greater psychological health.

The term "shamanism" may conjure up images of indigenous medicine men and women gathered around a fire or shaking a rattle. However, shamanism is a way that people from any culture can heal themselves and others, work with the past and future, relate in new ways to a higher power, and re-envision responsibilities to others and the collective. As is the case with Jungian psychology, shamanism is concerned with the unseen forces that influence us.

Shamanic and Jungian approaches complement each other. Shamanic traditions place the emphasis on having numinous transpersonal experiences: "experiences in which the sense of identity or self extends beyond (trans) the individual or personal to encompass wider aspects of humankind, life, psyche or cosmos."[1] In the shamanic approach, these experiences can lead to healing before understanding occurs. Conversely, in Jungian work, understanding often precedes healing. Jungians believe that when previously unconscious processes are brought to light and consciously examined, healing can occur. Jungian psychology categorizes experiences using a well-developed language and framework that can help us better describe and understand the energies we encounter when we do shamanic work. The Jungian framework includes but is not limited to concepts such as the ego, personal unconscious, collective unconscious, shadow, anima, animus, complexes, and archetypes. You will learn more about these concepts later in the book.

Even though they may look quite different on the surface, some Jungian practices are very similar to shamanic ones. One example is Jungian sand tray work and shamanic sand painting. You will also learn about other techniques that share core commonalities. Both traditions involve accessing energies, often embodied in symbols, images, and inner figures. A Jungian might access these energies through dreamwork or other engagement with the unconscious, while a shaman might access them through journeying to a transpersonal realm. Some might say the experiences you have when using shamanic and Jungian techniques are not real—that they are the result of the mind tricking itself. But the value of working with energy and symbols should not be underestimated. Although these techniques may seem foreign or unusual to you, I urge you to try them and see whether your experiences have value for you.

I believe that viewing a shamanic experience through a Jungian lens can deepen the benefits from your shamanic work and lead to a greater understanding of your conscious choices and unconscious behaviors. Sometimes, a transpersonal experience can be transforming. However, the effects of the transformation may be more profound and longer lasting if you employ the Jungian concepts and practices offered in this book. They will help you to gain understanding of the insights you develop and integrate them into your life.

You don't have to work with a shaman or a psychologist to use the practices and exercises in this book. All of them can be done alone, although you may wish to work with others as part of a ceremony or ritual. You will find descriptions of how to take shamanic journeys, which are experiences involving altering your consciousness and interacting with transpersonal realms, in Chapters Seven, Eight, and Nine. You can take these journeys while with a group and afterward, discuss your individual experiences and observe whether the individual journeys shared commonalities.

Once you have learned how to prepare for using shamanic techniques, I suggest you use the practice of journeying once or twice a week and, over time, do all the exercises in this book. Journeying and dialoguing (another important technique you'll learn about) may only take you 10–30 minutes a session. Many of the writing exercises in Chapters Three and Four, where you will explore your current story and write a new one, will take longer, but these can be done in increments. If you like, start with the exercises in Chapter Three that most resonate for you and when you have done several, do some exercises in Chapter Four. Alternately, you can work with all the exercises in Chapter Three and then move on to Chapter Four, writing a new story. You may find that as you use the shamanic and Jungian techniques in this book, your current story and your desired new story change. It can be very helpful to return to Chapters Three and Four and do some of the exercises again, or do ones you skipped, to see how your story has evolved.

I have deliberately placed the exercises that involve journaling and conscious analysis of your story ahead of the exercises that require you to access your unconscious mind. Using shamanic and Jungian practices without doing the work of discovering your current story and what you would like to change about it can cause you to become too enamored of the mysterious aspects of working with your unconscious mind without focusing on your everyday life. It's important to appreciate the power of the unconscious and to apply your new insights in a practical way.

In the last chapter of this book, you will find guidance on how to apply the ideas and techniques in this book in order to continue taking charge of your story and your life. However, to begin the process of discovering and rewriting your story, here are some questions for you to ponder now:

- Where did you come from before this lifetime?
- Who are you? What are you?
- Why are you here?
- Where are you going after this lifetime?
- How well do you know yourself?
- Do you believe in alternate realities? Have you experienced them?
- Do you believe in a Source or a greater power? If so, what is the nature of this power?
- Do you have a relationship with Source? If so, is the relationship reciprocal and satisfying?

The answers to these questions may not be immediately apparent to you, despite your efforts to analyze your thoughts and experiences. The dream I recounted earlier, for example, revealed wisdom hidden in my unconscious and taught me more than my conscious mind understood at the time. I came to realize, however, that dreams are not the only way to access hidden wisdom, and I have discovered that the practices you'll learn about in this book, such as working with nature and doing shamanic journeying, help me to recognize the parts of my story my conscious mind does not perceive. These practices have taken me to places where I discovered the potential for new stories, with plotlines and themes guided by my inner knowing.

You may find yourself having emotionally intense responses as you do exercises in this book. If these responses distress you, I encourage you to consult with a therapist who can help you learn techniques for managing your emotions so that you don't become overwhelmed by them as you delve deeper into self-discovery.

It is my hope that by using the techniques I offer in this book, you can discover your own hidden wisdom and write a new, better story for your life that allows you to feel connected to Source, to recognize your power as a storyteller, and to be of service in the world.

CHAPTER ONE

Transforming Your Life Through the Power of Story

Does life seem to speed up as the years go by? As you grow older, and when you contemplate your mortality and your purpose, you may wonder how much you have shaped your own story, and to what degree you were caught up in forces beyond your control. How often were you swept into currents that carried you to places you never dreamed of going or did not wish to visit? How often did you find yourself in situations that made you ponder how you got there, and how you might escape?

Many of us look back and wish that we had spent more time doing what we enjoy and less time doing what we felt we had to do. This book will help you make changes in your life sooner rather than later, allowing you to live as you would like, with fewer regrets weighing you down.

You may have some strong ideas about what you would like to change in your life. However, you may not know how to write a better script for your personal story and live according to this new, preferred narrative. You may feel you are powerless to affect your circumstances. If you do look back in self-reflection, though, you might discover the themes in your life's story, choose more empowering ones, and end up with a new, more satisfying story. The circumstances you find yourself in, the experiences you have, and the people you meet change when you take responsibility for the authorship of your own story and consciously step into the role of storyteller.

Once we claim our role as the storyteller, we need to make sure that our new script replaces the previous one rather than sitting on the shelf, unread and unlived. This is where most of us struggle. We think we know what we want to create, but our ideas don't translate to changes in our experiences, behaviors, and patterns. What is missing is our understanding of how to work with forces that are aspects of Source as a means of informing our new stories and bringing them to life. That is what this book is all about: reflecting on our lives and accessing information and energy that can help us to change our stories.

What Story Do You Wish to Write?

A woman had come to a major turning point and was reflecting on her story. She said:

> I had lived for decades according to the principle that there are rules and socially expected behaviors for men and for women, but then there's me, and I live outside these restrictions and limitations. I had gotten to a point, though, where things weren't working for me so well. I decided to divorce my husband and relocate. The consequences of these upheavals devastated my ego and cracked my soul. In response, I began to work with the concept of my life story to date—the story of my past that had brought me to the present moment in time. I evaluated my former image of myself as being supremely confident, fearless, androgynous, and independent, always able to imagine doors where none existed and open them. Although I marveled at this image, I also feared its illusionary allure. The themes of un-nuanced optimism, defiance, and cockiness running through my old story no longer served me.
>
> I wanted a new story in which I could see behind the obvious, rejoice in the lightness of being, accept the inevitability of disappointment, and have the resources to start anew whenever I chose to. I had come to understand that, although I could set my own rules, there could be serious trade-offs to deal with. In my newfound acknowledgment of my vulnerabilities and need for connection and community, I sought to craft a new life story going forward.

This woman needed to look back in order to imagine what her new story might be. Most of us don't take enough time to reflect on our stories and consciously create new ones. Instead, we get busy, anesthetize ourselves in a variety of ways, deny reality, or continue suffering. When our lives remain unexamined, we can become rigid and inflexible. When external crises arise, and they always do, we may break or collapse because we simply are not ready for change. We don't have the inner resiliency to bend with, readjust to, or absorb new situations. We don't know how to alter our story to accommodate these new circumstances.

As you examine your life story, you will begin to see which events you have highlighted and which you have discounted. When you look at different areas of your life, you will observe patterns and interconnections. You will become conscious of the themes running through your life, and aware of your habits and habitual responses.

The themes of your story serve as organizing principles for the events you have experienced. As you do shamanic and Jungian work, your story can become informed by wisdom inaccessible to the conscious mind, and you may discover new themes and new connections linking events and actions you have taken. Then you may begin to see your story as mythic—a story influenced by powerful archetypal energies that have always been present in the human experience.

Archetypal energies, such as those of the sage, trickster, eternal child, warrior, and so on, are not intrinsically positive or negative. How you use them depends on your choices, both conscious and unconscious. You may become the underdog who achieves success—but you may also become the brave warrior who forgets the vulnerability of his Achilles' heel, which leads to tragedy. Shamanic and Jungian practices help you discover and work with archetypal energies effectively so that you may write a more satisfying story for yourself.

In this book, you will learn about several shamanic techniques, including journeying to transpersonal realms, opening and closing sacred space, doing fire ceremonies, and creating a *despacho* (a ceremonial offering of gratitude). You'll also learn about sand painting, working with dreams, and dialoguing, all of which are modalities for working with the unconscious mind and archetypal energies. These latter techniques are derived from Jungian tradition or combine Jungian techniques with shamanic ones. Dialoguing melds Jungian active imagination with the shamanic practice of communicating with the consciousness of creation.

The Challenges of Exploring and Changing Your Current Story

You have written your current story in conjunction with Source because like all humans, you don't have the power to determine every event in your life. But you have more ability than you might realize to change your story to a more desirable one. To write a better story, you must first acknowledge what your story has been until this point, although it can be painful to see your story for what it truly is and be honest about your role in scripting it.

Even if you are able to look boldly at your story and yourself, you may find you are afraid to embrace transformation. Most of us are afraid of change. Perhaps we fear being shunned by society, our families, and our friends if we make different choices and take on new roles. Many of us are caught in stories told to us by others: stories about who we are, who we should be, and how we should live. Often, we decide that we don't want to continue being the people we have been, doing what we are doing, but we may be attached to our anger, jealousy, or fear and unwilling to release them. We may also resist letting go of possessions, power, or ideologies, or find it difficult to give up our sense of self-importance, habits, wounds, and desires. We wonder, "If I don't behave in these old ways, who will I be? How will my friends and family treat me? Will I still belong to my group?" The thought of looking honestly at our stories may be too agonizing for us to bear, causing us to live in denial and resist reflection and self-examination.

Our resistance to change binds us to our habits, and we create obstacles to discovering who we are. Often, we can't effectively express our concerns and resentments because we fear rejection and loss. We become indignant or defensive but do not know why we feel that way.

The practices described in this book will help you to develop better insights into why you act as you do. They will also help you to become more still and reflective. As a result, you will be able to make better choices and not fall back on habitual responses that lock you into your current story. For example, as you contemplate the patterns in your life, you will start to understand that by making a decision to alter your health habits, you may end up altering your relationship, work, and emotional habits. You might begin to eat better, which will help you to be less depressed, more confident, and ultimately, more assertive with your romantic partners and coworkers. Changes you make in one part of your story will affect other parts.

The practices will also help you to shed the energy of fear and let go of what is no longer serving you. Then you can open yourself up to the unfamiliar, seeing it as exciting and invigorating instead of scary. Liberated from your old feelings and ways of operating, you may also find that your desires, goals, and priorities change. It becomes easier to find your courage, discard what is no longer working, and establish new habits because you have brought in the energy of transformation and learned to work with it. Emotional neediness falls away and confidence takes its place as you begin to trust in the process of transformation. You recognize that you are the storyteller of your life and eagerly take up your pen to script a new and more satisfying tale.

What would you like to change about your story? What aspects of your story make you unhappy, uncomfortable, or even ashamed? Most people wish to change their circumstances in some way. Perhaps you want to eat differently, exercise more, or find ways to reduce stress. You might want to be less moody, anxious, depressed, angry, or obsessive. You might seek less conflict, more pleasantness, more connectedness, and more authenticity in your relationships. You might want to change how you feel about certain people or situations. You might hope to make more money, have a greater sense of security, and find more enjoyment. You might desire to be of service in the world and to experience your spirituality more fully.

Changing external circumstances is not easy, however. We've all seen the futility of New Year's resolutions. It's difficult to trust that we can transform, but we can. However, to change our stories, *we* must change. We must alter our perceptions and make conscious decisions about how to frame the events of our lives. Are we victims of bad luck, or underdogs who persevere and triumph? Are we unsuccessful wanderers, or free-spirited explorers and adventurers? Does the past dictate the future, or do we truly have the power to envision a new role and story for ourselves and bring it into manifestation with the help of Source?

This is a book about the importance of taking time to reflect on and discover the story you have been living, with all of its themes, events, metaphors, and subplots. It is a book about the importance of dreaming and imagining what you would like your new story to be. And it's a book that offers tools to help you conceive your new story and to bring it into being. By actively participating in a new story, you can choose your destiny rather than being tumbled along by the whims of fate.

Years ago, I did a research project looking at factors that affected outcomes in psychotherapy. Among other things, I found that those who expected the therapist to heal them had less successful outcomes than those who expected the therapist to guide them in healing themselves. Ultimately, the onus is on you to change your individual story, even though you may be availing yourself of other spiritual, psychological, and medical help. No shaman or psychologist can change your story for you.

All of us need to learn to ask for help when we can no longer cope by ourselves. But you have a choice: Would you rather ask others to fix you and take care of you, or ask them to help you discover and develop ways to take care of yourself so you can become independent once again? The latter is far more empowering.

Powerful Tools for Changing Your Story and Your Life

The tools I offer are spiritual in nature, and many are based on shamanic practices that are as old as the earliest men and women on this planet. Shamans say their practices were inspired by the god of creation and his or her many demigods. Whether or not you believe that, you will find that these practices are incredibly powerful.

Shamans believe we each have a soul's journey that encompasses our past lives and extends into the infinite future. They say that this soul's journey is a mythic one that incorporates themes carried over from previous lives. Regardless of whether you believe this to be true, it can be very helpful to think of your life in terms of forces that organize the events you experience and the choices you make, and that must be worked with if you want to alter the events of the present and future. When you see you are living a story with aspects that mirror the ones your parents and grandparents lived, you start to understand the importance of identifying themes that affect your beliefs and perceptions and, ultimately, your choices.

Changing your story is not easy, but the payoff is considerable. You discover life is less frustrating and wearying, and you experience greater love and gratitude. You feel that energies you are accessing support your well-being and your goals. Even when the inevitable challenges of life arise, you know you are in tune with your soul and with Source, and that knowledge gives you courage and comfort.

New behaviors, attitudes, and emotions are integral to writing a new story, and using the techniques described in this book will help you make changes in how you act, think, and feel. Self-reflection and self-discovery plant the seeds of transformation. When you better understand your past, you can better plan your future. Breaking patterns of behaviors will be easier. In your relationships, you will start to realize you can change yourself, but you can't make other people change. When this new insight lights your path, you will find you act differently toward others and, often, they will act differently toward you as well.

Momentum

One of the reasons it can feel as if we have no control over our stories is that the stories we are living have their own momentum. In physics, momentum is defined as mass times velocity. The weight of our experiences, the burden we carry because we can't let go of past resentments or hurts, is multiplied by the speed at which we go about our lives. It's hard to change when we are like the *Titanic,* a huge, weighty ship going forward at top speed. An iceberg may suddenly appear. To avoid it or brush up against it with minimal damage to ourselves, we must be lighter and more nimble.

When we slow down to reflect, we feel the weight of our experiences and recognize that we are not doomed to carry around pain, anger, fear, or regret. We change our momentum when we let go of the heavy baggage of the past and become more still. As we begin the process of gaining new insights and exchanging heavy energies—including shame, regret, and resentment—for lighter ones—joy, courage, love, compassion, and so on—we find it easier and easier to continue our work of self-reflection and letting go.

The insights you access by working with the exercises and practices in this book will change the weight of your experiences. They may no longer seem as important as they once did. You may shed the heaviness created by your regret, anger, frustration, shame, fear, or sadness. You will also find your momentum changes because you have learned to slow down, reflect, and make decisions consciously rather than merely reacting to situations. You will learn to work with energies effectively and minimize the influence of some of the forces affecting you. You can also bring in new forces to fuel your story. Switching directions will happen more quickly and easily.

Change Your Behavior at the Margins

Making changes "at the margins" means making small but meaningful alterations to your behavior. Such changes often lead to greater transformations, even as you are working on discovering fresh insights into your behaviors and bringing into your life new forces to help you manifest a better story.

The exercises and practices in this book will assist you in identifying hidden obstacles to your taking action. These obstacles may include attitudes, beliefs, and emotions that you're unaware of. As you move past them or dissolve them, it becomes easier to make changes. Even so, you may find it is difficult to make the grand transformation you desire unless you begin to change your behavior at the margins.

Changing your behavior includes changing how you spend your time. If, for instance, you want a deeper relationship with a higher power, you need to set aside time to work with that higher power. If you want to spend your time differently, you have to follow through on your intention to do so. Larger goals need to be broken down into smaller ones that you take action toward achieving; otherwise, your goals remain daydreams.

If you want to learn a foreign language, for example, you might be unsure of how best to do so, and then you might become annoyed and frustrated at having yet another thing to do. When you stop looking at your goal as one big endeavor, though, you start to see where you can make small bits of progress that add up over time. For instance, you might learn one or two new words of the language every day, thereby reducing your frustration and impatience.

Similarly, if you wish to be more authentic in your relationships, it's important to become more mindful of when you are inauthentic. With this awareness, you will be better able to speak your truth from the heart the next time you are tempted to please others by saying *yes* when you mean *no*. Your acts of change may not seem large—perhaps you will only be saying *no* to another evening spent doing chores instead of having an enjoyable conversation with friends or going out with your partner. Even so, such acts of change at the margins are crucial if you want to change your story and your life.

As you do more shamanic and Jungian work and become increasingly aware of the themes in your story, you will better understand your longings and choices, and you will continue to discover ways to make your story more satisfying. You will develop new goals based on new insights. For example, you might realize that yearning to learn the language of your ancestors, a language that was lost when they assimilated, represents a larger yearning to reconnect with the forgotten past—your own as well as that of your family. You might realize that you want to bring back themes from your youth that got left behind, just as your great grandparents' culture and way of life fell by the wayside when they integrated into their new community. This insight can lead to more changes that help you write a better story for yourself.

The Value of Experiential Knowledge

Shamans co-create with Source but know that Source makes the ultimate decisions. We are not separate from Source. In fact, we come from it and share its essence. Westerners often think, talk, and write about spirituality and consciousness from an intellectual perspective, removed from the actual experience of direct encounters with Source. Shamans recognize that wisdom comes from incorporating the lessons learned through direct experiences, not just from examination and dissection of their own or anyone else's experiences.

How can you shift your attitudes and beliefs so that it feels natural to begin changing your behavior, and so that you can go beyond changing at the margins and undergo larger, more profound transformations? How can you come to feel your connection to Source, your co-storyteller? It's not enough to simply read this book and absorb its ideas. Transformation cannot be a purely intellectual exercise. The wisdom you gain will come not from learning about shamanic practices and Jungian techniques but from actually using them. Then you can become aware of how you really feel, and your habitual thoughts won't talk over the voice of your inner knowing. You will be able to discard your old perceptions and beliefs and feel what it is like to embrace new ones.

The ideas and techniques presented in this book may feel foreign to you at first, but I hope you will be open to them and do the exercises provided. All can help you connect to the infinite, where you can access information and energy that can be valuable in writing and bringing into being a new story. Other traditions might help you make these connections using other means, such as prayer, meditation, qigong, or yoga nidra.

One practice that will complement your working with the practices in the book is writing in a journal, or journaling. As you do the exercises, you will be asking yourself a lot of questions. Keep a written record of all of your answers; they can be grist for your mill as you ponder your old story and dream your new one into being. Reviewing and contemplating your answers to the questions will make it easier for you to develop insights that can inform a new and better story.

The shamanic and Jungian techniques you learn about and begin to use will allow you to access the wisdom of your unconscious mind as well as that in the collective unconscious beyond your individual consciousness. You may feel resistance to this idea, but I encourage you to remain open to the possibility. Jungians believe that our unconscious has a personal and a collective aspect. Our personal unconscious consists mainly of those parts of our stories that we do not want to remember because they are too painful. Our collective unconscious connects us to the realm of the archetypes and their mythic influence. To craft a new story, we need to loosen the grips of these unconscious forces. The techniques you learn about and begin to use will help you gain insight into some of the dynamics of your unconscious mind and allow you to access its wisdom.

In this book, I provide many questions for you to consider—questions that, as a Jungian analyst and psychologist, I feel will help you better understand the insights and experiences you have as a result of using techniques and practices that take you out of ordinary consciousness. However, you may come up with some questions of your own as well.

Making deeper inquiries as you think about the answers you receive from Source will bring you deeper insights. For example, you might start with a question such as, "What do I need to know about my physical health?" and receive an answer that confuses you because you are trying to take it too literally, or you have a preconceived notion about what you should do. If an image of water in a clear lake comes to you in response to your question, "What do I need to know about my physical health," it could mean you need to spend more time around water to reduce your stress levels, or that you need to drink more water, or that you need to calm your emotions (water often represents the emotions). Asking more questions will help you to gain deeper insights and better understanding of the answers you receive. You can ask these questions as part of a journaling process or as part of a journey or a dialogue with symbols and energies. You can also ask questions while performing rituals and ceremonies, or working with sand paintings, dreams, and nature, all of which will be explained in later chapters.

Working with Symbols and Imagery

By expressing your story through art, movement, poetry, and other nonverbal or metaphorical ways, you engage both the rational (left) and intuitive/nonrational (right) hemispheres of your brain. The rational hemisphere is more involved than the nonrational one is when it comes to processing language and thinking logically. The nonrational hemisphere of the brain thinks in pictures and symbols, the primal language of Source and the universe. Be careful not to analyze the symbolic messages received too quickly, however, because the rational mind is used to perceiving in a limited way and may distort the message. As you work with the practices in this book, take your time and don't rush to verbalize and interpret what has come to you in the form of symbols, energies, and sensations.

In time, you will become more adept at interacting with energy and symbolic messages through the use of techniques such as journeying and dialoguing. Then, you can discard or replace the metaphors that you have outgrown or that don't serve you anymore. By changing your metaphors, you usher in forces that can bring to life a new story, perhaps one of an adventurer, a nurturer, or a wise elder. You can stop telling yourself and others that you're "swimming upstream" and adopt a new metaphor of "surfing the waves of uncertainty" or "going with the flow."

A woman went on a shamanic journey to ask for symbols that would help her create a new story. She described her experience in this way:

> One aspect of my story that I wanted help with was my relationship with my parents. On the journey, I received the symbol of a silver spoon, offering love and nourishment. Upon my return to ordinary consciousness, I was skeptical of this gift. It seemed too facile a symbol to capture the conflicted way I felt about my parents. To get more information, I decided to dialogue with the symbol [consciously ask the symbol questions, make observations, and then let the unconscious mind respond from the perspective of the symbol, in a back-and-forth conversation]. In the dialogue, I challenged the symbol of the silver spoon, pointing out that it could rapidly tarnish, losing its bright beauty. To my surprise, the energy of the spoon symbol communicated that I had hit upon one of its main messages. What I had seen as a flaw was really part of the symbol's deeper significance. Underneath the veneer of dark tarnish, the essential nature of the spoon remained unaffected. From the dialogue, I realized that although my relationship with my parents was tarnished very deeply in some places, underneath that, their love for me was steadfast.

This woman's journey allowed her to realize that her parents did, in fact, love her, and made it easier for her to be accepting when their behaviors disappointed her.

Finding and Reclaiming the Hidden Pieces of Yourself

The techniques you'll learn in this book, such as journeying and dialoguing, are highly effective for discovering and uncovering qualities and behavior patterns that may be hidden from your awareness. You may see these qualities and behaviors in others but not be able to recognize them in yourself. These hidden or lost aspects of yourself, which are buried in your unconscious, influence how you act, think, and feel. They are pieces of your story, your life, and your identity. If you reclaim them, learn from them, and incorporate your insights into your self-knowledge, you can write a better story.

Any quality you have disavowed and relegated to the shadowy corners of your consciousness has both positive and negative aspects. When you rediscover a quality you thought was negative, you may uncover its gifts and become conscious of how to access them while minimizing the more problematic aspects of that quality. When you embrace a positive quality you did not realize was within you, you become empowered.

It's difficult to change your story without bringing some of these qualities into your conscious awareness. Only then can you free the energy that you have been using to hide from your conscious mind the truths you have denied. This energy can then be channeled toward changing your life story. What's more, you will find it easier to stop wasting energy in endeavors that you don't value as part of your story. You will have fewer regrets.

Each aspect of your current story has, in one way or another, served a purpose. Even if you want to change or shed part of your current story, it is important to honor it for the role it has played. Although you can't change your past experiences, you can alter how you feel about them by scrupulously examining your current story and its origins and using the exercises and practices described in this book. You will likely choose to keep those patterns and roles that serve you well. But first, you must emotionally detach from them in order to appraise them with objectivity. In looking at your story, you must free yourself from both sentimentality and cynicism.

If you decide that some of your patterns and roles don't serve you or feed your soul, you can make new, better choices. As you change one aspect of your story, you might find that you want to change others as well. You might also discover there are parts of your story that are more important to you than you originally thought they were. For example, I have worked with women who felt inadequate and unsuccessful because they had not found a suitable life partner, and finding one was a pressing goal for them. After they did shamanic and Jungian work, this goal stopped being so important to them, and they developed a new goal to become strong and self-assured regardless of whether or not they found a life partner. After using shamanic and Jungian techniques to access wisdom hidden from the unconscious mind, you may find you have new ideas about what you would like to bring into your life.

A goal of this work is to bring greater integrity, that is, an unbroken condition or wholeness to your life, rather than allowing a disconnection between the actions you take and your conscious beliefs and intentions. Resolving your inner conflicts leads to greater equanimity.

As you do the exercises in this book, you may experience moments of transcendence in which you are able to see the larger picture of your life, glimpse possibilities otherwise unseen, and give birth to a new story you had never before imagined for yourself. You will be able to make conscious choices and see an ever-expanding number of possibilities as you become more attuned to messages from Source, encoded in symbol and metaphor and made accessible to you when you use the consciousness-shifting techniques in this book. You can learn to comfort your aching heart.

ACHING HEART

Waking, aching
yearning, burning
for an unknown balm
to soothe a hollowness no one else,
no thing, no idea
can fill
assuaged only if we can fit our lives
into the mold of pure being
until then,
forlornly dancing
to my aching, breaking heart.

The places that shamans access and work within, the invisible realms where you can interact with and dialogue with energy, are available to everyone, but you will find it easier to encounter and explore them if you continue to use the techniques in this book. It is best to surrender to the experiences instead of imposing your own ideas on them. Through patience and persistence, you can learn to bring to life a new and more empowering story.

CHAPTER TWO

Shamanism and How It Can Help You Change Your Story

Throughout history, the lore of indigenous peoples and the mystery traditions of the Greeks and Egyptians have contributed to the well-being of Earth and her inhabitants. Although such knowledge was once in the mainstream of people's lives, today it is relegated to the realm of the esoteric and is often dismissed. Such knowledge includes the tenets of shamanism.

When I look at the many shamanic traditions around the world and the work of modern shamans, I see fundamental similarities. For example, for all people on the shamanic path, direct encounters with Source and aspects of Source can lead to dramatic transformations and healing.

I believe that shamanic journeys and practices can enable anyone to access Source to help themselves and others. We don't need months of training to use shamanic practices. We do have to be respectful of their power. Using them occasionally can be beneficial for anyone interested in personal growth and transformation. However, the big changes happen when a serious effort is made to work with these tools regularly.

Shamans use specific techniques to alter their consciousness and journey to other energetic realms. There, they gain energy and information they can use to bring about changes in the everyday world. Some say these realms are imaginary; others say they are alternate realities that exist in other universes. Certain theories and phenomena within the science of quantum physics support the concept of alternate realities. According to Heisenberg's uncertainty principle, a subatomic particle can exist in any of a number of different locations, or universes, at the same time until its position is determined by an observer. From that moment forward, it only exists in one particular universe. This view, called the many-worlds interpretation, allows for the simultaneous existence of myriad universes, all of which are equally "real."

If the realms shamans journey to are, in fact, real places, then that does indeed support the shamanic view that they are transpersonal realms that can be accessed by anyone who shifts into a new level of consciousness and chooses to visit them. When shamans are in a non-ordinary state of awareness, commonly called an "altered state of consciousness," the reality of the senses fades to the background. Shamans then interact energetically with the sun, moon, stars, and Mother Earth. Such altered states of consciousness can be achieved through practices discussed in Chapter Five, such as mindful breathing and working in sacred space.

At times, shamans may have visionary experiences mediated by the use of sacred plants that have psychedelic or other mind-altering properties. Although the use of sacred plants can catalyze shamanic journeys and dialogues, you don't need to employ them to benefit from shamanic practices. You can create a shift in consciousness using the powers of your own mind.

In this book, I describe some experiences I have had, their energetic themes, and the conclusions I drew from them. I also guide you to transpersonal realms I have visited, and show you how to work with what you find there to alter your life story. My hope is that you can derive meaning from your experiences in these realms and use what you have learned, as well as the energies you have brought back with you, in ways that help you change your story. I also explain how you can undertake a shamanic journey and interact with energies you encounter in transpersonal realms by using a technique called dialoguing. Dialoguing is similar to Jungian active imagination—a process in which the ego engages content from the unconscious and then steps back to ponder what has been encountered and find ways to apply newly acquired insights to everyday life.[2] Dialoguing, like Jungian active imagination, is a form of engagement with content from the unconscious. Dialoguing specifically involves a back-and-forth conversation with a symbol, inner figure, or emotion, or even an aspect of nature that you came across in a shamanic journey or your work with nature. Some believe that shamans only listen to nature, which speaks to them. However, shamans will tell you they not only listen to what the wind and mountains have to say, but they also speak to them. Thus, a two-way dialogue is partly shamanic and partly Jungian.

Increasingly, we are realizing that all of us can be shamans to some degree, but it is helpful to know what shamanism is and what shamans have traditionally done. There are shamans who can assist you in using shamanic practices and who can journey on your behalf, but you don't have to work with a shaman to benefit from any of the techniques presented in this book.

What Shamans Do

Shamans believe in the power and consciousness of nature. They also believe in alternate realities and a space where things exist only as potential, before they manifest into tangible, everyday reality. Shamans work with energy. As healers, they correct imbalances in the body or mind. They also retrieve information and energy from the past and visit the realm of potentiality and possibility to explore other futures that might be manifested.

Shamans recognize and experience their interconnectedness with the natural world of plants, rocks, animals, and skies. When they are in an altered state of consciousness, shamans can interact with the spirits of ancestors and animals as well as the energies of places, such as mountains, rivers, and lakes, for aid in healing and transformation. Shamans then negotiate with the energies encountered so as to bring about a different reality in the present and future.

When shamans bring new things into manifestation and dissolve other things, they work with energy as it transforms into matter and matter as it transforms into energy. Often, their goal is to replace low-frequency vibrational energy with high-frequency vibrational energy for the purpose of healing.

Shamans say they can work with the physical world, including clouds, people, and rivers, because everything has a frequency and an energetic nature—even a mountain, which seems to be solid and unmoving. Scientists tell us that the known universe started with, and still contains, very high frequency vibrational energy. Over time, as some of that energy's wavelengths increased and frequencies decreased, it took the form of matter that became increasingly dense and more solid. The material world we know today is made of energy condensed into matter. Therefore, the universe contains a continuum of energy.

Shamans recognize that our bodies, like all physical objects, are made up of energy, and at the energetic level, we are all connected to one another and to the entire universe.

Scientists are still pondering the true nature of the relationship between mass and energy. At the subatomic level, a particle, which has mass, can behave like a wave of energy—and vice versa. We don't know why this is, but the recent discovery of the Higgs boson, or so-called "God particle," may someday lead us to understand the mysterious relationship between mass and energy at the smallest levels of reality. What is most important to remember, however, is that in using shamanic techniques, we are interacting with different energies and with different frequencies to affect the material world. We can work with the energy of the natural world, the energy of the human body, and the energy of thoughts and emotions.

When working with people who are caught in a whirl of fruitless thoughts or are habitually living "from the head," detached from experiencing life in a physical body, shamans might bring in lower-frequency energy to help ground them. Often, shamans will tap into high-frequency, transcendent energies to help them hear the voice of Source more clearly as they seek guidance. They also clear out heavy, stagnant energy that needs to move out of the body's energy field. Then, they bring in high-frequency energy, which causes the energy in the body's field to flow in a healthier and more balanced way.

To access high vibrational energies that can help with healing or birthing new stories, shamans need to raise the vibration of their own bodies. Through rituals, they release heavier, lower-frequency energy to Earth and the cosmos. In exchange, they bring in higher-frequency energy from the entire universe or entities within it, as well as from natural places on Earth. Shamans also raise their vibration when they harbor harmonious thoughts, or emotions such as compassion.

Because they are able to shift not only their own energy but also that of others, shamans have played important roles in their communities ever since the beginning of humankind. Traditionally, shamans have helped their people to find fertile land and fresh water and to locate animals for hunting. They have also influenced the weather by bringing rain during droughts and ending it during floods. They help heal their communities and individuals within the community. Shamans have been able to do these things because of their ability to interact with the spirits of the natural world in a way that embodies reciprocity and gratitude. They honor and interact with Earth and Source.

Shamans Today

Shamans come from a variety of backgrounds. Some are members of indigenous groups who maintain traditional values and teachings and have spent little time in the technological world. Others have ancestors from both indigenous and nonindigenous groups, or come from a nonindigenous background. Some shamans have learned to successfully work in both the traditional and technological worlds. While shamans still play important roles in traditional communities throughout the world, increasingly, they are also working with people in urban areas.

Shamanism is changing. In many indigenous groups, older shamans are not passing on their knowledge to younger generations. Young people are moving to cities and are often more interested in taking advantage of 21st-century opportunities than in learning the millennia-old teachings of shamanism. Some of the teachings are being shared with nonindigenous people, with resistance from some traditionalists who don't want to pass on their teachings to outsiders.

With the increased interest in shamanism, the number of shamans available to meet the demand has risen. Many of them are not trained shamans, but because they adopt names that sound exotic to people outside their communities, or claim training they have not had, people may mistakenly believe they are authentic. Even genuine shamans can be corrupted by the money that can be made by "selling" shamanism, and their motives for doing shamanic work can be perverted to seeking profits, being admired, and gaining power over others.

Shamanic powers are real. How they are used, and the motives for their use, have to be constantly assessed by shamans and those with whom they work. Many people are attracted to shamanism because they want to learn to do magic or produce miracles. I believe that some shamans who truly understand how to work with the forces of the natural world can bring about events that seem miraculous. They can do so because they have gained an awareness of consciousness and life that allows them to transcend the limits of consensual reality. However, a person can grow spiritually on a shamanic path and be of service without ever doing anything "miraculous." By continually increasing our conscious participation in life, we come to know that we are part of an ongoing miracle too vast for our comprehension.

The shamanic realms offer great opportunity for bringing about positive transformation in our lives, but practitioners need to be motivated by love and a desire to serve rather than by self-aggrandizement. They must also have done sufficient work to achieve personal growth, and developed enough self-awareness to know why they are choosing to do what they are doing. The most effective shamans acknowledge their abilities and technical skills without feeling or acting self-important. They know that Source works best through those who are clear channels.

The best shamans I have worked with don't call themselves shamans. They just work with energy, heal, retrieve things from the past, and predict the likelihood of possible alternative futures. Those with whom they work know who and what they are. Good shamans like to dance, sing, celebrate, and live life fully. They are guided by Source, not the opinions of others. They never take themselves too seriously, although they take their work very seriously.

Not all shamans are "good people" as most of us describe good people—kind, selfless, humble, considerate of others, and not using power for personal advantage. Some shamans have special connections to the spiritual realms but have not done important work at the level of body, mind, and soul. They may be alcoholic, narcissistic, or manipulative, or have feelings of entitlement. They, like all humans, have flaws. If you choose to work with a trained and experienced shaman, be discerning so that you are not taken advantage of. Even if a particular shaman has a lineage you find impressive, remember that you are dealing with someone who is as human as you are. Listen to your instincts, and don't work with this person if you are uncomfortable. Remember, as you use the practices in this book, you will get better at doing your own shamanic work. It is not necessary to have an "expert" shaman do it for you.

Goals of Shamanism

I believe that, at its essence, shamanism incorporates three major tenets or goals: knowing who we truly are; serving others from a place of love, gratitude, and compassion; and having a close connection with the sacred. Each of these shamanic goals reinforces the others. For example, as we learn to know ourselves, we can better know Source and serve others. Through a deeper connection to Source, we come to better know ourselves and feel motivated to serve others.

Knowing Ourselves

The process of doing shamanic work leads to knowing ourselves better. We reclaim parts of ourselves that have been repressed, lost, or forgotten. When our self-knowledge grows, we find it easier to move beyond our habitual roles and ways of perceiving the world. As we come to understand the holds that our current story and our emotional and psychological wounds have on us, we are able to disconnect the story and our wounds from the harsh, painful emotions wrapped around them. We learn to observe ourselves and others, as well as situations we encounter, with greater detachment and compassion. Then, we can be open to Source's voice and make new choices in order to find clarity and balance within ourselves as well as in our everyday lives.

Serving Others

When we are in mutuality with Source, we are connected to the infinite, and we feel an imperative to help others. The concept of being of service to others encompasses many things. For example, it can mean being authentic in our relationships, listening well, being kind to others, expressing gratitude, volunteering at a food pantry, or accompanying students on a school field trip. However, balance is required. We can spend so much time serving others that we neglect other aspects of our lives.

Perhaps the most profound gift of service is simply being fully present in the company of others. Giving our full attention and listening intently, without judgment, preconceptions, or expectations, are gifts that can be of tremendous benefit to others as well as to ourselves, regardless of whether external conditions have objectively changed. Being fully present requires being fully open and as accepting as possible.

Having a Close Connection with Source

A goal of all shamanic work is to quiet the rational mind to allow access to the voice of Source within us. We come into greater harmony with the cosmos when we honor Source. We do this by paying attention to Source's communications and listening to our intuition. As we become more still and quiet, we clear ourselves of accumulated physical, mental, and emotional baggage. Then we become more capable of perceiving the voice of Source and allowing it to inform our choices. The goal is not to give up our free will and expect Source to take over; rather, it is to make the best choices we can in the present moment by listening to the guidance of Source and our inner knowing and then taking responsibility for our actions.

TRANSFORMATION

An essence of the work
is learning how to make choices
unencumbered by our ancestral and karmic lineages—
constraints to which we are heedless,
limiting our freedom of action.
Is the goal to surrender all to Source?
No. It is to choose always anew,
In accord with our true soul's journey,
And to mind the promptings of Source
As we take responsibility,
Knowing our place in the cosmos.
Why do people enter the chrysalis?
What initiates a soul's metamorphosis?

To achieve the goal of being more present in the moment and open to the voice of Source, we need to recognize those situations where our thoughts, feelings, and roles take over and cause us to act unconsciously from a recurring pattern. We have to free ourselves of our habitual responses, thoughts, feelings, and actions. If we can interject a pause between stimuli that trigger our habitual patterns and our response to such stimuli, we have an opportunity to choose to be more fully present in the moment. We will become better able to broaden our perceptions and have experiences we would not otherwise have. When we have experienced a break from our ordinary reality, it is easier to recognize how important it is to reflect before acting if we want to change our lives and our stories.

Late one night years ago, I had the uncomfortable and frightening experience of feeling my heart wasn't working properly, due to what I now know was a treatable condition called atrial fibrillation. I didn't want to wake my wife and worry her, and I decided to perform some qigong exercises to see if that might help. I slipped out of our room, began the qigong, and suddenly heard a voice say, "Be still and know that I am God." In that moment, I realized that I was pushing myself too hard, taking on too much and trying to handle everything myself instead of trusting in Source to help me. I realized that Source was telling me that if I stopped "doing"—even doing qigong for health purposes at that moment—I could make myself more available to God's voice and agenda and not just my own.

We all contain the voice of Source within us and can access it when we decrease our mental chatter and shift our consciousness. But we also contain voices from our unconscious mind. It can be hard to distinguish among these voices. With practice, we can learn to determine whether a particular inner voice nurtures our self-awareness, helps us to be of service, and enhances our compassion. When it does, we know it is the voice of Source speaking through us and to us.

BLUEPRINT QUERIES

How can the speck contain the whole?
How can the cell be the blueprint for the organ?
Is it magic or is it God?

Is God the same as life or Source?
Would Source laugh at definitions of the ineffable?
Why climb Everest?

What if we suitably define what remains?
Will Source reinvent itself, or will we both transform?
Shall we know Alpha and Omega?

Once, I spent some time in Abadiania, Brazil, at the *casa* of João de Deus, or John of God, a powerful spiritual healer. On the morning of my last day there, I suddenly had a vision of cleaning my kitchen in a country house in preparation for a visitor. It was a simple kitchen with flowers and lots of light. Outside was a garden with more flowers. A guest arrived, Jesus, and I served a simple meal in the kitchen. We then went outside, and I showed Jesus my garden. He was genuinely appreciative. I felt humble that he would treat me as an equal, a brother. I cried.

In a visceral and deeply emotional way, this experience reminded me that the essence of Source is agape (ah-GAH-pay), or unconditional love, and that it is important to prepare a place for the Divine to visit so that we can present our kitchens, gardens, labors, and their fruits as offerings. I am still learning to become still and simply remain present with visions and messages from Source. I know that if I exercise patience, the meaning of what I see will become clear to me in time. Even so, after years of doing shamanic work, I still can relate to those who like quick answers.

Source's promise is that in each moment, we can begin again and create something new. We might be subject to economic, physical, or other seemingly insurmountable constraints, but if we can change our attitude toward our circumstances and realize that each moment is all that we truly ever have, our beliefs about our lives can improve dramatically. It's often very hard to move beyond our pain, but it does not have to define our lives. We are not our pain. Moreover, we are part of a much larger story shared by all.

In each moment, we breathe in and out, think thoughts or not, feel emotions or not, and act or not. Our attitude, and our faith in our ability to generate new ideas, new feelings, and new hope, moment to moment, can make all the difference in how we experience our current story.

ALL THERE IS

Each moment only
breath in, breath out,
thoughts, feelings in
thoughts, feelings out
some sticking, some repeating
but always with the possibility
of creating a new world of
attitudes, thoughts, feelings, actions
from the myriad possibilities
of our is-ness.

The choices we make today help determine which of many possible destinies we will experience. Once we have a strong connection with Source, we can tap into the destiny that best serves us and Source in this lifetime. Our destiny is not necessarily what our ego wants, but what we can co-create with Source. Unlike fate, which is what we experience when we go through life unconsciously, destiny is something we can influence through conscious effort. When we are on a journey of destiny that is right for us, we gain from our choices a sense of rightness and profound well-being. We feel more enlivened by life and more engaged in a bigger, richer, complex, meaningful existence. Then we make decisions and take actions that move us toward that destiny.

Cultivating *Ayni*, or Mutuality

To achieve any of the goals of shamanic work, we must first come into *ayni* (EYE-nee) a word in the indigenous Quechua language mainly spoken in the Andes. Ayni means reciprocity, right relationship, and harmony with the universe and all aspects of our being. In the process of healing ourselves and changing our stories, we need to bring the many parts of our being into harmonious balance, or ayni. These parts include our body systems, minds, emotions, intents, and spiritual selves. Ayni involves the right thing at the right time in the right amount. The external mirrors the internal, so when we find balance within ourselves, we experience balance outside of ourselves. When we have enthusiasm and passion, we begin to see it reflected outside of us.

Some years ago, I was working with fire as part of a shamanic ritual, and the fire had died down. I found myself thinking about my call to follow the shamanic path and its importance to me. I resolved to dedicate my life to this path. At the very moment I had that thought, the fire, which had earlier gone out, burst into flames—not just a coal or two suddenly flaring up, but complete reignition, which convinced me that I was being supported in this decision. I was in ayni, and the fire reflected what was happening energetically within me.

We are in ayni when we embody the three Quechua concepts of *yachay*, *munay*, and *llankay*. Respectively, these words mean "harmonious thoughts," "harmonious love," and "harmonious actions." Our cognitions, feelings, and behaviors do not conflict with each other.

With our intellect and our minds, we develop knowledge that allows us to explore what can be known. With our intuition and bodily knowing (or somatic awareness), we can explore the unknown. We can never know the Unknowable (Source), but we can encounter it and experience a connection to it, a connection that began when we came into being. Or, we can simply have faith that it is the Source of our individual essence. To achieve balance, or ayni, we should encounter Source in multiple ways.

Markers of being out of ayni at the personal level include not knowing ourselves, including our darker aspects, so that we too easily see ill intent in others; not serving others or giving back to our communities; and not allowing ourselves to be moved by nature or art. Markers of being out of ayni at the collective level include mistreatment of vulnerable members of society, widespread degradation of the environment, lack of accessible health care, and school systems that do a poor job of preparing our youth to become well-rounded, productive adults. We take ourselves out of ayni when we do not nurture a relationship with Source, and when we take spirituality out of our collective conversation, dismiss the importance of rational thinking, or do not value our emotions and intuitive abilities.

On a personal level, we gain harmony by getting rid of habits, situations, and relationships that no longer serve us and replacing them with ones that serve us better, and by experiencing ayni with all aspects of ourselves, even the ones that make us uncomfortable. We nurture ayni by being open to hearing the voice of Source. At the collective level, we move toward ayni when we honor one another and the planet on which we live.

As we come into harmony with ourselves and Source, we experience healing. Sometimes, healing means that emotional or physical symptoms abate. However, we can be in harmony and healed even when physical symptoms remain. Sometimes, healing means that we realize the purpose of an illness or symptoms and then let go, releasing fear and negative energy, so that we can be filled with lighter, less dense energy that is more conducive to wellness at the level of body and mind.

The Four Perceptual Levels

Shamans say that as we change our perceptions, we change our experience of being in the world.

We are constantly immersed in infinite interconnections. We perceive and gather facts about these interconnections, and our existence, in a variety of ways. Our physical body registers and processes information that comes to us through our senses. Our mind thinks and feels as we try to make sense of our experiences. Our soul perceives our experiences as well, and it makes sense of our lives by identifying themes and archetypal energies influencing us. When we perceive at an even higher level, the level of pure energy, our egos dissolve. The boundary between our individual experiences and that of all creation disappears. At this highest level of perception, we perceive that everything exists only as waves at various frequencies rather than as matter, and we feel no separation between us, Source, and all of creation. These four perceptual levels—physical, mental (or psychological), soul, and pure energy—are core to the shamanic worldview.[3]

According to shamans, the physical, material realm has the lowest vibrational energy, and the realm of pure energy has the highest. When we perceive from higher states of awareness, the information we access, and the meanings we make of the information, are more abstract and universal. This does not mean that a higher level of perception is superior to a lower one. Each of the levels contains elements of the others, and all are manifestations of Source.

Although we are able to perceive from the highest perspective, we are also spirits taking corporeal form. There are times when it is best for us to perceive from a lower vibration. As enriching as it is to perceive ourselves as part of a larger story with mythic qualities, to perceive that we are each on a purposeful soul's journey, it is better to perceive at the level of the body when we need to do yard work and wish to avoid a pulled muscle! Later, when having a cup of coffee and surveying our completed work, we can ponder the passing of the seasons and get in touch with our feelings and thoughts about them, and wonder about our destiny and how events such as the annual raking of leaves fit into that larger story. To live full lives, we need to honor all of the levels of perception appropriately.

The level at which you perceive can affect your choices about taking action or solving problems. For example, if you are at a physical level of perception, you think literally. You will see a stiff, sore neck as an indication that you are sleeping with an inadequate pillow or hunching over a computer. You will believe that the remedy is anti-inflammatory medication coupled with better sleeping arrangements, or perhaps a more ergonomic workstation. At the level of the mind, you will perceive the stiff neck through thoughts and emotions, recognizing that it could indicate emotional or mental rigidity. You will see it could be a sign that you feel you have to be wary in the workplace and "look over your shoulder" and "watch your back." As you consider remedies, you might think about changing jobs, addressing problems with coworkers you don't trust, or other possibilities for adjusting the work situation to reduce stress. At the level of a mythic soul's journey, the stiff, sore neck could reflect systemic tension arising from an unfulfilling life: You go through life with a "stiff neck," unwilling to try anything new or take risks. You might decide the ailment is a sign that you have to start finding ways to feel a greater sense of purpose or meaning. At the level of pure energy, your soul might perceive that a lack of harmony with Source is causing the stiff neck. The remedy could be to connect to Source in new ways through ritual, ceremony, and quieting the mind's chatter to be able to hear Source's voice.

All the perceptual levels support each other. Thus, while a sore neck may ultimately turn out to be a symptom of deeper psychological and spiritual concerns, instead of simply a physical ailment, an ergonomic chair and better relationships with coworkers might help, too!

When you see yourself as an energy being on a mythic journey of the soul, you see the world as filled with magical possibilities. When you make choices, you are less encumbered by the drama of your past.

Shamans have learned to change at will how they perceive the world, and thereby change their reality. Shamans journey to the places of as-yet-unformed potentialities so they can access energy that fuels a journey to a particular destiny. You can learn to do this, too.

When you are able to shift effortlessly among the levels of perception, you can better understand your experiences. When you are relaxed and not feeling the pressures of time and obligations, it is easier to shift between perceptual states and access each of the four levels of awareness to better comprehend what is happening. When you have access to the higher levels and choose to perceive your life from a higher vantage point, you can influence events at the lower levels. As you ascend the levels, you gain greater freedom of action, and change becomes easier. Your ability to consciously choose the level at which you perceive at any given time is a fundamental tenet of shamanism. Your perceptions affect your story and what you experience. Thus, it's important to recognize that perception has many layers.

The Lower World, Middle World, and Upper World

Shamans envision that we inhabit three worlds simultaneously, and that these worlds exist both within us and outside us. In the South American tradition, shamans call the middle world, which is the world of everyday experience, the Kai Pacha. From where we are in the middle world, we can interact with the Uku Pacha, or lower world, and the Hanan Pacha, or upper world. The Uku Pacha is the world of our unconscious, our psychological wounds, our ancestors, our past lives, and our as-yet-unrealized potentials. The Hanan Pacha is the world of our becoming, the world of the future, which contains many possibilities for our destiny in this lifetime. This is the world that contains all that was, is, or ever will be.

ETERNITY

Not forever
is everything
Nothing is forever
Accumulation isn't
essence is
things aren't
patterns are—
or are they?

The lower, middle, and upper worlds have primal energies that can give strength and guidance to your physical body and the energy field that surrounds your body. You can tap into these energies as well as the information contained in these worlds. Doing so allows you to write a new story.

The Quiet and the Matrix

Before creation, before the Big Bang, there was the void, which I call the Quiet. It is the Source of the universe, of all that has been created. Source, or the Quiet, is a form of energy and will always exist. Shamans believe the energy of pure light is the Quiet, or the Source of all things. Pure light, they say, has the highest vibration of any energy, and this light gives birth to and is a precondition for life. It is only through life that the love aspect of the light can be known. The energy of this light is too vast to comprehend and can never be destroyed, only transformed. The light that we see is merely a reflection of this pure light.

The Quiet permeates the matrix, which is the grid of energetic connections that unites all that is. In our everyday world, Source takes form as the sun and the moon, rocks, plants, humans and other living creatures, and all the elements of the natural world including earth, air, water, and fire. They reflect Source, which is light. We do not know why light, which has no mass, can give birth to matter. Our increasing understanding of the subatomic realm, such as our discovery of the Higgs boson, is providing us clues for unraveling this mystery.

All forms of energy derive from Source. Source permeates every reality, and every reality derives from it. As noted earlier, the essence of Source is agape, or unconditional love, which shamans would say should be extended to all beings and all things.

We can work within the Quiet and, with conscious intent, bring forth new stories for ourselves and our world. In the Quiet, we consider possibilities and give birth to a thought. Once the thought is shaped with our desire and attention, we create a spark between our consciousness and Source. Our idea emerges in the form that we have envisioned it, albeit with Source's modifications.

As the Quiet creatively expresses itself in myriad forms and types of energy, we can draw upon the various energies that are aspects of this larger force and allow them to nourish and inform us. The practices in this book can be used to connect to and work with these energies.

The matrix contains all facts and information—past, present, and future. When we journey there, we experience the interconnectedness of all things and access information that would otherwise be hidden from our awareness.

My first conscious interaction with the matrix occurred in the Peruvian jungle next to the Mother of God River, one of the tributaries flowing into the Amazon. At the time, I was over 60 years old and had never used a mood-altering substance other than caffeine, nicotine, or alcohol. Nevertheless, I was contemplating ingesting a potion made from the sacred plant of Ayahuasca, which has been used for millennia in the healing and spiritual rituals of South American shamans to aid the user in crossing a threshold of consciousness between the everyday world and the other dimensions and energies that surround us.

As I was thinking about drinking the Ayahuasca brew, I was somewhat apprehensive. I had heard that Ayahuasca can induce violent nausea and give rise to frightening experiences. I also wondered whether ingesting a hallucinogen was the right thing to do. Ultimately, I decided to have the experience.

The evening of the ceremony, the group I was with went into a hut in the jungle and prepared for the experience. Soon, the *Ayahuasquero,* Don Ignacio, started to sing his *icaros,* songs that communicate with the Ayahuasca plant and other spirits of the natural world to request, and give gratitude for, healing and protection. Each of us then received the Ayahuasca brew from him.

For a while, I experienced nothing out of the ordinary as I sat in a meditative posture. Then I started to see intricate patterns of colors shifting before my eyes. I had various experiences, some frightening and some not, and I continued to see geometric shapes shifting in front of me in a kaleidoscopic set of images. Suddenly, I heard a very loud noise. I had the sense that a membrane in the universe was breaking. After the membrane burst, I found myself in a blackness punctuated by an infinite number of globes of light, all connected to the others. I instantly knew that I was in the presence of the matrix. I recognized that it is alive and has awareness, and contains and connects the consciousness of all things that have ever been or ever will be. These things include not only human consciousness but also that of animals, oceans, flowers, and the entire cosmos. I realized that we, and all of creation, are all part of the matrix, and that everything in the matrix influences and is influenced by everything else. This was not an idea that I pondered but a reality I experienced as an inner knowing.

Many of us have had extraordinary experiences during meditations, dreams, or guided imagery, or when we encountered synchronicities or spontaneous images while awake and seemingly in an ordinary state of consciousness. We are even more likely to experience them if we do shamanic work. A man who had been participating in a series of shamanic workshops told this story:

Three days after my father passed away, I was jogging through the woods near my house. It was late Friday afternoon. One of my father's favorite weekly events had been to come to my house for dinner on Friday nights. Close to the point on the path where I usually leave the woods to return to my neighborhood, a large buck walked out of the woods and stopped about 10 feet away from me. I was breathing heavily, so he had to have heard me coming. I felt calmness and peacefulness emanating from him. In all the many times I had walked and jogged through these woods before, I had never seen any deer along that path—and certainly not a buck with a notable rack. We stared at each other for what seemed like several minutes in complete stillness. Finally, I broke the silence, said good-bye, and continued jogging to my house.

I have not encountered a deer in that area of the woods since that day. Although I believe that there are coincidences, even the skeptical part of me can't shake the encounter. I am convinced that my late father's spirit was present in the buck and that the encounter was his way of communicating to me that he was all right. This experience will stay with me the rest of my life.

Incidents such as this one remind us that we live in a world that is bigger than we can imagine—one that contains infinite information and lessons for us. At times, we perceive energies surrounding us, or glimpse aspects of other dimensions, of which we ordinarily are not aware. We might be intrigued by such experiences but, not knowing what to make of them, dismiss them as mere curiosities. As you use the practices in this book, whether they are journeys, rituals, or ceremonies involving nature and archetypal energies, you will come to realize that there is meaning in the most subtle messages. You will begin to pay closer attention to metaphors, symbols, coincidences, and synchronicities and to mine them for what they can teach you about your current story and the story you might create for yourself.

A Glimpse That Reveals a Wider View

A hologram is a two-dimensional surface that contains all the information necessary to generate a three-dimensional image. Another property of a hologram is that a tiny piece of it contains the complete holographic image and all its information. Just as with a hologram, each thing in the universe, including us, contains the essence of and reflects the whole. A glimpse of the Quiet reveals the whole and all of its qualities, including interconnectedness. We can experience the greater whole and the wider view by experiencing just a small part of it. As expressed by the visionary poet and artist William Blake: "To see a world in a grain of sand/ And a heaven in a wild flower/ Hold infinity in the palm of your hand/ And eternity in an hour."

Shamans attempt to interact with as many aspects of the energy of the universe as they can by activating areas within their own energy fields that encase their physical bodies. By so doing, they get in touch with similar energy fields outside themselves and interact with them. Each of us has a luminous field that, in a holographic way, provides access to all of the mysteries of infinity. Our individual consciousness reflects the greater, shared consciousness of Source.

When shamans speak of honoring Source, they are not talking about bowing to a superior, supernatural being. "Honoring Source" means acknowledging the sacredness of our interconnection with the Quiet and the matrix and seeing that we are tied to all that exists or that will exist. It means acknowledging and being in awe of the beauty and majesty, the vastness and the unknowability, of Source. Shamans express their understanding of the relationship between themselves and the Quiet when they affirm what they would like to manifest while accepting that Source may have different ideas about what should be brought into being.

Each time shamans use a technique for gathering information and energy, they make a point of honoring Source. In the next chapter, you will be asked to explore your own perceptions, ideas, and feelings about Source and your relationship to this force as part of the process of discovering your current story. Knowing what your current story is, including its themes, will help you to figure out what new story you would like to write for yourself.

Remember that you are not your story. If you become overly identified with it, you lose the ability to change it. Detaching from your story and viewing it objectively helps you gain fresh insights. The exercises described in the next chapter are designed to aid you in exploring and better understanding your current story and the roles you play in your life so that you have the freedom to write a new, more satisfying story, which you will begin to do in Chapter Four. Then, you will begin using techniques derived from shamanic and Jungian traditions and develop a clearer sense of what you can gain from engaging in practices that awaken your unconscious mind. You will also better understand the experiences you have in transpersonal realms.

CHAPTER THREE

Exploring Your Current Story

What is the story of your life? In answering, your first instinct might be to list in sequence the significant events you've experienced. However, if you define your story in this way, you may not recognize your authorship of it. It might seem that things happen to you without your having much control over them.

To claim your role as the storyteller of your life, it is helpful to observe that your story has patterns and themes. In this chapter, you will work with exercises that allow you to discover your story's themes, which serve as organizing principles for the events of your life.

Shamans look beyond the sequence of what happened and when. They see the themes of a person's life as energetic threads woven into a fabric, and pull out certain threads so that they can be replaced with new ones, reweaving the person's present and future. As you identify the themes in your story, you will come to better understand the idea of energetic influences on your story. A thread of caretaking, struggle, leadership, or curiosity may be a part of your fabric without your realizing it. One woman found in the process of discovering her story that the theme that most stood out for her was a fear of being swallowed up, or subsumed, and being forced back into old patterns.

Examining your story from different angles and telling it in a variety of ways makes it easier to identify such themes. In this chapter, you will do many writing exercises and answer many questions that will help you in this task. The insights you gain from doing the work in this chapter will make it easier for you to recognize which energies you want to bring into your life, and better understand the experiences you will have, when you start using the practices described later.

Each of these exercises will be helpful in exploring your story because each allows you to see it from a different angle. Start by doing the ones that resonate most for you. Take your time with them. After you begin to work with the shamanic and Jungian techniques and take journeys, be sure to complete all of the exercises in this and the following chapters. It will take some time to get through all the exercises in the book, but you will find they enhance your journeying and other shamanic experiences, and vice versa.

Some of the exercises may be emotionally challenging to work with. If you find it difficult to complete one, put it aside and think about it for a day or two before coming back to it. Do your best to answer the questions. In time, come back and reread what you have written and think about whether you would have different answers, having gained new insights as a result of doing the exercises.

The scientist and philosopher Alfred Korzybski stated, "A map is not the territory it represents."[4] Your life is more than a series of events that happen over the course of time. It is a story with themes and patterns. How you tell your story is up to you, but if you can tell it honestly and are willing to work with energies that affect your personal energy field, you can write an entirely new story with new themes and new patterns of events. It may be far more empowering and fulfilling than the one you tell now, even though you will not change the facts about what happened to you in the past. You will modify your interpretation of them, and your framing of them. The emotional charge of your wounds will be diminished, and your experiences can be infused with new emotional energies, such as pride in having survived difficulties, or joy in having created something positive out of suffering. The beliefs and emotions that color the tale may reveal themselves and even change as you explore your story.

Imagine that you have been an actor in a story written by someone else. You have acted according to a script, unaware that you could change it at any time. Now you are going to be the writer and director as well as the actor. A part of your awareness can step back from the stage or move behind the camera to see the events being played out. You can call "cut" and redirect what is happening. You are reclaiming your power to tell the story you have lived and direct where it goes from here.

You have not been the only director of your story until this point. Parents, friends, bosses, teachers, loved ones, and even time and inertia are just a few of your co-directors. It's hard being the director of your own story, but as you become more used to witnessing and directing what is going on in your life, you will find you are less willing to relinquish your power. As you begin the process of stepping back to observe your story, you will experience many emotions and perhaps many new insights as well, if you are paying close attention. Be sure to set aside time to completely focus on doing the writing exercises in this chapter.

What Is Your Story?

To begin exploring your story, write a short autobiography. It can be just a few pages. Write about the significant events that you experienced, the people you met, and your struggles, losses, and triumphs. Include facts about where you have lived and traveled, and what jobs you have held.

As you read over what you have written, notice whether you chose to write in first person ("I did this, and then that") or third person ("He had this experience, and then that one.") Now, rewrite it using the opposite voice. Next, read it over and notice whether you told the story differently. Did you leave out certain details or alter them in a particular way?

Now review both versions of the story and look for other patterns. Did you write about how you have interacted with others in your platonic, romantic, and work relationships? Did you express your feelings about those relationships—and if so, what were they? Did you write about your dreams and aspirations and what became of them? Were you surprised to notice how certain events coincided? You might discover, for example, that the timing of events in your relationships coincides with changes in your health, moods, or attitudes that affected you in other areas of your life, such as career, involvement in service to others, and so on. There may be ebbs and flows in various aspects of your life that you had not previously realized were related—times when you were very happy or not very happy, or times when you were actively striving versus being passive, for example.

While pondering this factual rendering of the events in your life, maybe you will see a series of challenges overcome, or unanticipated events shifting your life in a completely unexpected direction. Perhaps you will recognize that you have experienced a string of major losses occurring in a short amount of time, long stretches without a significant other, or several job or career changes that happened suddenly.

Pay attention to the patterns you see. Both conscious *and* unconscious habitual patterns influence what you experience. If you are often angry, you are likely to act out of anger and develop beliefs that justify your rage or irritability. These beliefs lead to your feeling angrier, which results in perpetuating the cycle of angry thoughts, feelings, and actions. If you have a pattern of avoiding situations, it could be due to feelings of inadequacy and fear of being exposed, or an attitude of "I don't need to take emotional risks in relationships."

Consider this version of your current story to be a first draft. You will add detail and nuance as you work through the other exercises in this chapter.

Creating a Timeline

As you try to recall significant events in your life, it can be very helpful to construct a timeline. You can select a particular interval, such as five-year increments, or you may find it easier to remember events by dates or by what age you were at the time. You can also build the timeline around periods of your life or significant events, with headings such as "Birth and Early Years in Kansas City," or "College Years." Then you can fill in what happened in the months and years between these events.

As you write, consider the times when you had important experiences regarding the following:

1. *Your Health.* Describe, for example, any health crises or major changes to your physical condition, including changes in adolescence, or after ending a period of physical activity (such as playing a sport in school).
2. *Your Relationships.* Include romances, friendships, and major changes in your family, such as a divorce, remarriage, birth, or death.
3. *Your Mood or Attitude.* Describe, for example, a period of depression, cynicism, or optimism.
4. *Your Vocation.* Include jobs you held and activities you participated in that you enjoyed greatly.
5. *Your Spiritual Experiences.* Include any religious practices, ceremonies, or rituals that were a part of your life at the time, such as attending catechism class, going on a spiritual retreat that strongly affected you, and so on.
6. *Your Service to Others.* Include service to your community, such as having done volunteer work for a charitable group or nonprofit organization, or having become involved in helping your neighborhood or city through government service or being active in your child's school.

Once you have looked at your linear story, and remembered more about what events you have experienced and when, you'll be better able to recall more about other less memorable events that nevertheless played an important role in your life because they were part of a pattern.

Exploring Your Emotional Story

In addition to examining the linear events of your story, explore your story from an emotional standpoint. What emotional highs and lows stand out? Like most people, you probably have had emotional experiences that still resonate for you. An emotional experience is one that, when you recall it, still stirs up feelings of joy, sadness, regret, anger, resentment, satisfaction, dissatisfaction, and so forth.

Emotional experiences that retain a charge for you organize your daily perceptions. They are the glue that binds you to certain habits. They color your perceptions and influence what you are attracted to, whom you interact with, and what you avoid. To move forward into a new story, you need to find ways to have your past emotional experiences affect you differently.

As a first step in lessening the grip of your past emotional experiences, write your story, focusing solely on your emotional experiences. Start with the earliest emotional experience you can remember, positive or negative, and work your way forward to the present. It might be useful to add these emotional experiences to your timeline for later reference.

When you write about your emotional experiences, record their initial triggers and the events that seem to reactivate emotional responses that originate in the past. Have others done something to you—or you to them—that has set off an emotional reaction in you? Have you experienced the unexpected death of a loved one, or a natural disaster, such as a flood or tornado? Have you been bullied or ridiculed, or felt ashamed because you judge yourself as inadequate or inferior? What is the origin of those painful beliefs about yourself?

Are there recurring patterns in your emotional experiences? For example, have you repeatedly been a bully, victim, or rescuer? Are painful emotions regularly triggered in you? What are your triggers? What has been your role in creating and sustaining your emotional experiences? Do you have behavior or thought patterns that trigger or exacerbate painful emotions, such as anger, fear, shame, or grief?

Writing Individual Chapters

You are now going to expand upon your story by writing a chapter on each of six aspects of your life. I've provided questions for each aspect to help you identify physical, emotional, cognitive, and behavioral patterns. If you feel uncomfortable answering any questions, it may be that you are on the brink of discovering something that will lead to your writing a far more satisfying story. Acknowledge your resistance but push through it. The questions are meant to help you reflect so that you might better understand your current story and how you might wish to change it. Remember that it is always your choice whether or not to change.

The six chapters are:

1. Your health and your attitudes toward your body
2. Your significant relationships
3. Your psychology, including your emotional temperament and moods
4. Your jobs or career, experiences as a homemaker, or how you are occupying your time in retirement
5. Your relationship to Source, God, or a higher power
6. Your ways of being of service.

Chapter One of Your Story: *Your Health and Your Attitudes Toward Your Body*
First, write about your body and your physicality over the course of your life to this point. How have diet, exercise, stress management, illnesses, and weight been woven into your story? For example, if you are older, you may realize that in your younger

years you were concerned with athleticism or appearance but, over time, you became more concerned with the condition of your heart, hips, and knees, or your blood pressure.

Now consider the following questions and answer them if you haven't already:

- How much of your story has been involved with tending to, or worrying about, your health? What type of health issues have you had to deal with?
- How mindful are you about the food you consume and its short-term and long-term effects on your body? Do you pay attention to what you consume and how much you eat? Do you eat too much or too frequently? Do you eat quickly or slowly, savoring your food? Are you in touch with your sense of hunger or your sense of fullness?
- What messages have you received about food, physical health, and weight? Where did these messages come from—your family, friends, the media, or someone or something else? Have you heeded those messages?
- Are you addicted to food or other substances, such as alcohol, caffeine, sugar, or nicotine? How do these substances affect your mood and energy? Do you avoid or abstain from them?
- What types of physical exercise do you do? Do you exercise enough to keep your body strong and functioning optimally? If not, why aren't you exercising more? Do you have emotional reasons for not exercising? What is the origin of your habits of exercising or not exercising? Did you exercise in the past, but stopped? If so, why?
- How efficient are your processes of digestion and elimination? Do you have digestion or elimination issues? If so, what was happening in your life when you first developed them? When do these issues flare up and become more problematic? How do you keep your digestive or elimination issues under control?
- How do you feel about your sexuality and how you express it? Do you experience sexual problems? Are you satisfied with the amount or quality of your sexual experiences?
- How well does your immune system handle challenges? Has your immune system served you in the past? Has your immune function changed and, if so, why?
- How does stress affect your physical state? What physical symptoms do you experience when you are under stress?
- Do you get adequate amounts of rest and sleep? What causes you to lose sleep or not rest? What happens when you haven't gotten enough sleep or rest?

Chapter Two of Your Story: *Your Significant Relationships*
In this chapter, write about your relationships with your parents, siblings, romantic partners, children, and friends. You might want to start with just a few relationships and come back later to explore less significant or obvious ones, such as casual friendships. Sometimes those seemingly less important relationships can hold important lessons for you.

After writing about your relationships, consider the following questions and answer them if you haven't already:

- With which people do you share the greatest emotional intimacy and trust? How long have you had these relationships? Have they changed over time? How have they changed?
- Are you isolated, or do you have strong connections with many people? What has influenced your desire and ability to create strong connections? What has influenced your desire to isolate yourself? Are you comfortable with how connected to others you are?
- Do the people who are close to you treat you as you would like them to? Are you looking to others to give you what you could be giving yourself, such as approval or nurturance?
- What is the balance of give and take in your relationships? For example, is there an imbalance between how much you listen to others and how much they listen to you? Do you give in expectation of receiving something back in equal measure? Are you uncomfortable receiving gifts or attention from others? If so, why?
- What ties to your parents or other family members no longer serve you? What ties to old friends no longer serve you? Why are these relationships no longer serving you? Why do you hold on to them?
- How similar are your goals and desires to those of your friends? Are you comfortable with how different or similar your goals are to theirs? Why or why not?
- Do you put yourself down when interacting with others, or speak about yourself in a self-deprecating way? What response do you expect from others when you do this?
- Do you feel socially inadequate, different from others, or not part of the "in group"? Do you believe others see you as "the odd one out"?
- If you have expected others to notice you or rescue you, are you comfortable with retaining that hope? What, if anything, is the payoff to holding on to those expectations?

- Do you try to "fix" other people? If so, how do they respond to your efforts?
- What are your expectations about life and other people? Are they reasonable and realistic? What are your judgments about other people or groups?
- Are you jealous of or bitter toward certain people? Are there any past relationships that still cause you to feel anger or resentment?
- How do you feel about hearing, initiating, or passing on gossip? Do you feel differently if the gossip is about someone you care about than if it's about someone you are not close to? If you gossip, why do you gossip? What is the payoff?

Chapter Three of Your Story: *Your Psychology*

Write the third chapter of your story about your psychology—that is, your thoughts, perceptions, attitudes, and moods. Here, you are digging deep to recognize and acknowledge how you think and feel not just at the surface but in your unconscious mind, where lay hidden the wounds of your past and those qualities of yours that you have trouble accepting.

Afterward, consider these questions, and notice if there are psychological topics you didn't explore when writing this chapter (for example, maybe you only focused on your emotional struggles and not on the times when you were feeling positive, or maybe you had difficulty identifying your emotions):

- How much fulfillment have you experienced? How does it compare to the amount of aching, yearning, and wanting you have experienced?
- What is your most common emotional state? Are you usually happy, sad, irritable, depressed, or anxious? What are the dominant emotions in your story? Would you like to experience those emotions less frequently and less intensely?
- What makes you joyful?
- What makes you angry, resentful, or upset? What are you anxious about or scared of?
- When you are criticized, how do you respond? Are you able to listen to the criticism and take it constructively? How has your response to criticism worked for you?
- Are you a perfectionist? If so, what events influenced your perfectionism?
- Over what types of issues do you tend to ruminate?
- What repeating patterns show up in your self-talk? Are your thoughts pessimistic, optimistic, unrealistic, hopeful, or something else? Do these thought patterns serve you, or would you like to change them?
- Do you expend a lot of energy feeling strong emotions about certain matters,

whether it is a problem another person is having or the performance of your favorite sports team? Are these emotional experiences distracting you from and draining energy from other aspects of your life that should take priority?

- Are you overly identified with certain ideologies, causing you to put excessive emotional energy into your opinions and judgments?
- Do your emotions settle down when you take action? Why don't you take action more often than you do?

Chapter Four of Your Story: *Your Work, Career, or Livelihood*

Write your fourth chapter about your work, paid and unpaid—your jobs, your career if you have one, and the life's work you do, even if you aren't paid for it. If your life's work is, or has been, to raise a family, or if you are a schoolteacher but think of yourself as a writer as well, acknowledge that in this chapter. If you are retired or have moved on from various jobs, careers, or pursuits, don't forget to include them as you write this chapter.

Now consider the following questions and answer them if you haven't already:

- How much have you let others' expectations affect your working life and your choices about career and livelihood?
- Have you felt unappreciated or overlooked when it comes to your work?
- Are you a leader or a follower?
- Do you like what you are doing and how you are spending your time?
- Do you like your coworkers, partners, or bosses? Have relationships with coworkers, partners, or bosses in the past affected your story? What were the themes in those relationships?
- How long have you been doing the work you are currently doing? How long would you like to remain doing this work?
- Do you feel you have balance between the work you most wish to do and the work you do for purely practical purposes, such as to earn money?
- If you'd like a different job, what is keeping you from making a change?
- Are you making enough money or being sufficiently rewarded for your efforts in some other way?

Chapter Five of Your Story: *Your Relationship to Source*

In the fifth chapter of your story, write about your relationship to Source, God, or a higher power—however you think of the creative force of the universe. If you have no particular relationship with a higher power, write about that.

Now consider the following questions and answer them if you haven't already:

- How do you understand the concept of a higher power?
- How has your life been affected by your beliefs about God or a higher power?
- Are you able to connect with a higher power and feel rejuvenated and comforted by that contact?
- Do you participate in a traditional religion, attending services or taking part in the rites of that religion? Are you renewed spiritually by participating, or do you participate out of habit or for social reasons?
- Do you engage in spiritual rituals and ceremonies outside of a traditional religious context? Do you find them meaningful? If so, what forms do these rituals and ceremonies take? How frequently do you engage in them? What do you derive from performing them?
- Do you consciously choose to communicate with Source? If so, how do you communicate, and how often? Does Source communicate with you? When and how does Source communicate?
- When you communicate with Source, are you asking for things, expressing gratitude, or both? How do you feel about your communication with Source? Would you like it to change in some way?
- What feelings come up for you when you are contemplating Source? How do you deal with those feelings?

Chapter Six of Your Story: *How You Are of Service*

In this sixth chapter of your story, write about whether and how you are of service in the world. We can do good for others because we know it is right to do so, or so that others will applaud. However, the quality of our service will be vastly different if our hearts and our souls are heeding a call to serve rather than being driven by a personal desire to be seen as a "good person."

Now consider the following questions and answer them if you haven't already:

- How are you of service in the world? For example, are you in a vocation that involves being of service?
- How much time do you spend being of service? Is helping others a priority for you?
- Do you feel that you have enough time and resources to be of service? Are you frustrated because you are not doing more? Are you frustrated because you feel you are doing more than you can manage?
- How does being of service make you feel? Is it an obligation or a joy, or something in between?
- What is your motive for being of service? What are the payoffs? How do your

acts of service make a difference in the world?

In addition to the six chapters I've described, you might wish to write additional chapters on such topics as how you:

- manage your time
- deal with money
- relate to sexuality
- relate to authority and power
- deal with other aspects of your life that are important for you at this time.

Time management is an especially important topic because it reflects how well we follow through on our intentions. If time seems to slip away from you, you are not acting as the storyteller in your life.

Sometimes, our habits are unconscious. To see if this is so for you, write an hour-by-hour description of your typical day. If your weekend days are quite different from your workdays, describe a typical workday and a typical weekend day. Is your story congruent with your activities? For example, do you see yourself as someone who has no time for adventure and exploration because you need to take care of your family, but your typical days include very little time spent with your spouse and children? Often, people don't realize how much time they spend on a particular activity because their days are broken up into small intervals. You may think you spend 10 minutes here or there doing something you don't value, only to discover you actually spend 10 minutes on the task 10 times a day, which is significant. Are you happy with how you spend your time?

- How many hours per week do you use your computer, phone, or other electronic gadgets? Do these activities enrich your life, or do they use up time that you could better use for something else?
- When you watch television, what do you watch? How frequently and for how long do you watch it? What purpose does it serve in your life? Does it relax you or distract you from activities you would find more rewarding?
- How many hours per week do you spend going to movies or cultural events, listening to music, reading, being involved in family activities, working, eating, exercising, daydreaming, sleeping, making love, and anything else that you do in a day? Are you satisfied with the amount of time devoted to these activities?
- How frequently do you do multiple things simultaneously, such as talking,

texting, and listening to music? Are you able to be fully present to each of your activities and your life in the midst of your multitasking?

Perhaps you value certain activities or things, but spend your money as if you have very different priorities. It's common to be unaware of your spending patterns, which might reflect unconscious beliefs and feelings.

You might ask yourself the following questions:

- Do you spend more than you earn? How much do you spend on things that do not have lasting value for you? How much do you spend on travel and experiences you will always remember?
- Do you find it difficult to spend money on yourself?
- What themes about borrowing, earning, receiving, spending, and investing money have played out in your story? Are you satisfied with those themes?

Sit in the Director's Chair

As you reflect on what you have written so far and your answers to the questions that have been posed to you, try not to be self-critical. Just note without judgment what your story has been and now is. Self-condemnation can be paralyzing and is seldom a vehicle for positive change. Moreover, if you shut down, attack, deny, or become defensive when others criticize you, you may have trouble accepting alternatives to your current story.

For instance, you may perceive that you are a victim, but people close to you may see you as someone who has had opportunities but did not make the best choices. Only by exploring your story honestly will you be able to write a new and better one. If you can listen to criticism and recognize how it can be constructive, and look at yourself objectively, the information you glean can help you move into a new story instead of simply fantasizing about your life improving.

It is important to develop the ability to discern when self-criticism or criticism from others is warranted, accurate, and useful and when it is simply demoralizing or even destructive. When you can appraise yourself honestly, without harsh judgment, you can create emotional distance from your experiences, which will help you envision a new set of experiences and take new action. You can become aware of what you have done as an actor, but choose not to step onto the stage and continue the drama. Instead, you can sit in the director's chair and observe the larger picture, seeing how the events of your life fit into a larger whole and how the chapters in your life are interdependent.

For example, you may see that if you don't take care of your body, you won't have energy to take action for change and bring your new story to life. You may also see that if you don't change how you interact with others in your personal relationships, you will repeat your old emotional patterns, which will play out in several chapters in your life. And you may see that if you don't change an unsatisfying story, you will not feel a sense of purpose or connection to a creative and nurturing Source.

To pursue your sense of purpose, you need to be true to yourself, which is difficult for many people to do. A barrage of media images influences people's perceptions and beliefs. It can be hard to resist taking emotional shortcuts—that is, responding to situations by repeating someone else's response instead of taking the time to determine what you feel you ought to do. In time, you can lose touch with your feelings and beliefs, and lose the ability to say what you truly want to say. When you explore your story, make sure that your responses to it are authentic.

When investigating the various chapters of your current story, look closely at each piece of data to see how it fits in with the others. When examining your story about your health, for example, look at all your body systems. When examining your psychology, look at all of your behavior and moods, including their triggers. When examining your vocations, look at all of your jobs.

Observe the themes that run through individual chapters, as well as the ones that run through more than one chapter. For example, if when examining your psychology, you discover you are not being honest with yourself about your emotions, you might realize that you are also not honest with yourself about your physical habits, your relationship patterns, or your behaviors on the job. Maybe you eat when you are not hungry in order to numb yourself to uncomfortable emotions rather than face them. In your important relationships, such as with a parent or your spouse, perhaps you swallow your discontent rather than expressing your true thoughts or feelings. In your job, you might not speak up and make suggestions for improvements because you feel your opinions and ideas don't have value. Perhaps you are afraid that other people, such as your employer, will see your ideas as valueless. Think about replacing this unsatisfactory theme of repressing your difficult emotions with another one, such as authenticity or confidence.

Take some time to answer the following questions, as they will help you recognize patterns in your life and begin to identify your current story's themes:

- How would you characterize yourself, the central figure in your story? For example, are you kind, generous, or focused on yourself? Are you reserved, withholding of affection, or distracted?
- How much of your story has been influenced by external expectations—from your family, authority figures in your life, and your culture? How much have media messages influenced your story? Are you comfortable with the amount

of influence others have on your story's themes, or do you wish to have more power as the storyteller?

- Have you maintained your current story because you are reluctant to affect another person's story? Who has benefited from your keeping your story the same? What is the payoff for you if you change? What is the payoff if you don't change? Which payoff seems larger?
- What successes have propelled you forward? Have these successes in any way hindered your development into a more well-rounded person?
- Are you content with the amount of time you spend complaining about your life versus the amount of time you spend trying to improve it?
- Do you look for satisfaction by seeking out stimulation and novelty—for instance, through sexual experience, drug and alcohol use, or generating and engaging in dramas in your relationships? How has that worked for you?
- How much stillness, rest, and relaxation do you have in your life? How much of your life is filled with media stimulation or sensory stimulation? Do you get a lot of intellectual stimulation or emotional stimulation? Are you comfortable with the amount and type of stimulation you have in your life? What practices, if any, have helped you balance rest and quiet time for contemplation with stimulation and activity? Have you used those practices regularly? Why or why not?
- Do you ever allow yourself to simply enjoy being present in the moment without having to do anything? Or do you need to fill all of your time with activity? Do you do this to avoid being alone with yourself?
- Are you able to look at yourself honestly and address your weaknesses or flaws without feeling embarrassed or ashamed? Are you too self-critical? Do you have a hard time acknowledging your strengths? If so, why is that?
- Do you feel that you can usually trust other people? What events have shaped your ability to trust others?
- When you consider the areas of your life that you feel aren't working for you, where do you think your problems stem from? Do you feel responsible for creating those problems, or do you feel someone or something else is responsible? Why?
- Do you feel that the benefit of speaking your truth aloud to others is greater than any potentially negative consequences of doing so? What has influenced your feelings about speaking your truth?
- What adjective would you use to describe your life? For example, has it been happy, sad, bittersweet, tragic, or charmed?
- What is the overall theme of each individual chapter of your story? Does each

have a different theme, or do you see the same theme serving as the organizing principle in more than one chapter? Which themes have worked out well for you? Which have not?

- What has been working well for you in your current story, and what hasn't?
- When do you like to be in charge, and when do you like to be told what to do?
- When do you like to be the center of attention, and when do you prefer to stay on the sidelines or in the background?
- Which chapters of your life are marked by feelings of anxiety and fear? Which are marked by anger? Serenity? Joy?
- Do you have clarity about your dreams and goals?
- Is there a particular obstacle that seems to show up in every area of your life?
- When others disagree with your opinion, how do you feel and respond? Are you open to changing your beliefs when presented with new ideas and information?
- Are you interesting to yourself? What would need to change, or what could you do, so that you would be more interesting to yourself?
- Have you resigned yourself to accepting your life as it is rather than daring to make changes? Are you uncomfortable with the compromises you have made?

Beginning to Identify and Work with the Energies That Create Themes

Shamans speak of a soul's journey that contains certain energies that manifest as themes in your life and strongly influence which people, events, and situations become a part of your story. As you'll learn, the concept of an archetypal energy, which comes from Jungian psychology, matches up well with shamanic ideas about energies that influence our stories. While there are many energies that affect us, including gravity and electromagnetism, in this book the focus is on archetypal energies, which serve as themes or organizing principles.

When you use shamanic and Jungian techniques, you can work with archetypal energies, bringing some in or amplifying them and letting go of or reducing the influence of others. These energies may change both in intensity and in how they are expressed in your life. When you begin to minimize the impact of one energy and bring in a new one—for instance, letting go of the energy of the warrior and bringing in the energy of the diplomat—you start to change your story. You may wish to change your story at the level of events, too, hoping to lose weight and gain more physical energy, procure a better job or relationship, or experience less depression or malaise. These tasks are easier when you bring in energies that support your new efforts.

Working collaboratively with the archetypal energies that are affecting you can alter the way you perceive current and past situations, too. For example, perhaps you have been laboring under the archetypal energy of futility, represented in classical Greek mythology by the character Sisyphus, who struggled to roll a large boulder up a mountain only to have it roll back down again every time he nearly reached the summit. This energy may have caused you to miss opportunities and waste your efforts. If you bring in another powerful archetypal energy to supplement it—for example, adventurousness—you will perceive the events of your life differently. The "failed" relationships or job losses will now be a part of an adventure involving risk, daring, and perseverance. When new opportunities arise, fear of being subjected to yet another Sisyphean effort can give way to a sense of excitement as you step into adventurousness and feel confident knowing that you won't give up easily.

You may also wish to change your soul's journey, not because it has become dissatisfying but simply because you have outgrown the old one. Perhaps you no longer wish your primary role to be that of the father who ensures the safety and well-being of his children but rather that of the experienced paternal figure who guides them as part of a story of a journey toward wisdom and balance. Perhaps you have been an advocate for survivors of a particular disease or traumatic experience and now wish to find meaning in a new role or story.

When you identify too strongly with your story, the persona (or mask) you adopt can trap you. A general who is no longer on the battlefield might maintain the energy of the warrior, but if that energy is brought into relationships with a spouse, sons, or daughters, the results can be very dissatisfying. The movie *The Great Santini* with Robert Duvall vividly depicted a man stuck in this type of role. Think about the roles you have taken on as part of your story. Have you held on to them for too long?

Now imagine your story as a journey of the soul, mythic in that it reflects universal themes. How would you summarize it? Is it the story of "the underdog who triumphs over adversity"? The "free-spirited adventurer who became lost and dispirited and then had a revelation that allowed her to reclaim her pluck and her sense of direction"? Is there a simple plotline to your story?

You've identified some of the themes in your life already. Here are some common ones you might have discovered:

- I've been tired most of my life.
- I've had frequent health crises that have sidetracked me.
- People I count on inevitably let me down.
- When things really start to go well, I always sabotage myself.
- I'm more capable than others, but nobody recognizes it.
- I'm less capable than others, and everyone notices it.

- I'm always putting my foot in my mouth and saying or doing the wrong or inappropriate thing.
- Some people were born under a lucky star, but I wasn't.

As you can see, there are many ways to describe the themes of your life. You can talk about them in psychological terms, identify the common emotional experience, or express them metaphorically, borrowing from ancient or current myths. Now think about how you would describe these themes in terms of energy. Are you being influenced by an energy of sabotage, for example, or an energy of blundering?

The questions below will help you to further identify your story's themes, which together make up your soul's journey. As you answer them, once again, think about what type of energy or force is associated with the themes you're identifying. For example, if you perceive yourself as a modern day "comeback kid," you might say that you're being influenced by an energy of reinvention.

- With which figures in popular culture, history, literature, or film do you identify? Why?
- Which labels or roles resonate for you, stirring up feelings of pride and belonging? (examples: mother, father, teacher, or student.)
- With which classic dramatic plots in literature and film do you identify? (examples: the kid from the wrong side of the tracks who wins the girl who is out of his league, the star-crossed lovers Romeo and Juliet, the triumphant underdog, or the lost soul who finds her voice and leaves behind those who prevented her from recognizing and wielding her power.)
- With which great myths (Greek, Roman, Norse, Asian, African, Native American, or other) do you identify? (examples: Prometheus, the Greek Titan who took what was not rightfully his and was endlessly punished, or Achilles, who was a great Greek warrior but whose vulnerability led to his downfall.)
- How have you characterized yourself? For example, are you a winner or loser? A stoic or a complainer? Are you cranky or genial? Are you a warrior or a healer?
- When have you felt most at peace and most comfortable with what you are doing and experiencing?
- When have you felt the most energized, passionate, and excited about your life?
- When have you felt, "This is what I was born to do"?

More Ways to View Your Story

By now, you have worked hard to explore your story and its themes. Even so, there may be parts of your story that you have overlooked or considered unimportant that would give you insights you never had and may even benefit you immensely. You may begin to see the possibilities for changing your present life and your future trajectories that you wouldn't have imagined before.

What follows are various practices to help you delve deeper into understanding your story and explore the many ways to tell it.

Discovering Patterns in Your Timeline

Because you have already considered the various chapters and themes in your life, looking again at the significant events you experienced, laid out in a linear fashion, may trigger new insights about themes and repeating patterns. Revisit the timeline you created. Then, ask yourself the following questions:

- Did you experience a period of freedom and exploration, or a period of anxiety and conformity? If so, when did it occur? What else was happening in your life at the time?
- Are there correlations between certain types of events and problems with your health?
- Were there periods when your mood or attitude changed? What led to those changes? What changes did you experience after your mood or attitude transformed?
- Were there times when you felt closer to Source, and if so, what was happening at those times?
- What types of events felt most significant for you—Losses? Changes?
- What are the themes of your earliest memories? For example, your memories might fall under the themes of "No one was there to nurture or care for me," "I am always at the center of a drama," or perhaps, "I knew that there are winners or losers in life, and I was determined to be a winner at any cost." (Specific childhood memories may remain with us because they encapsulate a theme that has become dominant in our lives.)

  As you identify patterns and connections, start thinking about how you would characterize them according to theme. Pay attention to which themes dominated your life, or chapters of your life, during different periods.

Notice Your Daydreams

Another way to get beneath the dry facts of your current story and start recognizing the themes is to look at the wanderings of your mind. As you imagine scenes in the future, do you see yourself winning, putting other people down, being recognized as superior, or being misunderstood or overlooked? Daydreams, which are often pleasant but which can also be unpleasant, give you glimpses into which aspects of your current story you would like to change and which archetypal energies you would like to bring into your life: that of the hero, the lover, the rescuer, and so on.

Daydreams can also reveal the soul's journey you would like to take. They can help you envision how you will change your story. Be cautious about becoming stuck in daydreams, however. Shamanic journeying can help you to let go of the fear of risk-taking and manifest your most appealing imaginings in your everyday life.

Looking at Your Story Objectively

Sometimes we can be like the proverbial ostrich, burying our heads in the sand, unaware of what's going on in our lives and how we are being perceived by others. Sometimes we don't want to know. We are afraid that others' opinions of us are unfavorable, and we prefer to avoid that painful truth.

A useful exercise is to look at and listen to yourself from time to time as if you were an objective, outside observer. Stand in front of a mirror and note what you see. Who is looking back at you? Your appearance is more than just your physical attributes. It includes how you carry yourself. Be completely honest and see yourself as you are, not as you would like to be seen by others. Complete the thoughts, "This person is a _____ ," "Looking into these eyes, I see _____ ," and "This is the face of a person who _____."

Listen to a recording of your voice (for example, on your voicemail) or watch a video of yourself speaking. Do you like the way you sound? What is the quality of your voice? Are you confident or tentative? Do you sound stiff and uncomfortable, or natural and genuine? Do you speak as if you are being rushed? If so, why is that? Are you lighthearted and humorous, or serious? Make an honest appraisal. Are you speaking to gain the approval of others, or are you speaking in ways that please you and reflect who you truly are?

In stepping back to observe yourself, you may not like some of what you discover. Perhaps you will realize that you feel unseen and unheard, and that you may well *be* unseen and unheard because you present yourself in a timid, apologetic way. Also, you may find it difficult to embrace aspects of yourself that you have been told are unattractive. Most qualities can be either positive or negative, depending on how you look at them. You might perceive assertiveness as aggressiveness, or vice versa. You might look at what you formerly thought of as tactlessness and decide to relabel it as "being refreshingly forthright." Rather than deny the qualities and the themes you discover in your story, embrace them so that you may explore them and learn to integrate them into your life in a positive way.

You can become more objective about your story by recording it on paper or on a recording device and later, reading it or listening to it. You might also record it on a device with video function, where you can see your face as you record your video. Each of these techniques will provide a different narrative experience. Play back the video while "sitting in the director's chair," observing your facial expressions, tone of voice, body language, hesitations, and so on.

The nonjudgmental, observing director sees what the actor can't. As you reread your story, or watch or listen to a recording of you telling it, you may be able to see yourself without the bias of your ego. However, it may be difficult to accept what you are seeing. You might think you are tolerant and loving, but as you listen to yourself, you might realize that you think very negatively about certain individuals, professions, religions, political parties, genders, sexual orientations, races, or people who have a particular economic status. To know yourself and your story requires examining your thoughts, feelings, and ways of relating with an objective eye, which requires self-compassion. Otherwise, it is easy to slip into denial. Feelings, thoughts, and responses such as defensiveness, fear of ridicule, a belief in one's inadequacy, or anxiety about social status are commonly hidden from the conscious mind by the ego, which does not like to accept them. However, once these are brought to the surface, you can make conscious decisions about what to do with them.

Imagine Others' Perspectives

Use your imagination to tell your story from the perspectives of others. If your son or daughter had to write a short biography and description of you, what would it say? What would your closest friend write about you? Write a paragraph or two from the viewpoint of people who are or have been important in your life. Think about what the following people would say when asked to describe who you are and what your story is:

- Your mother
- Your father
- Your siblings
- Your children
- Your romantic partner
- A former romantic partner with whom you had a bad breakup
- A good friend
- An estranged friend

- A mentor
- Source

Afterward, ask yourself whether you have gained any insights into your story. Why do you think you either did not see these aspects of your story, or you considered them unimportant? As you review the paragraphs you've written, consider how much of your story has been influenced by your parents' expectations, authority figures you have encountered, other people in your life, and the culture in which you live.

Once again, review what you have written, looking not only for facts but also for themes, metaphors, and organizing principles. Where are your attention and energy going? What aspects of your health and body are you focused on? Which relationships are you putting energy into? Are the everyday situations you find yourself in blinding you to the big picture of your life?

EPHEMERA AND ETERNITY

Against life's backdrop
buildings, objects, things, people come and eventually, go
Ideas, ideals last longer
but they too disappear.
Ozymandias poignantly poised
dissolves into the sands of time.
Only love endures forever
Source's essence.

Use Creative Representations

You can gain a fresh perspective on your life and more easily see its themes if you express your story by using art and poetry, which engage both the rational and nonrational aspects of your brain. If your life story were a color or shape, what would it be? Have you experienced a "blue period" or a "rose period"? If your story were a dance, what would the choreography look like?

How does your current story smell, taste, and feel? What animal best symbolizes your overall story? What animals best symbolize individual chapters, such as your health or your relationships? What images come to mind when you think about your relationship to Source, or your work and career? What songs, melodies, or rhythms do you hear when you think about your emotional temperament or moods, or how you are of service to others? Is the music that represents your life mystical or aggressive? What is your theme song?

In addition to letting your unconscious mind deliver to you images and ideas that reflect the nature of your experiences, you can work with artists' tools to depict your life. With pen and paper, write a poem that describes your current life or an aspect of your story. Draw or paint a picture of your life. You might also write a song that describes your soul's journey. Working with images in your mind or through art will help you to gain additional insights into your story.

Identifying Metaphors

After you have worked through the exercises described above and begun to identify the themes in your story and the symbols that encapsulate them, take a closer look at the symbols you have discovered. What is their metaphorical significance? If an image of an animal came to you when you were contemplating some aspect of your story—such as how you interact with others, perhaps—what does it signify? If when contemplating your career, the image that comes to mind is a stagnant pool, what does that tell you? Are you "on top of the world" when it comes to your health but "down in the valley" in your relationships? Do you feel like a deer caught in the headlights, or as if you were on a runaway train? Do you feel that you are losing your mind, or dancing like a marionette?

Look, too, at the metaphorical meanings behind events and circumstances. Suppose you have diabetes. You might consider how the failure of your pancreas to adequately regulate your blood sugar relates to how you experience the "sweetness" of life. Depending on your specific health conditions, you can ask yourself what is unbalanced, inflamed, congested, stiff, or stagnant in your body and in various aspects of your life. Now is the time to put into words what these symbols, images, and impressions reveal.

Remember, all of us cowrite our stories with the help of Source, and we can always look to Source for guidance in understanding our current story and designing our new one. We can tell our stories in sentences and paragraphs, but Source speaks to us in symbols, feelings, and sometimes, individual words, phrases, or sayings. Source does not write long explanations, and Source doesn't always give us unambiguous directives. To communicate with Source, we must be open to forms of communication that are metaphorical or symbolic. Then we can see the universality in our experiences.

In addition to looking for metaphors in your current story, you can look at the symbols in your dreams and identify their metaphorical meanings. Symbols and metaphors in your dreams can help you realize ways you have adapted to situations and how your unconscious might be pulling you in different directions. Later in this book, I will teach you ways to dialogue with symbols and metaphors. Such dialogues help you recognize the quality of the energy that is attached to an aspect of your story and work with it. For example, you can release the energy of fear that wraps around and infuses your story. Another energy, such as courage or compassion, may take its place, keeping your story alive in you in a new way. You can experience your memories differently.

According to the worldview of the shaman, your relationship to Source and your soul's journey inform all the chapters of your life story. If you are aware of your relationship with Source and the themes of your soul's journey, you can choose to alter them, thereby transforming what happens in the other chapters of your story. Then you are being a conscious storyteller, effectively working with archetypal energies, and you are able to function capably when the inevitable challenges of life arise.

Because you are not the sole storyteller, you must accept that some of the lessons and realizations you gain along your soul's journey will not show up when you expect them to. You can't always know why you have the experiences you do, or why opportunities suddenly seem to dry up, never to reappear.

Once, when I was immersed in a shamanic journey, I came close to the secret of the Holy of Holies. I had a vision in which I was flying, and I looked down and saw a city thousands of years old. I sensed it to be a Mycenaean city, which was characterized by walls and buildings that formed squares inside circles inside squares, like a mandala. As I observed the city from above, I found my awareness being drawn below ground, deeper and deeper, into a place that I knew to be the Holy of Holies. Just before I was to enter it, I became distracted and was suddenly pulled back into ordinary consciousness. When I started to journey again shortly afterward, I found myself outside a chamber that was guarded by the Knights Templar. I knew the chamber contained the secret of the Holy Grail. As I was opening the door, I was distracted a second time, and I returned to ordinary consciousness again. I was tempted to give in to frustration or disappointment. However, I had to accept what had happened. We don't have total control over what we experience when journeying.

Years later, I again encountered the Holy of Holies, and I have learned some of its meanings for me. It is an awareness of our oneness with Source. It is being fully conscious in every moment and recognizing the specialness of our opportunity to experience life as humans: relating, learning, and giving. Experiencing the Holy of Holies was exquisite, and it happened unexpectedly. Source reveals itself in its own good time, when the seeker is ready.

THE VISIT

The Holiest of Holies
not a place but an experience
dreamt of but unknowable until it happens
being in the presence of Source
acknowledged with dignity and respect.

Even one as small in the firmament as I
wanting to honor Source as a guest
and prepare a meal to share
and show my gardens
and my stewardship.

Attaining Closure

As you look at your story, keep in mind that it is not necessary to resolve every troubling issue or emotion. Sometimes, it is best to agree to disagree with someone, or note the existence of a particular mood rather than trying to change or fix it. Attaining closure—that is, letting go of the emotional drama surrounding your issues—is important because it allows you to experience ayni and come to peace with the fact that you can't be perfect. Without closure, your unresolved issues become wounds that can fester, and they will give rise to feelings that perpetuate the cycle of anger, hurt, frustration, and paralysis. Can you imagine that even without curing your tendency to remain silent when you should speak up, or your habit of distracting yourself from uncomfortable circumstances, you can be at peace with your story although it may involve some suffering?

To change your negative feelings about past events and current situations, you need to release your judgments of them. It can be very hard to give up the perception that a wrong has been done to you or someone you care about. You may wish to be forgiving but find it too difficult to get past having been betrayed by a coworker, relative, or former romantic partner. You may wish to let go of all your judgments but find you simply can't do that when it comes to your assessments of certain people, or groups of people who hold beliefs or values that contradict yours.

Of course, there are times when we have to be discerning and set healthy boundaries with others while taking a stand against unethical behaviors. However, we have to beware of making harsh, negative judgments about people and situations.

Relinquishing your habitual ways of acting, thinking, and feeling can be quite a challenge. You may struggle to let go of jealousy, self-importance, power, or possessions. Letting go of your current story can be as painful as experiencing any other loss or death. You might wonder who you will be if you change your behavior. Yet, you must let go to move forward.

It's vital to honor your current story by acknowledging the role it has played in your life. Doing so will allow you to have a sense of closure. Then you can step into a new story, whether or not you have some unresolved issues, because now your emotional agitation will have been quieted. When you make peace with your past, you no longer spend too much time living in it through memories of what was and what might have been.

There is a possibly apocryphal story that in Southeast Asia, people catch monkeys by placing a banana in a box with a hole in the bottom and hanging the box from a tree. The monkey reaches in and grabs the banana but is unable to withdraw its hand. The clenched fist holding the banana is too big to fit through the hole. To escape, all the monkey has to do is release the banana. Sometimes, the monkeys hold on for a long time and are then captured. People, too, often give up their freedom by holding on to things too long. When we let go of that which does not serve us, and recognize how we have trapped ourselves, we can make a new choice and surrender to our best destiny. If we don't let go, Source might take things away from us until we do so.

What baggage in your life could you jettison to gain more peace of mind and freedom of movement? Can you let go of the past that binds you and imagine a future that holds more happiness and tranquility?

HE WHO BINDS HIMSELF TO A JOY
by William Blake

He who binds himself to a joy
Doth the winged life destroy
But he who kisses the joy as it flies
Lives in eternity's sunrise

Remember that each aspect of your current story has, from some perspective, served a purpose. Even if your conscious reflection leads you to wish to change your current story, there is great value in honoring it and the events, situations, and themes that comprise it. Although you can't change your parents, your wounds, or your past experiences, you can change your attachment to your memories and the way they live inside you energetically. You can let go of the banana in the box.

Later, you will learn about two important archetypal energies, death and initiation, that can help you achieve closure with your previous story and step fully into your new one. You'll also learn about ceremonies and rituals you can use to consciously change the energies that have affected you to this point. In the meantime, remember that however painful a particular event or situation was, it may turn out to have awakened you to some vital truth, or sent you in a new direction that will take you to a better place than where you were before. When you can honor a situation for how it served your growth, and when you can allow aspects of it to die, you create conditions for a viable new story to be born.

PEACE

An is-ness
a stillness
a serenity
not disturbed
by regret or worry
Elusive
hard to grasp
requiring acceptance
and lessening of judgment and expectation.

Here are two examples of releasing the past as a result of working with our stories. One person said:

> When I wrote the story of my life to the present day, with segments covering my youth, adolescence, teen years, early adulthood, etc., the details flowed effortlessly and formed a picture that allowed me a view of myself as if I were outside looking in, as a sort of third-party observer. I was the person in the story, but I was reading it as an observer. When I was observing from this vantage point, parts of my life were revealed in ways I'd not seen nor understood before. One story recounted my experience at age 13, when my best friend was burned and horribly disfigured in an accident. As I contemplated that story from an observer's perspective, I learned that my strong empathy for people, as well as an inordinate sense of obligation and responsibility for the happiness and well-being of others, was fueled by the shock and trauma of that experience.
>
> My life of achieving and accumulating brought with it rewards and comforts but also propagated the illusion that happiness and security came in large part from owning things and having enough money in the bank. By age 50, after having it all by this standard, I found that true inner peace and happiness were still missing. By recounting my childhood and teen years, I gained a clearer understanding that my values and goals as an adult were sourced from insecurities formed from my parents' financial struggles and my embarrassment that we had less than others around us. My striving was a means to cover insecurities that didn't need to live in me.
>
> Writing the story and then reading it allowed me to see my life experience from a detached perspective. It showed me how the experiences lived in me

today, and what needed to be honored and what needed to die before I could move on to a new story. It provided insights, raised questions, and uncovered pieces in need of healing. Most importantly, it provided a better understanding of the old story that is essential to the creation of a new story.

The second person described the following experience, which incorporated a practice called dialoguing, which you will learn more about in a later chapter:

> I had written my life story many times before, but I was surprised that something new and different emerged this time—a powerful sense that I had been poisoned in utero by my mother's alcoholism and tobacco use. (I have a congenital heart disorder that has been linked in studies to maternal smoking.) I understood as well that the pneumonia I had developed twice as an infant was an indication that I was fighting for survival from my earliest days.
>
> I thought of a dream figure (Gabriel) I had encountered who was cutting off men's heads. When I dialogued with the figure, I asked him why he was killing so many men. His rejoinder was that he must kill because I would not. I realized, "Of course not! How could I kill? I've fought too hard to survive." Yet, I also understood that I lacked what I had heard described as ruthless compassion—the ability to compassionately observe myself and others with clarity detached from sentimentality. Gabriel had come to give this—and much more—to me, and I would need it to (for starters) kill off the parts of myself that had developed to protect me from the ruthlessness I deeply feared in myself and others.

As you work with your current story, you will gain motivation and objectivity to use in writing a new one. In the next chapter, you will return to the exercises you just completed and begin fashioning a new and better story. Then you will learn how to bring it to life energetically using shamanic and Jungian techniques.

CHAPTER FOUR

Writing a New and Better Story

Now that you have examined your current story, it's time to think about the new story you would like to bring into being. What story would serve you and Source better than your current one does?

When it comes to what constitutes a "good" new story, there are no absolutes. Each of us is unique—we have different personalities, proclivities, and circumstances—so our ideas about what makes a story satisfying will be unique to us. However, a satisfying story usually involves good health, minimal psychological distress, relative calm and equanimity in the face of life's vicissitudes, mutual and satisfying relationships, a job that provides some satisfaction as well as financial benefits, a nourishing connection to a higher power, and opportunities to help others and make a difference in the world to some degree.

To begin writing a new story for yourself, do the exercises in this chapter that you sense might be the most helpful for you at this point. Take your time with them, and if you become stuck and unable to complete an exercise, give yourself a day or two before coming back to it. You can do all of these exercises before beginning to use the shamanic and Jungian techniques in this book, or complete some of them, start to use the techniques regularly, and continue working on the exercises. In fact, the insights and energies you gain as a result of using the techniques in this book may dramatically alter the new story you wish to write.

Before you start to bring your new story to life, make sure it is in synch with the desires of your deepest self. It should incorporate your conscious and unconscious desires, which you will begin to identify as you work with this book. Soon, you will come to understand how very powerful your unconscious longings, feelings, and beliefs are. You will learn ways of drawing them into conscious awareness and ways to heal yourself. Then, there will no longer be a conflict between your conscious and unconscious mind or between your conscious desires and your unconscious desires.

The themes and the events of your life will change in accordance with this new story you write, influenced by the will of Source. Although you are not the sole determiner of the circumstances you find yourself in, you may be surprised by how naturally your circumstances change when you write a new story informed by fresh insights and you alter the energies that are influencing you.

As you work with the exercises in this chapter, let your imagination run free. Don't worry if specific images elude you or you have difficulty envisioning what new situations and people you would like to be a part of your life. Be as general or as specific as you like in designing this story for yourself; just be certain that you are not attached to exactly how and when the story unfolds and are open to input from Source.

Remember, over time, small changes at the margins can add up to major shifts. Be patient with yourself as you work toward bringing your new story into being. It may take multiple experiences with the practices in this book to alter the energies that are determining the themes of your current story.

To begin writing your new story, describe briefly how your story will develop from this moment onward. Suspend your judgment about whether your new story is probable or realistic. This new autobiography should start with the present and stretch into the future. It can be just a few pages long. When you are finished, read it and ponder it. Then, rewrite it in first person if you wrote it in third person, and vice versa, so that "I will speak up when I feel I'm not being respected" might be written as "She will speak up when she feels she's not being respected." In doing this, you may not notice any real differences in the two versions of the story. Then again, there may be some differences that surprise you and that can shed light on what you want to create for yourself and whether you feel able—and entitled—to create it.

Consider this version of your new story to be a first draft. As you work with the exercises, you may embellish it or change it. As the story begins to unfold, you may discover other alterations you would like to make. You are stepping into your power as a storyteller.

Creating a Timeline

Write out a timeline for the future, dividing time into intervals (for example, five-year increments). Start with the present and near future. What do you imagine yourself experiencing in the next five years? What will you be doing 5–10 years from now? What will be the story of your retirement years or "golden" years? What themes will play out during these intervals, and how will they play out? What events do you expect to experience? What do you have to do now to bring about the future events you desire?

Exploring Your Emotional Story

Reflect on the story you wrote in Chapter Three about your emotional experiences and how they continue to affect your life today. The more you become aware of your emotional experiences, the less influence they will have on you. You can reduce the power of your triggers to reactivate past emotions.

Write a new story about how you respond in more effective ways to your emotional triggers. For example, suppose your father habitually compares you unfavorably to one of your brothers, and your customary response has been to feel hurt and exclaim that your father loves your brother more than you. In your new story, you could describe how you could respond with less agitation. You might write, "When my father says, 'Why can't you be more like your brother?' I respond by saying, 'I know you're very proud of him.' I recognize my father's fear that people who do not work for a major corporation in a full-time job will not have security, and I do not take on his fear when he expresses worry that I don't have a job similar to my brother's.'" In this new story, you can spell out both the action you will take as well as the way you will reinterpret and reframe the experience so as to avoid being pulled back into the old behaviors, thought processes, and emotional patterns that no longer serve you.

One way to reduce the hold your past emotional experiences have on you is to explore where a particular emotion resides in your body. Reflect on a particular emotional memory. Notice whether there is a place in your body or in the energy field surrounding your body where you feel it, perhaps as a heavy, dark spot or a sensation of aching, throbbing, or shooting pain. Draw your attention to this area and observe it. Notice whether it changes as you continue to observe it—and notice how it changes. If it does not change, keep your focus on this area. Then, as you inhale, envision that you're drawing in white, healing light. As you exhale, envision sending that healing light to the spot in your body or energy field where you are experiencing the emotion and breaking up, healing, or purifying that area. Repeat until the area changes. Observe how it alters. When the area has been cleared, come back into ordinary awareness.

This technique promotes detachment from your emotionally charged experiences of the past so that habitual, unconscious reactions become less common and less intense. You will more easily handle people and situations that trigger memories of past events that made you feel uncomfortable. You will also be better able to make new better choices in the present moment, free of the influence of your old emotional conditioning.

Writing Individual Chapters

As you did in Chapter Three, expand upon your basic story—this time, however, expand upon the new story that begins in this moment, not the one you have been experiencing until this point. Write the story in chapter form, focusing on the aspects of your life explored earlier. Imagine what your new life looks like.

As with your current story, your new story should have six core chapters:

1. Your health and your attitudes toward your body
2. Your significant relationships
3. Your psychology, including emotional temperament and moods
4. Your employment, work as a homemaker, or, if you are retired, whatever occupies the time that would otherwise be spent working
5. Your relationship to Source, God, or a higher power
6. Your ways of being of service

Begin by writing the chapter on your health and your body. Describe how you will handle such issues as diet, exercise, weight, stress management, illnesses, and any chronic conditions you might have, such as high blood pressure or an autoimmune disorder. Perhaps you have a physical problem and you would like it to affect your story in a different way. How do you treat your body in this new story? What are your feelings toward it? What thoughts about it will you maintain, and which will you discard? Can you accept your body as it is now? Will you be able to accept your body as it ages? Can you maintain the level of health and stamina you have today, or even improve on it?

Write a new chapter about your relationships with parents, siblings, romantic partner, children, friends, and coworkers. What would your relationships be like if you were energized by rather than depleted by them, or if you were more accepting of yourself? What would your friendships be like if you experienced greater balance and reciprocity? What would it look like to have healthier boundaries? Would you like to have fewer expectations of your relationships, or would you like to get more out of them? If your new story includes dealing differently with your feelings about people who are now deceased or otherwise no longer part of your life, describe how you will perceive those relationships from now forward. Remember that this chapter is about you. Don't try to delineate how others will change. You have little or no control over that. You can, however, make new choices about how you relate to others and how you choose to look at your interactions with them.

Write a new chapter about your psychology, including your moods. If you were to experience greater happiness, how would your life look different? What would it be like to have the ability to detach from stressful situations? What would your life be like if you were less judgmental and more accepting of unexpected outcomes?

Write a new chapter about your livelihood. What could you do to have a greater sense of accomplishment or fulfillment? Would you like to change vocations? If you are not able to devote the amount of time you would like to your preferred vocation, can you imagine how you could accept your current situation and work toward spending less time simply making money and more time pursuing the right livelihood for you? How would it feel to go to work to a job that's very different from the one you have now? If you have been a homemaker, or a full-time parent or caretaker, will you continue in that vocation or change it? How might you pursue your new livelihood, given the many responsibilities you now have? If you are retired or unemployed, or will be in the future, how will you spend the time that would otherwise be spent working? How would it feel to wake up and not have a job to go to because you are retired?

Write a new chapter about your relationship to Source, God, a higher power—or however you think of the creative force of the universe. Would you like to expand this relationship? If so, how would you do it? What practices would you engage in regularly? Are there rituals or ceremonies, or particular activities, that would help you to communicate with Source and feel heard, or that would help you hear the voice of Source? What changes would you experience if you expanded your relationship with Source?

Write a new chapter about how you will be of service in the world. What will you do differently? Do you really want to make any changes in this area? Why? How would you like your attitudes about being of service to evolve? Can you imagine simple ways that you could be of service—ways that don't require a great deal of planning or strategizing?

Other chapters you might like to incorporate in your new story could include how you will:

- relate to money
- relate to sexuality
- relate to authority and power
- manage your time
- deal with other aspects of your life that are important for you.

Each change you make in your new story will require that you spend your time differently and prioritize what you value and wish to pursue. Therefore, write an hour-by-hour description of how you would like a day in your new story to unfold. What would happen during the course of a typical workday, or a typical weekend day? Can you see yourself devoting large chunks of time to what you say are your priorities? Can you imagine finding time, even if in small increments, to devote to what matters most to you?

As you did in the previous chapter with your current story, you will engage your new story in different ways. You do this by enlisting both the rational and nonrational parts of yourself to gain insights that will help you to write a new story. Begin by noting the themes, or energies, that would be associated with your new story.

A Mythic Soul's Journey

Your new story can be a mythic soul's journey that incorporates classic, universal themes such as triumph through perseverance, adventurousness reclaimed, or reinvention as a result of reclaiming a quality that has been lost for too long. To identify what patterns and themes you would like as part of your new story, take some time to answer the following questions. There are many, but each can be valuable in helping you dig deeper and discover themes that you will find satisfying.

- What major changes to your story do you desire? How would you categorize these changes thematically?
- How would you characterize yourself as the central figure in this new story? For example, will you be kinder, more generous, or more focused? Will you have healthier boundaries with others?
- How much have the expectations of others, such as your family, influenced the new story you have imagined for yourself? Are you comfortable with how much they have influenced your vision of your future?
- How much have media and cultural images and messages influenced the new story you have imagined for yourself? Are you comfortable with their amount of influence?
- Will your expectations about life and other people remain the same? If not, how will they change? How will your expectations about others influence your new story's themes? For example, if you have expected others to notice you or rescue you, and are adopting a new theme of self-reliance, what are your new expectations about other people and your interactions with them? What sorts of adjustments might you need to make to account for other stories that overlap with yours? For example, if someone you love is living according to a theme of caretaking or being the underappreciated martyr, and you are adopting a new theme of self-reliance, how will that change your interactions with your loved one?
- If in the past you have been reluctant to make changes in your story because you are reluctant to affect another person's story, why are you willing to make them now? Can you commit to your new story despite how it may affect another person? If not, what do you need to do to change your new story or let go of your reluctance?
- What disappointments or hurts from your past do you still have strong

feelings about? What is the advantage to having held on to resentment, disappointment, anger, or regret? What is the disadvantage?

- How will your past successes affect your new story? Will you build on them, and if so, how? Do you feel comfortable letting go of your identification with any past successes so that you might be more open to new pursuits? If not, why not?
- How would you take action in your new story to bring about change? How might you change the habit of complaining instead of taking action? What themes would your actions take? For example, would they fall under the themes of creative problem solving or patient perseverance?
- If in the past you looked for satisfaction by seeking out stimulation and novelty—for instance, through sexual experience, drug and alcohol use, or generating and engaging in dramas in your relationships—will there be dramas around sex, drugs, and relationships in your new story? If not, why not? What will change?
- How much stillness, rest, and relaxation do you want to have in your life? How much media, sensory, intellectual, and emotional stimulation do you desire? Are there any practices you wish to incorporate into your life to help you balance time for rest and contemplation with time for excitement and stimulation?
- In your new story, how will you respond when you become aware of your weaknesses or flaws and how they affect you? How will you respond if you discover strengths you didn't know you had? What themes encapsulate these new ways of responding to your weaknesses and strengths?
- Will you be more trusting or less trusting of others? Why?
- When you have the opportunity to speak your truth aloud to others, will you do so? Why or why not?
- What adjective would you use to describe your life in this new story?
- What is the overall theme of each individual chapter of your new story? Does each have a different theme, or do you see the same theme serving as the organizing principle in more than one chapter?
- What has been working well for you in your current story? How will you make it a part of your new story?
- Will you have more opportunities to be in charge in your new story than you have had in the past? Will there be times when you take a backseat and let others lead or be the center of attention, and times when you won't? When will you step forward and when will you step back?
- Do you have clarity about your dreams and goals?

- Is there a particular obstacle that seems to show up in every area of life that you now feel will no longer stand in your way? Why will it no longer be an obstacle?
- In the future, when others disagree with your opinion, how will you feel and respond? How will you be more open to changing your beliefs when presented with new ideas and information?
- Will you be more interesting to yourself in this new story? If so, why?
- What compromises are you willing to make to live according to your new story? What compromises are you not willing to make?
- In what ways will your attitudes toward earning, saving, and spending money change in your new story? What themes about abundance and finances would you like to bring into your new story?
- How will your connection to Source and your ability to communicate with Source be different in this new story? What themes would describe your relationship to Source in this new story—for instance, is it a give-and-take relationship? Is it characterized by appreciation, or perhaps reverence without fear?
- What other themes and energies come to mind as being important to bringing your new story to life rather than letting it remain merely a wish or daydream?

Tryon Edwards, a 19th-century American theologian and author, said, "Thoughts lead on to purposes; purposes go forth in action; actions form habits; habits decide character; and character fixes our destiny." This quote highlights how we create our stories by focusing our attention on certain things. How have your thoughts shaped your current story? What thoughts would be consistent with your new story? Can you identify a theme or energy that might have a strong, positive influence on your thoughts and thought processes?

The Director's Chair

To bring your new story into better focus and see it in greater detail, you can use the techniques you worked with in the previous chapter: creating and working with timelines, noticing daydreams, looking at your new story objectively, using creative representations of your new story, and imagining others' perspectives. In so doing, you might recognize that you have incorporated long-standing patterns and habitual roles into your new story. If these patterns and roles serve you well, then you might choose to keep them. However, before you solidify your new story, you need to step back from these roles and patterns so you can evaluate them compassionately but clearly. If you decide that some of your patterns and roles don't serve you, then you can make new choices. Remember that your story can have you in its grip, and that your task is to loosen the grip so that you can be free to choose a new story and bring it to life.

Working with Timeline Themes

Look back at the timeline you created. What events did you imagine you would experience in the future? What themes encapsulate those events? What life stages might you experience in the future? What archetypal energies, or themes, do you need to bring into your life in order to live according to your new story? What archetypal energies need to be less influential?

Notice Your Daydreams

Allow yourself to indulge in a daydream you have had before. Has it changed? Think about the themes in your typical daydream. Do you like them? Would you really be happy if this daydream came true? Are your new daydreams different from those in your current story, and if so, why do you think that is? Curiously, many of us would continue to daydream even if we achieved what we say we most desire. Perhaps it's in our nature to always seek novelty and never be completely satisfied!

Now allow yourself to indulge in a daydream based on the new themes, energies, and specific ideas you have chosen to incorporate into your new story. How does it feel to step into this daydream? When you experience the emotions it evokes in you, do you wish to make any changes to it?

Perceiving Your Story Objectively

One exercise for discovering whether your new story will create the feelings you desire is to stand in front of a mirror and affirm the person you are becoming, saying, for example, "This person is becoming _____(fill in the relevant description)," "Looking into these eyes, I see _____," and "This is the face of a person who_____." If you are uncomfortable doing this, try to identify the energies that would help you shift your feelings. For example, allow yourself to believe that you are a person who is becoming appropriately involved with others instead of always taking care of their emotional needs, or that you are looking at the face of a person who does not need to take credit and receive accolades for the important things he does in service to others.

You might also use a video device to record yourself narrating your new story. When you play back the video, be the nonjudgmental, observing director who can see what the actor can't. Set your ego aside and be self-compassionate as you note what you say and how you say it: your tone of voice, facial expressions, hesitance, body language, and so on. Without judgment, note any part of your new story that elicits in you feelings of resentment, frustration, irritation, resistance, fear, or sadness.

As you continue to hone your new story, it will be helpful to know about any conflicts between what you say you want to create and what your unconscious resists. Remember that defensiveness, fear of ridicule, anxiety about social status, and the like are commonly hidden from the conscious mind, which does not like to accept these thoughts and feelings. By bringing in new energy through the use of shamanic and Jungian practices, you can let go of archetypal energies connected with themes such as "the dutiful son who never complains," "the imposter," and the like.

Imagining Others' Perspectives

Now see your new story through the eyes of others. Think about the various people who are or have been important in your life. What comments would the following people make about your new story?

- Your mother
- Your father
- Your siblings
- Your children
- Your romantic partner
- A former romantic partner with whom you had a bad breakup
- A good friend
- An estranged friend
- A mentor
- Source

When you have finished writing about how these significant people would see your new story, ask yourself how you feel about their perspectives on and responses to your new story. Do you feel conflicted, inspired, restricted, or intimidated, for example?

Think about whether you are caught in stories told to you and about you by your parents, friends, and society, which define how you should live your life. These stories may feature themes such as "the golden boy who redeemed the family honor," or "the disloyal daughter who did not devote her life to caring for her parents." You must liberate yourself from unwanted or limiting family and cultural stories and patterns before you can freely choose a new story or pattern. Consider the ways in which your new story is in line with the expectations of others—your parents, society, authority figures—and the ways in which you are choosing to be independent of these influences. Do you imagine your mother telling you that you are being impractical, or your mentor telling you, "That's a terrible idea! It's all wrong for you!"? Can you imagine yourself allowing others to object to your new story without you rejecting it and reverting to the old one? If you imagine them not accepting your new story, imagine what your response to their resistance will be. How will you act in this new story when you feel a lack of support?

Now, consider how your new story would look if it were written by Source. What possibilities might lie before you that you had not considered before? What miracles might manifest as part of your new story?

Using Creative Representations

As you did when writing about your current story, use alternative methods of expression—colors, shapes, images, movement, and sounds—to represent your new story and its chapters. How does your new story look, sound, feel, smell, and taste? By engaging your senses as you think about your new story, you tap into energies that support bringing this story into being. The imagination can actually attract archetypal energies that can help you become more confident and experience healing.

What animal or animals represent your new story and its chapters? What would your new story look like if you expressed it in dance or other physical movement? Draw a picture of your new story. Write a poem or a song that encapsulates it. If you feel your career is a tiny creek that gets lost in the heavy underbrush of a forest, what would you want your career to look like? What comes to your mind's eye? Is it a steadily flowing river with lush banks where people stand admiring your clarity, power, and movement?

What fresh perspectives do you gain when you consider these visual representations of your new story? How are these symbols similar to or different from the ones that represent your current story? Does making these comparisons help you to further develop your new story?

A metaphor or message about what to incorporate into your new story can come to you when you least expect it: listening to and watching the rhythms of waves, or becoming still as you experience the beauty of a loon's call, a foghorn, a far-off train whistle, a sunrise or sunset, a dream, or your imagination. Be open to missives from Source.

You can start to shift various aspects of yourself by changing your metaphors when you speak about yourself and your life. For example, if you habitually tell yourself and others, "I'm always slogging through a quagmire," you can change that internal thought to "I'm swimming through my day." "I'm crazy busy" can become "I am busy and enthusiastic." Think about how these descriptions of your life fuel your current story, and how new metaphorical descriptions might be more appropriate for your new story.

Beginning to Manifest Your New Story

Manifesting your new story begins with action. As I said earlier, changing at the margins is a beginning, but it is only a beginning. By using the techniques in this book, you will actually shift your personal energy field and the trajectory of your future, even as you heal the wounds of your past. Rewriting your story at the level of the mind, or psychology, is only a start, too. As you rewrite it thematically and visualize new myths for yourself, you will be making your new story into a soul's journey that you experience consciously. You can let go of themes such as weariness, betrayal, or inauthenticity. You can bring in themes such as strength, trust, and authenticity. These thematic energies can serve as powerful magnets, drawing in people, opportunities, and situations that reflect those energies. In this way, your new story starts to manifest at the level of the literal: the events that you experience.

As you make small changes around the margins, as I described earlier, pay attention to what feels good about your new story and what doesn't. A story that is working well can be altered as you grow. It is not a rigid template to fit yourself into. Be flexible and open to Source's ideas for your story.

At this moment, you may only have a vague sense of how it will feel to step into your new story. How will you find an outlet for your desire to serve, or begin to reclaim your playful nature? You can never really know how you will react to what is unfamiliar, or what feelings, insights, and desires will arise when you walk a new path. Be creative and open to the surprises that appear when your new story begins to play out.

LETTING GO

The struggle unremitting:
no movement, no resolution.
Suddenly, a letting go
a surrender
to the Source from which all springs.
Not knowing the outcome
but accepting
and trusting in whatever happens.
When do I let go
and you take hold?

Addressing Obstacles to Manifesting Your New Story

To increase your chances of fully living your new story, and reduce the possibility that you will resist transformation, you need to let go of any fears about how people will perceive you. Instead, you must wholeheartedly and unapologetically embrace the true desires of your soul. Practice what I call "ruthless compassion": Let nothing stand in the way of being compassionate toward yourself and accepting your soul's longings. Your self-compassion should be unrelenting and unadulterated by any guilt or shame, so that you can see yourself and others clearly.

When you write or tell your new story, notice whether you perceive any obstacles to bringing it into being. You may consciously or unconsciously feel there has been some payoff to maintaining your current story. While you might not wish to forego this payoff, the price of not changing may be much greater than you are willing to pay. It's easy to forget the high cost of not changing because there is some comfort in the familiarity of the old story. If you practice ruthless compassion for yourself, you begin to see the cost of resisting transformation.

You may notice that making a change in one area of your life causes shifts in other areas of your life that you may or may not like. For example, if you lose weight or become more fit, you may discover you have more energy and feel more confident, but you might also find that friends treat you differently. You may not be comfortable with the latter change, which you might not have anticipated. You could choose to respond by bringing into your life new friends who support your new story: for example, people who socialize around activities and conversations rather than around food. You could also respond by exploring how to change the way you interact with the friends who treat you differently now that you are more health conscious. If you resist acknowledging and addressing the change in your friends' treatment of you, you may find it difficult to maintain the change you have made in your story.

Another obstacle to your new story might be a lack of acceptance and closure with regard to your old story. You have to emotionally detach from the old story and recognize that you did the best you could at the time. However dysfunctional the old story was, you don't want to hold on to guilt or shame that would serve as an obstacle to change. You can let go of the old energies through rituals and ceremonies, which you'll learn more about later in the book.

In addition to difficulty in detaching from your new story, you might find yourself holding too tightly to your conception of how you will get the support you need to bring your new story into being on a particular timetable. As one woman said, "When I most want the answer from Spirit, it doesn't come. I can tell that I'm putting my own desires into what I experience. When I'm tired, not trying too hard, or not expecting anything from Spirit, I am sometimes moved beyond anything I can explain." When she let go of her need to control the process, she was able to receive the resources that helped her move into her new story.

Yet another obstacle that can derail your efforts to live your new story is the desire to be perceived as special—the best friend, best mother, best lover, best business person, and so on. It's common to believe that if you are "the best," or special, it will be easier to get your needs met. Needing to be special may take the form of having to be "number one," receive coveted awards, or achieve fame, prestige, or effusive praise. It may also take the form of needing to be seen as the most victimized or most downtrodden person in the room. It's important to assess the cost of trying to be special. Is your quest to be special obscuring what your true needs are?

If you suspect this theme of having to be special is affecting you, consider the following questions.

- Why is it important for you to be seen as special? If you need to be seen as more beleaguered than others are, what is the payoff to seeing yourself or having others see you that way?
- What would happen if you gave up trying to be special? What would your life look like?
- Close your eyes and pay attention to how you feel when you imagine not having to bear the burden of being "the best" and constantly competing with others to maintain your position. Or, if you need to feel more downtrodden than others are, imagine what it would feel like to be no more or less downtrodden than anyone else is. What do you feel like as you imagine these scenarios?
- What needs would be unmet if you were no longer "special" or striving to be seen as special? What would be the consequences of not meeting those needs? Would there be other ways to meet those needs?

When you no longer need to be special, you gain freedom. You can move forward into experiencing new themes that make for a more satisfying story.

Desires and Obstacles

Do you know what you want? Are you afraid you can't have it? Wanting can be painful because of the fear that desires will never be satisfied. It may be that you don't let yourself acknowledge what you would like to have in your life.

WANTING

The pain of wanting
can fester and kill
when what is wanted
cannot be.
But when the bearer of desire
shines the light of eternity onto the wanting
it transforms into a mirror that reflects the truth
and heals.

If you do know what you want, you have to believe you can acquire it or experience it. Otherwise, you won't recognize opportunities to satisfy your desires or, if you do, you will approach them pessimistically.

Take some time and list some reasons why you think you can't manifest your new story and experience the life you want for yourself. What would stop you? How often do rationalizations such as "I'll do it when I have more time, money, or energy" or "when I retire" or "when the kids go to college" keep you from changing? Could you begin changing at the margins right now, and take yourself out of your comfort zone? Take a step toward doing something big that you have put off until something else happens.

When you consider the obstacles you believe lie in your path, ask yourself whether you might get around them or move through them. Have you been unrealistic in writing your story, and not accounted for limiting factors that can't be overcome? An example of a limiting factor is a physical limitation: A 50-year-old man wanting to run a 100-meter dash in 10 seconds flat is not being realistic about his body's limits. But even limiting factors can be accommodated, and new stories can evolve in spite of them. A 50-year-old man can get in shape and compete in a track meet for people of similar age. He can rewrite the story of "the would-be athlete who disappointed his father and the team" as the story of "the man who persevered in pursuing athletic competition, and enjoyed it because he let go of his need to achieve athletic success to please others."

Check to see how many of your obstacles reside in you and your attitudes, and not in your environment. You can overcome obstacles in many ways. For example, you can almost always find time to do something differently, but you have to recognize that there is more than one way to reach your goal. Do you hold on to beliefs such as "I can't find happiness unless I am in a committed romantic relationship" or "I can't start a new career until I have saved enough for my children to go to college"? What if you could be happy without putting conditions on it and needing something to happen first? What if you could achieve two goals that seem to be mutually exclusive?

You can also let go of any negative, limiting beliefs that are holding you back, such as "I'll never find true love," "No one will ever accept me for who I am," or "My worth is determined by how much money I have." If you choose to be ruthlessly compassionate with yourself, it becomes easier to soften rigid beliefs that serve as obstacles for you, perhaps in more than one chapter of your life. For example, "always the bridesmaid, never the bride" may be a limiting belief that affects not only your relationships but also your vocation. Rid yourself of the belief and you may find new opportunities presenting themselves, and you may experience new responses to those opportunities.

Perceptions can be obstacles, too. The riddle about a goose in a bottle illustrates the power of assumptions. Suppose a baby goose is put inside a bottle, and the goose grows to full size. How can you get the goose out without breaking the bottle?

The answer depends on your concept of the bottle. If you are locked into thinking about the bottle in a certain way, that limits you. If you think of the bottle as a "normal" bottle, the idea of a goose growing up in it and later emerging as an adult is absurd. However, if you think of a huge bottle, perhaps laid on its side, then it's not so impossible to imagine how to get the goose out of it. In the same way, you can imagine new possibilities in your life, and ways to work around obstacles.

Then again, you might be reluctant to embrace opportunities and to live fully. Perhaps you would rather keep alive the dream of possibilities rather than trying them out in the world. You sabotage your journey when you submit to judgments, expectations, and fears that serve as inner obstacles.

JUDGMENT

Judgment's gaze
withers, divides, rigidifies,
contracts life
Acceptance allows
expansion and growth
Ice melting
returns home
to the lake's depth

By releasing preconceptions, judgments, expectations, and fears, you open yourself to new, perhaps yet undreamed of, possibilities. But to bring a new story into being, even with the help of Source, requires effort and discipline. It's necessary to transcend the inertia that can sabotage your efforts to change, particularly as you get older. Experiment intentionally, trying out new ways of feeling and thinking. Reflection opens the door to contemplating new stories. It is possible to let go of your old expectations about how others, and the world, should be, and learn to work with your current reality to make it better.

EXPECTATIONS

Regrets, resentments, and fears
are conceived
when expectations
impregnate what is.

You can waste much time and energy worrying about what might happen and lamenting its potential bleakness. Fear can poison your life and drain you of your vitality. The following story, a Jewish folktale recounted in greater detail in the children's book *Solomon and the Ant: And Other Jewish Folktales* (Boyds Mills Press, 2006), illustrates the poisonous power of fear.

A sultan was choosing between two highly skilled physicians to be his new personal physician. To prove his superiority, the first physician proposed a contest in which each contestant would attempt to poison the other. The one who survived would win the position of court physician. The sultan acquiesced to this scheme, but the second physician demurred, saying that he could not take another's life. Nonetheless, the contest began. The first physician tried various ingenious ways to poison the second, but the second physician consistently counteracted his efforts. The first physician grew weak and ill because his fear of being poisoned led him to avoid eating or drinking. Finally, he snatched a glass of milk the second physician poured for himself, reasoning that it must be safe. The second physician expressed satisfaction that his colleague had finally consumed some nourishment. At that, the first physician became convinced that the milk had been poisoned, and he tried increasingly desperate cures for himself. By morning, he was dead. The sultan asked the second physician what poison he had put in the milk. The second physician replied that the milk had been wholesome. The first physician's fear-based frenzy had caused his heart to give out. Fear was the greatest poison.[5]

FEAR

Fear comes unbidden.
Rapid heartbeats accompany shallow breathing,
sweaty palms.
Fear of the other, nature,
our bodies,
people who can hurt, kill.
Shame, danger, negation.

To start living a new story, we need to let go of fears about what might happen and what roadblocks we will encounter. It is easier to do this when we use shamanic and Jungian techniques and work with information and energies we encounter in transpersonal realms.

Some obstacles to our new story reside in our unconscious and must be discovered, overcome, and perhaps transformed into energy for positive change. Shamanic and Jungian practices help us to look at these hindrances differently. I have always liked the story about a person who, fretfully anticipating what will happen, looks down the road and sees a pack of troubles approaching. Some of the troubles fall by the wayside and some are diverted and go down other roads. The ones that actually get to the worrier might bear little resemblance to those seen from a distance. Rather than feeling like a victim of forces and fates beyond our control and anxiously anticipating what might happen to us, we can start to look at our story differently. Then it becomes easier to make choices that give birth to new, more desirable stories.

It is sometimes a mystery as to when and why we become motivated to make significant changes in our lives. Whenever we decide we need to make a change, we should start by preparing the ground and planting and tending the seeds so that they can emerge when we and Source decide it is time.

Sometimes, major shifts occur after we uncover a profound insight, release a stale energy that has been influencing us for too long, or bring in a new energy that nourishes us and helps us to grow rapidly in the way that sunlight can quickly turn a seedling into a flower. Now that you have done so much seminal work on uncovering your story and sketching out a new one, it is time to familiarize yourself with shamanic practices and begin to use them to change your story.

CHAPTER FIVE

Preparing for Shamanic Practices

S hamanic practices involve working with energies, some of which can be very powerful. Unlike trained and experienced shamans, we are so familiar with being in
everyday consciousness, seeing the world of the senses as the only reality, that we are
usually unaware of these energies. We have to shift our consciousness so that we can
experience and work with the energies that surround and infuse us. Preparing for
shamanic practices involves actions that make that shift possible.

All shamanic work opens you up to what is hidden in your unconscious mind, a
mind that is intermingled with the larger, collective mind that we share with Source.
You must reduce the frenetic activity of your conscious mind so you can more easily
access what is hidden from your everyday awareness.

Every time you wish to do a shamanic journey (known as "journeying") or do a ritual
or ceremony, prepare for the practices as a shaman would. Start by opening sacred space,
a ritual that signals to Source that you are ready to shift your awareness and perception
and begin consciously interacting with Source, communicating energetically through
symbol, metaphor, feeling, sensation, and so on. Next, you need to cleanse your energetic field so that any heavy, dark, or dense energies clinging to you dissipate. When
your energy field is lighter and your vibration higher, it is easier to communicate with
Source, which is pure energy. Then you should use a simple breathing practice that will
alter your brain wave patterns, reducing your mental chatter. You might also wish to do
this preparatory sequence when dialoguing or working with your dreams.

Let's look at each of these preparatory practices in detail.

Opening Sacred Space

Sacred space can be any space you approach with reverence and designate for working
with transpersonal energies. You are immersed in sacred space at all times because
Source is everywhere, infusing all that exists, but in *opening* sacred space, you inten-

tionally connect to loving and supportive energies and avoid any dark, heavy, dense ones that might prevent you from accessing the information and high-vibrational energy you seek. When you do your shamanic work in sacred space, you are influenced by the timeless realm of infinity, where anything is possible. You operate within the place of eternal new beginnings.[6]

To open sacred space, you ask various aspects of Source for their assistance in the work that you will be doing. Traditionally, you do this by calling in aspects of Source associated with each of the four directions—South, West, North, and East—and from below (Earth) and above (Heaven). Then, after you finish your shamanic work, you will close sacred space, thanking and honoring the energies that have worked with you. By showing these energies respect, you invite them to continue to surround you and protect you from low-vibrational energies that can weigh you down, dampen your mood, or even, according to shamans, cause illness.

The invocation presented below for opening sacred space is derived from Andean mythology and adapted from a version by Alberto Villoldo. Many traditions attribute different energetic and psychological qualities to the four directions, Earth, and Heaven. In the invocation that follows, the South is associated with regeneration and healing our wounds; the West, with moving beyond our fears of death and life and separating from the karma of our families of origin and ancestors, as well as from the energies of past lives; the North, with detaching from habitual roles, seeing time as circular and infinite, and connecting in a conscious way to sacred lineages; and the East, with the world of the future, new possibilities, and bringing new ways of being into the world. Earth is our living Great Mother. She supports us and reminds us that all things on the planet are related and connected. Heaven, Sun, Moon, and Stars also influence and sustain us and, as aspects of the Great Spirit (Source), remind us of the many in the one and the one in the many.

Turn to face the South. Lift your arm, with your palm facing outward, and invoke the South using the words below. Then, turn to face the West, and invoke the powers of this direction. Repeat for the North and East. When calling on Mother Earth, kneel to touch the ground. When calling on Heaven, reach toward the sky.

> *To the winds of the South!*
> *Great serpent, life force,*
> *Come teach me your ways.*
> *Wrap your coils of light around me,*
> *teach me to shed my past the way you shed your skin,*
> *to walk softly on Mother Earth.*
> *Teach me your beauty way.*

To the winds of the West!
Mother jaguar, tracker in the darkness,
Come teach me your ways.
Help me to move beyond fear.
Teach me to metabolize the energies that no longer serve me,
to live impeccably.
Show me the way beyond death.

To the winds of the North!
Hummingbird, great journeyer,
come, teach me your ways.
Help me to drink deeply from the sweet nectar of life.
Help me to find stillness in the midst of my activity.
Grandmothers, grandfathers, ancient ones,
come, and warm your hands by my fire.
Whisper to me in the wind.
I honor you who have come before me,
and you who will come after me, our children's children.

To the winds of the East!
Great eagle, great condor,
come to me from the place of the rising sun.
Teach me your ways.
Help me to view things from different perspectives
and to bring new ways of being into my life.
Keep me under your wing.
Help me to glide with joy on the ever-changing currents of life.
Teach me to fly wing to wing with the Great Spirit.

Mother Earth!
I am here not just for myself but for the healing of all of your children:
the four-legged, the two-legged, the creepy crawlers,
the finned, the furred, and the winged ones,
the stones and the plants,
all my relations.
Thank you for all that you give me, and teach me to be a good steward.

Father Sun, Grandmother Moon, and the Star Nations!
I honor you and ask for your presence and help.
Great Spirit, known by a thousand names
and yet ultimately unknowable.
Thank you for bringing me here
and allowing me to sing the song of life one more day.

Over time, as you become more familiar with opening sacred space, you might find yourself modifying the invocation so that it becomes personal to you. The intent is important, not the words you use. If you are working in a group, use plural rather than singular personal pronouns. Also, let your intuition guide you as you imagine which energies might work with you in sacred space. The energies you choose to invite to participate in your experience might include ascended masters, guardian angels, spirit guides, and totem animals.

Each time you do shamanic work, begin by opening sacred space. When you are finished, close sacred space by facing each direction in turn, as well as Mother Earth and Heaven, and thanking all the energies that have participated in your work.

Cleansing Your Luminous Body

Shamans believe we have a luminous energy body that surrounds and infuses the physical body. What happens in the luminous body affects what happens in the soul, mind, emotions, and physical body. So, after opening sacred space, the next step in preparation is to clear your energy field by cleansing your luminous body.

Sit quietly and focus on your breathing to center yourself. When you exhale, imagine that you are releasing unwanted, heavy energies. When you inhale, imagine that you are drawing in the cleansing energy of creation.

Now visualize your energetic luminous body. You may notice dark or heavy energy somewhere within it—you might see it or sense it in some way. This energy affects your well-being. Clear it away by focusing your intention on it and holding the intent to dissolve it. It will begin to break up and move away from you.

As you visualize the energetic field that surrounds your physical body, you might also sense electromagnetic energy. You might see electrical lines intersecting in a grid surrounding you. However you imagine or visualize them, allow yourself to imagine playing with them. When I have seen broken lines, I have imagined connecting them. You might visualize straightening and calming lines of energy that wiggle and curve if it feels right to do so. Allow your intuition to guide you.

Another way to clear your energy field is to imagine dark or troubling energy draining from your luminous body through a tube at the level of your navel that drains into

Earth, where the energy is used by nature and transformed. Don't be concerned that the energy you are releasing is too dark or negative. Think of it as fuel for a fire—the fire does not care whether the words on the paper feeding it are part of an angry rant or a mathematical treatise. It is all burned impartially.

Alternatively, you might visualize holding a ball of energy between your hands, which you fill with your heavy, unwanted energy. Periodically fling the filled ball onto the ground where Earth and the cosmos can reabsorb and transform it, and start filling a new ball. Repeat until you feel you have let go of all that you need to release.

After you have cleared your field, envision fresh energy from Source filling the places from which you released stagnant, unwanted energy. Observe how it feels to bring this light into your energy field.

You can also use the following guided visualization to cleanse your luminous energy field. You may wish to work with it before embarking on a shamanic journey, or you might simply do it as a cleansing exercise. It was inspired by an experience I had when I was on a small plane flying to a lake in northern Wisconsin. It was a very hot day, and the plane was overloaded. During the flight, the propeller on the right side of the plane stopped, and the plane started to lose altitude. While I was pondering the possibility of an emergency landing, I spontaneously had the dissolution vision that follows. Afterward, I became aware of my surroundings again, and I felt purified. The plane was dropping lower and lower, and the pilot was just able to make it over the trees and land safely at an alternative airport. Since that flight, I have revisited this vision many times. You can use the dissolution visualization below for healing, to cleanse your energy body, and to release stagnant or heavy energies that no longer serve you. This visualization may open you up to new energies and to transpersonal realms.

If you like, record yourself reading this visualization exercise aloud and listen to the recording as you do the exercise rather than rely on your memory. To begin, open sacred space, cleanse your energy field, and focus on your breathing in order to enter non-ordinary reality.

GUIDED VISUALIZATION: DISSOLUTION

Inhale and exhale naturally as you focus on your breath, letting any thoughts that enter your mind fade away unexplored. Open yourself to the dissolution experience, and envision that you are in a cave. You take all of your clothes off and lie down. Moisture dripping from the ceiling has an acidic, corrosive quality that painlessly dissolves all of your flesh, your organs and body systems, and eventually, your skeleton. Your essence and awareness are contained within globules of moisture that roll to the front of the cave.

When the sun comes out, the globules evaporate and rise into the clouds. Your essence and awareness are now high above the ground in the form of water vapor. You feel the wind cleansing you as you move across the sky. You are further purified and cleansed by the sunlight. The water vapor condenses, and your globules of moisture begin to fall from the sky as rain. You become a part of the ocean, which further cleanses and purifies your essence. Then, an ocean wave splashes onto land. You sink into the sand, where you are further nurtured and cleansed by Earth.

Then, another rain washes the sand into the ocean, where you are cleansed again, and then lifted into the air as the water containing you evaporates. You go back into the wind, which, along with the sun, cleanses you. The wind carries you back to the entrance to the cave. There, a flash of lightning reintegrates your physical body. You feel yourself being re-formed. First, your skeleton, and then your organs, and body systems—nervous, endocrine, vascular, and so on—and the rest of your body: all that is necessary to make a human. When you have returned your body to wholeness, the visualization is complete.

Close sacred space when you are finished. And as with any exercise in this book, it's a good idea to think about your experience and write about it in a journal, and come back to it again later to glean any further insights.

Mindful Breathing

The first thing we do in this life is take in a breath, and the last thing we do is let go of our final breath. Despite the fact that we must breathe to survive, we rarely think about this crucial physical act. Mindful breathing is an important part of preparing to use shamanic techniques. It helps us to feel connected to the forces around us. Do mindful breathing after opening sacred space and cleansing your energy field. These practices will help you further shift your consciousness and slow down your thoughts, allowing you to better hear the voice of Source.

As you breathe in, you can imagine bringing in the energy to start fueling your new story and letting go of the energy fueling your current story. Be mindful of the sensation of drawing in and releasing breath. Think of your breathing as an exchange between yourself and the heavens, Earth, and the universe, bringing you in synch with the rhythms of nature and Source. When you are in synch, the energy that surrounds you supports you and makes it easier for you to bring about changes, just as a natural breeze makes it possible for a sail to billow and propel a boat. Before journeying or performing any ritual, close your eyes and focus on the physical sensations of drawing in breath and releasing.

You can also make breathing into a ritual: Imagine what energies you are taking in and which you are releasing, and meditate on how you are connected to all that surrounds you.

One simple breathing ritual is to breathe in for seven counts, hold your breath for seven counts, exhale for seven counts, and hold your breath again for seven counts. Repeat for several cycles. You can change the length of the count as necessary to one that is comfortable for you. You can also use the yogic technique of alternate nostril breathing: Press against the right side of your nose and, slowly and deeply, breathe in through your left nostril. Then press the left side of your nose and slowly exhale through your right nostril. Do this a few times, and then switch sides. Afterward, observe whether using these breathing rituals helps you focus your awareness in the present moment, or helps you feel more connected to energies that can support your new story.

Each of these techniques—opening sacred space, cleansing your luminous field, and doing mindful breathing—should be used whenever you are going to engage in shamanic practices. One of the most basic and important practices to prepare for is journeying, where you will encounter energies and interact with them through a process called dialoguing. Journeying and dialoguing, which you will learn about next, will give you access to the insights and energies that will allow you to make significant changes in your story.

CHAPTER SIX

Journeying and Dialoguing

A shamanic journey involves intentionally suspending your ordinary way of relating to the world in order to travel to transpersonal realms. Although some believe that such journeys are imaginary, I believe they are real. The shamanic view is that they are trips to another dimension or reality that we all can experience—that is, to a transpersonal realm. Here, you can dialogue with whatever you encounter to gain insights (the practice of dialoguing can be used in other contexts as well, as you will learn).

Traditionally, shamans might speak to the mountains or rivers and listen for an answer, but you can extend such communication into a longer dialogue—and have a conversation not just with nature but with symbols, sensations, emotions, and other forms of energy.

Both journeying, which is a core shamanic practice across cultures, and dialoguing, which involves two-way communication with symbols and energies, offer ways to access wisdom, information, and energy that can help you in your everyday life. (In the two chapters that follow this one, you'll discover more about some of the energies you might encounter and work with.) These energies can take different forms but commonly appear as figures or symbols with which you can dialogue. Although the energy and insights you bring back from transpersonal realms can be quite powerful, they will not do the work of transformation for you. You have a responsibility to work with them in your everyday life. That way, your transpersonal experiences will be more than simply interesting; they will actually serve as catalysts for transformation.

Here are one person's comments on journeying:

> Journeying has served as a gateway for me to learn simple truths about the real and essential me. In some regard, the revelations have not been new. That might sound like a contradiction; what I mean is that while we cognitively

"know" things about ourselves, we often don't accept them as the truth. To do so would invite in the responsibility to live in accordance with that truth. Journeying has allowed me to see aspects of myself, to see their undeniable reality. And always, the experience is bathed in a flow of love and compassion. My journeys are accompanied by an inner knowing that Source is present, which makes the journeys more real and the messages more accessible.

The energies and insights accessible in transpersonal realms might be difficult or even impossible to attain in a state of ordinary consciousness. When journeying, you can access and interact with the energy of your unconscious mind. According to Jungian psychology, your unconscious mind contains both your personal unconscious and the collective unconscious. Within the collective unconscious are the prototypes of all ideas, stories, and myths, including that of the sage, who offers wisdom, or the fool, who reveals human folly. The collective unconscious also contains the prototypes of universal experiences, such as water as being a cleansing force and fire being a transformative one. In addition, it includes information that exists outside of linear time: You can encounter knowledge from a past you have not lived and a future that has yet to be.

In transpersonal realms, the past, present, and future exist simultaneously. It's as if you were at a crossroads, looking at cars moving in many different directions. You can see alternative futures for yourself and align yourself with a flow of traffic moving toward where you wish to go, a destiny you wish to experience. You can also take a road to the past and revisit memories that have left you with energetic detritus—feelings of shame, fear, regret, grief, and so on. Rather than simply thinking about and analyzing what goals you would like to make, or what past wounds you would like to heal, you experience the future and past as if they were real today. You can access the energy of future conditions and events, so that you experience what you long to see manifest. In so doing, you actually bring that energy back with you to the present, where it sets you on a new course.

Journeying also allows you to encounter and bring into your personal energy field energies that alter the quality of your memories. Then, they will no longer haunt you. In this way, you change how the past lives inside you. The memory that caused you grief, sorrow, anger, or regret may now also help you to feel courageous, wise, and strong.

The new energies you bring in will serve as organizing principles that change your vibrational energy. As a result, you will no longer feel so compelled to engage in your old, problematic behaviors. It will be easier to make new choices and to take different actions.

SCULPTING

Incarnate yet concealed, quarried but unshaped
my essence yearns to be revealed.
Water erodes
wind flays and polishes
fire cracks and anneals.
Who is the stone carver—is it me or is it life?
I need to select my carving tools with care
be especially gentle with some
and apply them all with love.
My chisel, hammer, and file
must not be too gentle or too harsh:
never seeking fracture, only joyous revelation.
I strive with clear-eyed compassion
to uncover my essence
seeking to understand the meanings
of my layers of defenses
and the machinations of my evasions.
Feelings of being too little, too weak
indulgence in mindless activities and illusory fantasies—
all attempts to elude contradictory insights
and unalloyed reality.
I thank these and other fear-borne mechanisms
as yet unnamed
for their protection
and I free them from indenture.
An eternal essence progressively revealed
as life and volition carve away detritus
accumulated in this and other lifetimes—
layers that are analyzed for meaning
and then let go.
An essence shining, accentuated by the dark,
emancipated at last, yet connected to all.

You can use all of the practices and ideas described herein to help change your story and sculpt a new life for yourself. There is no one correct way to journey and do the practices I describe, and what you will find when journeying is not predetermined.

Although the transpersonal realms are shared by all, your experiences in them will be unique to you. What you discover will be invaluable in birthing and living your new story.

There is no way to journey "incorrectly." One workshop participant, who had experienced journeys several times before, had used shamanic practices often, and thought of himself as a very visual person, had the following experience:

> During a guided journey to the upper world, I saw the top of a tree in a large green field. From there, we were instructed to find a silver thread and follow it upwards. I very easily ascended through a layer of white clouds and found myself above the clouds, with blue sky visible as far as I could see. This image was perfectly clear to my mind's eye. My attempts to ascend on a ladder to higher levels were difficult to envision. I was not able to see any other beings or characteristics of the place that I was seeing, even though other people who were being led on the same journey later reported all sorts of profound encounters with dead relatives and messages they received.
>
> My experience of the upper world journey was frustrating. I felt stupid and inept, believing that others were able to easily journey and experience this work readily, whereas I could not. Why was I so dense and unable to experience what the others had in spite of more years of study and trying? Yet I had definitely seen the blue sky and clouds below me, and I had no other memories of that scene to serve as prompts, nor had I been told that I would arrive above the clouds and see blue sky (that is, I had not been given a hypnotic suggestion). I had to wonder where that image I had experienced came from, even as I was struggling with my own lack of ease in doing the journey work. The realization that I had seen something that didn't simply arise from my fantasy encouraged me to continue trying to pursue this work without personal judgment about the nature or quality of my experience.

Be open to surprises on the journey, and do not let your analytical mind interfere with the experience. As the workshop participant who had difficulty envisioning the upper world said:

> The journey work does not come "naturally" to me. It does not come easily and does not yield consistent, expected results. Nonetheless, my mind's eye has brought me visual images that I can't deny having seen. The images were not memories of things I had seen before. I don't know whether they came simply from my imagination or were true experiences of a transcend-

ent, transpersonal place. However, I have come to trust that I did have an undeniable experience. It was not just daydreaming and fantasy (or I would have cooked up more elaborate mental images, I suppose). And some of the characters I encountered have left me with a sense of awe, gratitude, trust, and encouragement. I have come to believe that these were genuine experiences of other dimensions of reality, which is what I had hoped to discover.

You may experience profound insights and shifts in your energy field very quickly after you begin journeying. Regardless of what you experience in your initial journeys, you will find it most valuable to take your time with this important work and make a habit of journeying. You must journey frequently to become truly proficient at it, and even then, as the workshop participant who did an upper world journey discovered, you may find that some journeys are more difficult than others are.

After any journey, take time to ponder your experiences instead of hurrying to make sense of them. Sit with your newfound knowledge. Consider the meanings, which may be multilayered, and observe what it feels like to have a new organizing principle affecting your life.

A man who started to use journeying and dialoguing to change his story said:

> The power of journey work is that you may introspectively observe who you really are and make connections through a dialogue with various split-off aspects of your personality or dissociated parts of yourself that in ordinary consciousness you would not normally have access to. This form of therapeutic engagement is much more raw and penetrating than just thinking about your values and conflicts, or free-associating to images and thoughts. It is the silent dialogue the soul has with itself.

Dialoguing

One of the most important parts of journeying and all the practices in this book is to dialogue with, and establish a relationship with, various energies you encounter, which can take the form of symbols, sensations, people, animals, or feelings. For example, during a journey, you might dialogue with a symbol that represents for you the energy of adventurousness. When performing a healing ceremony for yourself, you might dialogue with a dark, heavy energy that resides in your energy field and has manifested as an illness or physical ailment. In your mind's eye, you may be able to see the energy taking a specific form, or you may perceive it as a colored light, a heaviness, or a sensation.

How to Dialogue

Dialoguing is a powerful technique for understanding various aspects of the figures you encounter and integrating their energy and wisdom into your energy field. These four questions should be used in every dialogue:

- What message do you have for me?
- What do you want from me?
- Will you give me _____ ? (Fill in your request.)
- What can I do for you?

A successful dialogue involves a conversation between your ego consciousness, which initiates and carries on the dialogue, and the symbol, sensation, figure, or ailment that answers your questions verbally, symbolically, or somatically (for instance, when you ask the figure a question, you may receive the answer in the form of a physical sensation). The dialogue is experienced in the present moment. You do not analyze your experience while you are having it, but it is helpful to reflect upon it afterward. At a later time, you can always begin new dialogues with the symbols, sensations, figures, or ailments if you would like to learn more.

Whenever you are dialoguing, your witness consciousness needs to be active as well. The witness, or observer, is the aspect of your awareness that objectively listens to the dialogue and mediates when necessary. It is the part of you that notices when you are afraid to ask a difficult question or listen to an unsettling answer, and can encourage your ego consciousness to drop its fear and continue dialoguing. Your witness consciousness also is able to glean insights when it partners with your ego consciousness in reflecting on the experience after the conversation is over.

To dialogue, start by asking a question. Then merge your awareness with the figure or image you want information from. Become one with it and let it speak its truth. When it is finished conveying its answer, let your ego consciousness reflect on what the figure or image said. Then your ego consciousness may choose to ask another question of the figure or image with which you are dialoguing, and once again you will merge your awareness with it and let it speak its truth. Shift back and forth between dialoguing and reflecting, and continue the dialogue until it feels complete. You will also need to be able to shift your awareness to your witness consciousness to gain insights that might escape the notice of your ego consciousness. You may wish to journal as you dialogue: As you switch from one section of the dialogue to another, you might write down what was just said or what you just experienced. Alternatively, you can complete the dialogue before journaling about it.

When your dialogue is finished, thank that with which you were dialoguing. Afterward, informed by the dialogue and input from your witnessing consciousness, you can better decide whether to make changes.

Another way to dialogue is to use a "working stone," that is, a rock or other physical object that represents the energy or symbol with which you will be working. This technique can help you separate your ego consciousness from the energy itself, identify with the other energy and answer in its voice, and more easily participate in the exchange of questions and answers.

Select a stone for which you have an affinity. Hold it in your hands and sit on a chair across from an empty chair that is facing you.[7] Blow into the stone, imagining that you are transferring into it the energy of the thing with which you wish to dialogue (a symbol, an ailment, and so on). Place the stone on the chair opposite you and ask the first of the four questions, "What message do you have for me?" Then pick up the stone and sit in the other chair, facing the spot where you were sitting previously. Take a breath and merge with the energy of that with which you are dialoguing. Respond to the question as if *you* were the embodiment of the energy—as if you were the animal, the symbol, or the figure. When you as the embodied energy have answered the question your ego consciousness asked, get up and place the stone on the chair where you were just sitting. Return to the other chair—the one where you were sitting when your ego consciousness initiated the dialogue. Ponder the answer and see if other questions occur to you. If so, ask another question and continue this process until you feel satisfied that you have learned what you needed to learn. Don't forget that your objective, witness consciousness is available to you to review what you are experiencing and give you further insights.

If you have trouble becoming one with what you're dialoguing with, imagine what it would be like to become that symbol, figure, or object. For example, if you want to dialogue with a wolf you encountered on a journey or in a dream, imagine how a wolf looks and smells. Look into the wolf's eyes, feel its fur, and examine its mouth and teeth. Observe how it breathes. By imagining the sensations of being next to a wolf, you may find it easier to imagine becoming it—inhabiting it and merging your energy with the wolf's.

When you are finished dialoguing, thank whatever you dialogued with for the conversation. Blow the working stone clean: Imagine dispelling the energy you were working with as you exhale into it, so that it will be clear of the old energy when you use it again.

Now take time to digest what you have learned. Make a record of your dialogue; that way, you won't forget important aspects of it, and you can refer to it later. Then, incorporate into your life the lessons and insights you have gained. And at a later date, dialogue with that energy again. In subsequent conversations, observe whether you and the energy have changed your perspectives. For example, you may feel differently toward the energy, and it may have changed its relationship to you.

When you first begin to dialogue, you may find the process awkward and difficult. Try to suspend your judgment, and don't resist the process just because you have a thought like "I'm just making all of this up." Simply be open to the experience, and you will develop a greater comfort with it. Eventually, you will easily be able to dialogue in your mind with an energy or symbol. Even then, it's useful to periodically use your working stone to see if you gain new perspectives from employing that technique.

Acting on the Guidance You Receive

Whenever you dialogue, listen carefully and be respectful of the energy with which you are conversing. Remember, however, that no one—no person, and no entity or figure you dialogue with—can tell you what you must do. Use discernment in weighing whether or not to follow the guidance you have received. Listen to what your witness consciousness has to say on the matter. If you feel that taking the advice will help you live a life more in keeping with the best destiny for yourself that you and Source can co-create in this lifetime, do so. If it doesn't feel right to you, ask more questions during the exchange, or dialogue with the energy or symbol later. In fact, you can dialogue with it as often as you need for the purpose of receiving valuable insights.

Listen to your witness consciousness, and don't act on advice that doesn't feel right to you even if you feel the message comes directly from Source and must not be questioned. It is possible that you are mistaken about the origin of the message. Even if the directive that makes you extremely uncomfortable does derive from Source, it is important not to be reactive and rush to obey it. You may require more information and energy to follow through on the guidance, and you may have misinterpreted it. When your instincts tell you to slow down and get further information, listen to them.

The energy you encounter and dialogue with always has important information for you to consider and may contain profound wisdom as well, but you may not understand it at first. Note that the information received might come in the form of an image or symbol with which you need to dialogue further to discover the nuances that might not be immediately apparent.

Any resistance you feel may be due to instantly judging the energy and being unwilling to explore its many aspects. You may be afraid that envisioning a new story will force changes on you that you are not ready for. You may not want to hear or face certain truths and may be tempted to short-circuit the process, or dismiss it as not being useful after you have received information or guidance that you don't like. Remember, in dialoguing, you are receiving information that you can choose to use or not use. No external entity or energy is imposing its will upon you, or pushing you to process the information and make changes. You may need time to let go of your resistance and begin exploring what you learned in dialoguing.

Dialogues don't need to be confined to energies you encounter on journeys. A dialogue can also take place between you and any symbol that comes into your consciousness, whether through a dream, a vision or daydream, or a synchronistic experience. Dialogues can take place between you and symptoms of illness, or you and one of your inner selves. You can dialogue with the part of your body that is experiencing pain, or the aspect of you that wants to rest and the aspect that wants to get physical exercise.

Dialoguing with Inner Figures

Everyone has inner figures. For example, we all have an inner critic and an inner wise person, an inner mother and inner father, and an inner feminine and inner masculine figure or energy. You are likely to discover inner figures when journeying or dreaming, and you may also simply become aware that they are within you. By dialoguing with inner figures, you can better understand how they affect you. Dialoguing with an inner figure can aid you in coming to know yourself, change your story, be of service, relate differently to Source, and express more kindness, compassion, and peace.

Whenever inner figures appear, engage them and ask them what messages they have for you right now and what they want from you. State what you want from them. Ask what you can do for them. By giving voice to all of your parts, you honor them and hear them, so they don't have to make their presence known covertly. Then, it will be easier to make desired changes and not be so strongly influenced by archetypal energies that you're unaware of.

Sometimes, an inner figure will not answer you. When this happens, it may be because you need to take action and experience something, or change in some way, before you can truly understand the message it holds for you. If you are not sure why you are getting no answer, try dialoguing with the inner figure at another time. Once during a shamanic journey, I encountered a wise inner Carl, who had an ironic sense of humor. I asked him why I had to go through so much turmoil in my life. He merely smiled, offering no response. Later, I invited him to dialogue again further, and our exchange went as follows:

> **CARL:** Why can't you tell me why I have to go through upheaval and drama in my life?
>
> **WISE INNER CARL:** You need to experience life and the transpersonal realms yourself, and draw your own conclusions about what those experiences mean. As you do this, you will realize that you create much of your inner con-

flict by clinging to your judgments and expectations about what should be, rather than accepting situations and people and working more collaboratively with them.

CARL: I hear what you're saying, but it's hard to change my expectations and judgments. What do you mean about working more collaboratively with situations and people?

WISE INNER CARL: You must work collaboratively with them and not force people and situations to conform to what you want them to be. You need to do a better job of being open to input from others and Source and must learn to distinguish between when exerting your will serves the process and when it doesn't.

CARL: It seems I need to learn to be patient and accept that things need to unfold in their own time. Also, I'll need to stop denying what is happening, or trying to make other people behave as I would like them to. Forcing matters often leaves me frustrated, but it's challenging for me to let go of this habit.

WISE INNER CARL: Change is a process. Once you get the hang of interacting with others more collaboratively, and stop trying to force situations, you'll find life getting easier. You will also gain a wider perspective and your problems won't seem so large.

CARL: Thanks for the conversation and your wisdom. I know I will be talking to you in the future, because I'll need time and patience to develop a new habit of being more collaborative and accepting.

WISE INNER CARL: Thank you for the conversation as well. We can talk again.

I don't know why the wise inner Carl did not answer me the first time I made my inquiry, but I knew that in a future dialogue, he might respond again, offering valuable insights. Now, having dialogued with him, I know that the wise inner Carl was trying to get me to recognize that sometimes, I need to simply let events unfold rather than trying to force situations to conform to my expectations or my timetable.

Communication with inner figures is a critical part of birthing new stories. For example, a person with a traumatic past might have many inner figures that are in conflict. One inner figure might want to be "good" and remain silent to avoid attracting any attention, while another inner figure might want to express itself with loud, angry outbursts. When two inner figures are in conflict, dialogue with each, as both will have insights for you. Afterward, you may find that the conflict between these aspects of yourself dissolves or lessens considerably.

When interacting with energies within you, listen thoroughly to them. Be considerate, attempt to understand their viewpoints, and thank them for offering you insights, just as you would with another person. Even though the inner figures live within you, they often have ideas and desires of their own that deserve respect.

Ask yourself whether you have inner figures, or parts of yourself, that are not in harmony. If your answer is yes, engage the figures and ask them how long they have been in conflict. After giving you their insights, they may calm down and come into balance with each other. The part of you that longs to speak up may start to harmonize with the part of you that is rightly concerned about repercussions. In the future, each time you experience something that would previously have sent you into conflict—"Should I protest or remain silent?"—you'll be much clearer on what the right decision is for you in those circumstances.

Sometimes, inner voices can be hostile not just toward each other but toward you. Although it may be difficult for you to listen to them, they need to be heard. You don't have to agree with them, but in dialogue, it is important to communicate why you don't agree and hear what they have to say in response. You may choose to give an especially hostile voice no more airtime until the two of you can reach a way of interacting that is more comfortable for you.

Each of us contains inner figures that seem younger than the wisdom figures we also contain. The younger figures are usually more easily swayed by emotion, while the older wisdom figures have a calm acceptance of life. As you dialogue with them, notice how much older the wiser part seems. Does it feel as if you are speaking with an elder and a child, or a middle-aged person and an adolescent? Ask your younger self what it needs to do to mature. Then visualize the younger figure merging with, or interacting with, the older one. How does that feel? What does that look like?

From time to time, dialogue with these two disparate selves again. Check to see how old the younger part feels now. Does he or she seem more mature? Again, visualize your older and younger selves merging or interacting. How does it feel when this happens? Do you feel more grown up, for example? Growing up does not mean giving up youthful joy and exuberance. It does mean letting go of the moodiness and self-centeredness that sometimes characterizes younger, less mature people.

After you dialogue with an inner figure, thank it and record what was communicated. Think about how you can incorporate into your life the wisdom you attained as a result of the dialogue. Later, check in with yourself to see if your dialogue resulted in your experiencing more peace in your inner and outer relationships.

Dialogue with your inner mother and inner father, too. Ask your inner mother whether there are any qualities of hers that live in you that need to be released, or whose influence needs to be reduced by bringing in new qualities or energies. Then ask her what qualities of hers you need to keep, value, and draw strength from. Say good-bye to her and thank her for helping you. Then dialogue with your inner father and ask the questions of him, thank him, and reflect on the insights you received. Afterward, think about what it would be like to have the conversation with your actual parents—and consider having it with them, and then comparing their responses to that of your inner mother and inner father. One woman said that this exercise helped her "to differentiate between me and my parents, to see them and accept them as they are, to embrace and keep some of their attributes, and to simply let others go."

However, don't try to use the dialoguing process with figures representing actual people, whether it is your parents, your ex-spouse, or anyone else. Shamans believe to do so would be unethical because you might affect the energies of those individuals as well as your own energies. Instead, you might dialogue with an emotion or symbol that represents your relationship with that person or a situation you shared with this individual.

Here is an example of a dialogue with an inner figure that a woman came to understand was the energy of resistance that dwelled within her. The woman had sensed that she had an inner energy that was holding her back from achieving her goals, and she wanted to learn from it. She was surprised to realize that the energy was not only a saboteur but also was very wise. It explained to her how to quiet its voice and minimize its influence on her. The woman was left with the task of integrating the information and energy from her inner resistance.

WOMAN: Who are you? What is your agenda with me? And why is it that no matter what I want to do, I find a way of not doing it?

ENERGY: I am a voice from your past. You have never confronted me to hear my message, so you have left matters unresolved and have not changed.

WOMAN: What is the payoff for me if I don't confront you?

ENERGY: You get the ability to believe you could do something, and you don't risk failure because you don't take chances or fully commit to a course of action. You don't have to be disappointed by the revelation of your true self. You fear that your potential is not as great as you think, and that you don't have the energy, ability, desire, or courage to reach your potential. By not confronting me, you remain safe from disappointment, shame, humiliation, and the knowledge that you are more ordinary than you like to see yourself as.

WOMAN: If so, why do I still have the desire to be creative and do artistic things?

ENERGY: You made superficial changes in your appearance, art, and creativity, but then you stopped changing and resisted true transformation. You only go so far in the direction of who you would like to be because of your fear of disapproval and failure. You have let me get the upper hand. You have the desire to change but not the courage to take risks. Take a leap of faith, acknowledge the good and bad in you, and find a way to equalize yourself with other people—not to feel inferior or superior. If you move forward, you will be less angry. Even if you fail, you will be less likely to blame others for your failings. You will need to face me, and oppose me, if you want to get on with your life and replace me with another voice.

WOMAN: It has been uncomfortable to hear what you said, but I am glad you were honest with me. Thank you for the dialogue.

ENERGY: Thank you for talking to me. I have much wisdom for you.

Although hearing these truths made this woman bristle, she continued with the dialogue anyway and brought back from the experience valuable insights that she was determined to apply to her life. She realized she had chosen to keep her resistance alive so as not to fail, and she had collaborated in her own self-sabotage. Her next challenge was to apply the knowledge she gained and start taking more risks. She understood that future conversations with the energy might help her further.

It will be your responsibility to apply to your story any insights you gain as a result of using the techniques in this book. After a journey in which the importance of play came up for her, a woman dialogued with Source about "play." Here is what she learned, and how she acted upon the insight she attained:

In a dialogue with Source, I was led to ask the question, "What do I have to lose if I do not have 'play' in my life?" After waiting in silence for a response from Source, I drew a blank. I couldn't hear or feel or sense anything within me. Then, I realized that there was a blocking force, something that had been holding me as a prisoner. It was as though I had a tiny glimpse of the slave driver called "workaholism" that had been tormenting me all of my life. I got the sense that I had made a pact somewhere in my life, and I could only serve my master as long as I kept "play" at bay.

I felt tremendous sadness in my body—a whole life being deprived of joy through play. As I wept, I had the impulse to fall to the ground, curl up in a fetal position, and sob uncontrollably. I acknowledged this silent menace that had kept me from experiencing play and the joy that it brings.

About a week later, I felt a strong urge to swim in a lake near my home. With much confidence and energy, I donned my bathing suit and leaped into the water. I had not remembered having that much fun since I was a child. Since that time, I have made several visits to the lake during the warm summer months. Each time I play in the water (with no cares of how silly I might look—like a kid with sand all over me), it stimulates great joy within me. I relax, I breathe deep, and I take in the beauty of the sky and the water. I feel at one with myself and my surroundings. It is as though I am reclaiming my inheritance.

This woman realized that she needed to play, but to change her story, she had to act upon the insight she received through her patient dialoguing.

Now that you understand the process of dialoguing, you can use this technique whenever you travel to transpersonal realms and connect with the collective unconscious. You can also dialogue with Source and with the matrix of energy that weaves together everyone and everything in the universe. What you discover—even, perhaps, what you discover on your very first journey—may play a major role in helping you change your story.

CHAPTER SEVEN

Taking Shamanic Journeys

When you decide to begin a shamanic journey, set an intention for it. Where would you like to go? What would you like to learn or gain? Certain realms are more helpful than others for accessing particular insights and energies, as you will see. One man who began a practice of journeying had this insight about setting an intention before journeying:

> The intention attracts the experiences and information that come to me in the process of journeying. I can see clearly that more practice with the method will increase the ease I have in doing it. To see what is being offered requires that I am open to receiving the input. And then, seemingly out of nowhere, a new idea or image appears to me containing information that I can consider. My challenge is how to be strategic and intentional in my inner work in order to access other information when it might be valuable.

During your journeying experience, it's important to be open to the unexpected, regardless of your original intention. The man who learned about setting intention encountered a figure that he was not expecting:

> On a journey to the upper world, I suddenly found myself above the clouds. I looked around for other people and encountered a figure approaching from the distance wearing a brown robe (like Obi-Wan Kenobi in *Star Wars*). As he approached, I asked if he was my teacher. He drew nearer, and I saw Jesus's face under the hood of the robe. Without words exchanged between us, I knew that he was there to teach me as I needed. After the journey was completed, a friend remarked that it seemed strange that a Jewish person should have Jesus appear as a teacher, but I had no problem viewing him that way.

Upon deeper reflection, you may find that what you encounter is far more valuable than you first realized. What seems odd or random might turn out to be a very important symbol or figure in terms of the insights it has to offer you.

As a journeyer, you can travel to many transpersonal realms, including to the place before creation, to the matrix, and to the lower and upper worlds that shamans have described. Each realm you travel to has energies and information that can affect the body, mind, and soul. Journeys to the place before creation can connect you to the primordial energy of the universe, where anything is possible. Journeys to the matrix connect you to the consciousness of all things that have ever been or will be.

When you journey to the lower world, the realm of your past as well as of your as-yet-unexpressed potentials, you can see how energies from your past or your ancestors' pasts live within you today. Such a journey may free you from your wounds and genetic and karmic predispositions. It can also provide you with resources and energy for more fully living in the present. A journey to the upper realm, the place of your becoming, your future, can help you lock into a future destiny—one more pleasing to you and to Source than your current trajectory. Connecting with this alternate destiny can help you to understand what you must do in the present.

A journey is a sacred undertaking. Be open to what you experience, be fully present, and be careful not to impose your ideas upon the images and messages encountered on the journey before you have spent enough time in observation. Don't prematurely attempt to analyze or understand your journeying experiences, and don't give great weight to your initial emotional response. Simply witness what you experience. When you allow your ego to try to control what happens, you can lose the wisdom you encounter on your journey.

During a shamanic journey, a woman saw a mouse and perceived that it was her power animal, that is, a representation of an energy that was affecting her by serving as an organizing principle for her story. The woman was disappointed because she felt that mice are inconsequential and annoying, unlike some more majestic animals. Consequently, she resisted interacting with it and forfeited the information it could have conveyed. If she had dialogued with the mouse, she could have asked it what message it had for her at that moment and why it had appeared at that time. Perhaps the mouse would have told her that while others might overlook her, she possessed the ability to pick up on information that others might miss. Perhaps it could have given her a message about appreciating her quietness or her ability to pay close attention to details and nuances.

A man came across a porcupine while he was journeying and interpreted it to mean that he was prickly, hurt people, and kept them away. Rather than avoid the porcupine, he dialogued with it to learn more about its message for him and discovered it was he

117

who was hurt most by his isolation and defensiveness. However negative your initial reaction to a symbol may be, dialoguing with it can provide you with important insights, so be sure to engage it.

If you become discouraged because nothing seems to happen in the various places where you journey, be gentle with yourself. Everyone I have known has had meaningful experiences when they have been willing to be patient and keep trying.

Two of the energetic realms, the lower world and upper world, have particular figures that serve as guardians, and you should ask their permission before journeying into these realms. If the response is favorable, state your intention for the journey and ask for Source's or the guardian's help and guidance. If the guardian indicates that it is not a good time to journey, dialogue with this figure to find out why, and whether you can do anything to make today an appropriate day for journeying. If at that point the response is still "the time is not right," ask when would be an appropriate time, and don't journey until then. If the guardian tells you not to take the journey, it is only because it is looking out for your best interests, so acquiesce and be patient.

Begin your journey when you are rested. Being tired can interfere with your ability to travel to transpersonal realms. You might wish to experiment with listening to recordings of shamanic drumming or rattling as you journey, and compare the experience to how it feels when you journey in silence.

To begin, open sacred space, cleanse your energy field, and do mindful breathing as explained in Chapter Five. Create an intention about what issues you would like to work on and where you would like to journey. Be open to whatever you will experience there. Close your eyes and breathe deeply. Relax, and then begin.

When you are finished, give thanks for your journey. Close sacred space. Take your time interpreting your experience, and journal about your thoughts and feelings. As you come to understand what you encountered, incorporate into your everyday life any messages you have received or insights you have gained.

The first two journeys you will take, to the Quiet and to the matrix, can easily be done from memory. The others involve more details, actions, and questions, so you may want to record yourself narrating them and play back the recordings while you are journeying to guide you. If you do this, be sure to leave pauses in the spots where symbols, figures, and sensations are likely to arise, allowing plenty of time for the revelation that will occur in the transpersonal realm.

Journey to the Quiet

The Quiet is the place before creation, the realm of unformed potentialities from which an idea emerges, takes form, and is energized. Once when I was on a journey seeking alternative destinies for myself, I suddenly found myself traveling at great speed through a dark tunnel and then through the center of a clear, faceted crystal that felt hard, stable, and pure, like a diamond. From there, I emerged into the Quiet. I find that visualizing this pathway can be helpful. Your experience of the Quiet may be different from mine, but you will know the Quiet by its essence: unconditional love for all beings and all things. The Quiet can be a wonderful balm for the vicissitudes of our lives.

We can never fully know the vastness of the Quiet, the place we come from and will return to someday. We can interact with it and glimpse how we and it are one and the same. We can realize its loving nature and trust in the changes that the Quiet, working together with us, can bring about.

To journey to the Quiet along the same route that I do, set your intent for the journey. Open sacred space, cleanse your energy field, and do mindful breathing. When you are ready, you can begin the journey.

JOURNEY TO THE QUIET

Picture yourself going through a tunnel that leads to a diamond-like crystalline structure. Move through the crystalline structure, sensing your energy body being cleansed as you go. When you exit through the other side, you will emerge into the Quiet, the place before creation. Sense how you feel in the presence of the Quiet. Ask any questions you have, but be sure to include:

- What message do you have for me?
- What do you want from me?
- What can I do for you?
- Will you give me _____ ? (Fill in your request.)
- Is there anything that I need to know that I haven't learned yet while here?

Before leaving, you might also ask the Quiet for help in manifesting your new story.

After your dialogue is complete, thank the energies that interacted with you. When you are ready, come back the same way you went—through the diamond-like crystalline structure and then through the tunnel back to the here and now.

When you have returned to ordinary consciousness, close sacred space. After your encounter with the Quiet, notice whether you feel changed in some way. Journal about your experience with the Quiet.

WHOSE SENSES?

Love's color:
opaque;
sound: impenetrable;
appearance: cloudy;
taste: bittersweet;
touch: gripping;
essence: Quiet.

When one man took this journey, he found that the Quiet's message for him was to be patient and to let life events happen without trying to force them to happen. The Quiet wanted him to learn to be more still so that he would be more open to the Quiet's influence. The man asked for help in becoming still and being more discerning as to the Quiet's voice. The Quiet wanted the man to embrace life more joyfully and to celebrate it.

Here is what one woman had to say about her experiences with the Quiet:

I saw that the Quiet is filled with all of the souls of all of the people and animals and things of the universe. I could see that each soul was unique, and yet each soul overlapped with every other soul, and each soul was simultaneously the center of the universe, which was the stillpoint, or God. So everything has God at the center and at the center of everything is God—and not only at the center but at the edge and within. There is nothing that is without God, and yet God is nothing.

I saw "God" as the collective mind and creativity of all that is in the universe, which means that all within the universe are creating the universe and that all the souls are creating with a "yes." I saw that God is the great "yes," and everything that is not "yes" is not God. And that's where evil comes in.

One time, I was listening to some beautiful music. Without the intention of going to the Quiet, I nevertheless found myself there, and I was suddenly surrounded with the warmth and light of God's love for me. I was overcome.

Many times when I go to the Quiet, I ask the question, "What message do you have for me today?" Without fail, I receive a message I need—a simple, obvious message that makes all the difference for the day. When I anticipate a challenge, I ask, "How can I add value today?" I always receive wisdom in response.

All problems are solved in the Quiet. The Quiet says, "I love you," and I say back, "I love you." The Quiet says it's not important if I am not loved by anybody—even my spouse —it's only important that I love. It only matters that I love.

I have developed a daily practice of going to the Quiet. Every morning before breakfast, I exercise for a half hour or more, and then I meditate. I begin by seeing myself in a beautiful place, usually at the ocean, where I experience the sound, sights, touch, taste, and smell of the ocean, the waves, the wind, the trees, the sand, the sky and all the life forms there. I invite my guides to join me and together, we rise up through a tree into the sky and beyond, through the universe, through a clearing crystal and into the Quiet. I sit in the stillness for a while and then ask, "What message do you have for me?" The answers come from deep within. They are always what I need to hear. They comfort me, inform me, support me, and bring me in touch with a wisdom, insight, love, and mystery I have never known before. Usually, it comes in the form of words, but often in pictures.

This woman had many experiences of the Quiet, and applied the insights she gained to alleviate her anxiety about the pressures she was under as a student:

I was taking a graduate course and experienced a lot of anxiety whenever I started doing the required papers. One day, I felt stuck, so I went to the Quiet to help me calm down and let go. I asked the Quiet, "What message do you have for me?" and I saw a huge, riveted iron gate in front of me. It was so heavy and so big it appeared as if it would never move, but I pushed gently against it, and it opened as easily as if it were the lightest gate in the world. There in front of me was a sky filled with endless small clouds, each representing a person willing to share their wisdom and support and knowledge, so that right in front of me was all that I needed! Then I noticed that the posts holding the gates were free standing, so I could just as easily have gone around the gates to access the same resources! After that meditation, I went back to that place whenever anxiety began, and the rest of the semester went smoothly because I knew I could always have access to whatever I needed.

You can journey to the Quiet any time you like. It will help you achieve healing and feel your energetic connection to the infinite. On subsequent journeys to the Quiet, you don't have to follow my route. You can travel there in whatever way feels most natural to you.

BALM

I'm already dead—
I died a long time ago.
Then who is here pondering?

Triage and good trauma care save the body
but a psyche ravaged by
accusations, indifference, and shame
needs the balm of infinity.

Journey to the Matrix

During a journey that I described earlier in this book, I found myself spontaneously part of the matrix that connects all things. It was a glowing net of connections linking an infinite number of luminous spheres of awareness. Everything that has existed, now exists, and might exist, including rocks, plants, animals, and humans, is part of the matrix, and shares individual consciousness with that of the entire matrix. The matrix arises from the Quiet, and the Quiet interpenetrates the matrix and coexists with it. Both have love as their essence.

The matrix is highly dynamic and contains an ever-expanding amount of information. In every instant, we are all embedded in the matrix. Paradoxically, few of us realize this because of the distractions that come with being incarnated in a physical body.

You can seek particular kinds of healings and experiences from the matrix. For example, you can ask the matrix to give you more of the types of energy you need and remove other types of energy that are not beneficial to you at this time.

To journey to the matrix and experience your connection to it, you can simply decide that this is the experience you want to have and allow your unconscious mind to guide you. However, you may find it helpful to set your intention, open sacred space, cleanse your energy field, do mindful breathing, and follow the instructions here.

JOURNEY TO THE MATRIX

Imagine being surrounded by a luminous, egg-shaped field of energy. Picture this egg-shaped field being connected by energetic lines to an infinite number of other energy fields, each representing an awareness or consciousness. Stay plugged into this interconnected matrix for a while, and then bring your awareness back to the here and now. Sense how you feel. Are you calm, excited, energized, or drained?

You may wish to ask the matrix the same questions you would ask of the Quiet:

- What message do you have for me?
- What do you want from me?
- What can I do for you?
- Will you give me _____? (Fill in your request.)
- Is there anything I need to know that I haven't learned yet while here?

Before leaving, you might also ask the matrix for help in manifesting your new story. Then, return to ordinary consciousness.

Close sacred space when you have finished your journey. Take time to reflect on your experiences and journal about them.

You have the capacity to be transformed by the love within the Quiet and the matrix. When you realize this and allow the transformation, you are likely to change your story in fundamental ways. You can learn to serve others out of joy rather than obligation. In addition, your behavior toward the planet is likely to become more caring. Usually, these changes happen gradually because it takes time to alter engrained habits. If you are lucky, when you start to communicate with transpersonal places such as the Quiet and the matrix, you will find passion for your new story ignited in you so that it becomes impossible for you not to live it.

After you journey, remember to write down your experiences—that way, you can work with them later.

Journey to the Lower World

This journey is commonly called a soul-retrieval journey. It takes you to the lower world, which is the realm of the parts of your soul that have been split off or never fully expressed. It is also the realm of your past lives. This transpersonal realm is the meeting place of your personal unconscious and the collective unconscious described by Carl Jung. The purpose of this journey is to:

- discover parts of your soul that have split off as a result of wounds you have suffered and that have never been fully expressed;
- rewrite contracts that have governed what you have experienced and what choices you have made;
- retrieve energy and information that can help you to bring to life your new, more desirable story.

There are various forms of soul-retrieval journeys. I adapted this version from one I learned from Alberto Villoldo. Like the journey to the upper world, it is a more extensive journey than the ones to the Quiet and the matrix. You may wish to record yourself narrating it and play it back while you are journeying to make it easier to remember where you will go and what you will do once there. As you record the directions, be sure to leave pauses in your narration to allow your unconscious mind to bring forth the energies you will be working with during the experience.

There are a few things you ought to know before using this journey to help you become fully immersed in the experience and prevent your mind from trying to analyze the journey as it is unfolding. First, you will encounter a guardian, or guide, toward the beginning of the journey. He, she, or it may not grant your request to continue to journey. If so, it means that you are not ready to encounter a difficult truth that has been hidden from your conscious mind. Respect the guardian's protectiveness, for it is an aspect of your own mind protecting you from pain. After you do more healing work, you may find that when you take this journey again, the guardian will let you know that you are ready to continue. If the guardian does grant your request, the guardian will serve as your guide throughout the journey.

Be open to how this guardian will appear to you. One woman described her expectations about the guardian, and what she actually encountered, in this way:

Although the shaman I worked with asked me not to anticipate what would happen when taking a lower world journey, how could I not? If someone asks you not to think of pink elephants, what else can you think of? When it was explained that a guardian, or guide, would show up, I knew instinctively who my guide would be. He would be an angel, full of light and truth. His face would radiate love and agelessness. I had it all pictured. I was ready to go. My angel guide and I would go get my soul back.

I closed my eyes. I heard the shaman's rattle. I think I was also tired that day, and I allowed the sound of the rattle to shake away any thoughts and worries of now. As instructed, I waited on the shore of a lagoon for my guide. I was in a different place from what I had pictured when the concept of a guide was explained to me.

My guide slowly walked toward me. She was an old, old, old woman who was short and had a face that was brown and very wrinkled and full of love beyond anything I can explain in words.

As this woman discovered, it's important to be open to the experience and the unexpected way in which it might unfold.

In this journey to the lower world, you will be visiting four chambers: the chambers of wounds, contracts, grace, and treasures. Don't linger too long in the chamber of wounds, identifying with your suffering, or you may become engulfed by your emotions. When you are ready, you and the guardian will move on to the chamber of contracts. There, you will discover and learn about the contracts your soul made before you were born or in this lifetime. Your contract might be revealed in writing, by a voice, in an image, or by a knowing. Note that a soul contract has two parts: what you will do and what you will get. An example is: "I will keep my connections with people superficial in order to avoid getting hurt."

While you are in the chamber of contracts, you will decide whether you want to terminate your current contract and replace it with a new one that would better serve you and Source and support your new story. If so, you'll write your new soul contract and leave it in the chamber. You can always revisit this chamber and rewrite your contract again.

In the third chamber, that of grace, you will meet and interact with a soul part that has never expressed itself or that has split off from you because of an unpleasant or even traumatic experience. The soul part, which might seem beautiful or ugly to you, represents an aspect of yourself that has the capacity to come into being and be useful to you. In retrieving it, you can reclaim its qualities, such as being vulnerable or feeling safe. This soul part may or may not accompany you on the rest of your journey and become incorporated into you and your energy field once again.

Finally, you will visit the chamber of treasures, where you may find a symbol representing a particular insight you can use in your everyday life as a reminder of this lower world journey. You might be able to bring it back with you to ordinary consciousness for help in manifesting your new story. If not, you can dialogue with it to find out why. Perhaps you have to do more work before you are ready to receive that energy or insight.

Finally, you will encounter your power animal and learn what gifts it can offer you from the animal realms of existence. You may or may not bring its energetic gifts back with you, depending upon your and the power animal's readiness.

Create an intention to travel to the lower world and learn something that might help you write a new story. Be open to discovering unhealed wounds, restrictive contracts you've made, and as-yet-untapped resources. When you are ready to begin your journey to the lower world, open sacred space, cleanse your energy field, and do mindful breathing.

JOURNEY TO THE LOWER WORLD

Let your mind bring you to a place in nature that is pleasing to you. It could be a place you are familiar with in your everyday life, or it could be entirely imaginary. From this place, travel down through the soil and bedrock to an underground cavern that has water running through it. Enter the water and let it take you to the shore of an Eden-like garden. Observe your surroundings with all your senses. What types of flowers and other plants do you see? How do they smell? Observe any wildlife that is present. Can you hear birds singing in the trees? Touch the rocks and taste the water.

Become aware of the approach of the guardian of the lower world who will serve as your guide. Notice the guardian's appearance. Ask it if it is a good day for you to journey. If the answer is yes, prepare to journey farther. If the answer is no, ask if there are conditions you could meet that would allow you to continue. If the answer is still no, remain in the garden for a while and rest before returning to ordinary reality the way you came.

If the guardian tells you this is a good day for you to journey, follow it and walk up a path on a hillside that has chambers along its left side. Enter the first, lowest chamber. This is the chamber of wounds, where you will find a wounded, unhealed part of yourself. Observe who and what is there. What does this wounded, unhealed part of yourself look like? Dialogue with it if it feels right to do so. Don't stay too long in this chamber if you feel yourself being overcome by emotion.

You can ask questions of any figures in the chamber if you choose and then, when you are ready to leave, ask the guardian, "Is there anything I need to notice that I haven't observed yet?"

Depart from the chamber of wounds and continue with your guide up the hill to the next chamber, the chamber of contracts. Enter the chamber, look around, and note who and what is there. Do you see, hear, or feel something that tells you that you have a contract you have been honoring in your life? What is that contract? Decide whether you want to terminate this current contract and replace it with a new one that delineates what you will do and what you will receive, and that will better serve you and Source and support your new story. If you wish to write a new contract at this time, do so and leave it in the chamber. You can always revisit this chamber to rewrite your contract. Before you leave, ask the guardian, "Is there anything else I need to observe or learn here?"

Leave the chamber of contracts and go up the hill to the third chamber, the chamber of grace. In this chamber, you will meet a soul part that has not had an opportunity to fully express itself through you. Enter this third chamber and interact with the soul part. Ask what message it has for you, what it wants from you, and what you can do for it. Tell it what you would like from it. Listen carefully for any subtle differences between the message it has for you, what it wants from you, and what you can do for it. What can this soul part tell you about the transition from your previous story to your new story?

If you desire, ask the soul part whether it would like to come with you. If it says yes, but has conditions, dialogue with it to see whether you are willing to meet its conditions. If you don't want the soul part to accompany you, or if it says no, leave it in the chamber. Before you depart, be sure to ask the guardian, "Is there anything else here I need to observe?" Listen for the answer. When you are ready to go, leave the chamber with your guide and the soul part, if it is willing to come with you, and continue up the hillside.

Enter the fourth and last chamber, the chamber of treasures, also called the chamber of gifts. Look for an object that will be a reminder in your daily life of this journey and be helpful in manifesting your new story. As you did with the soul part, ask what message it has for you, what it wants from you, and what you can do for it. Tell it what you would like from it. If you wish, ask the object whether it would like to come with you. If it says yes but has conditions, dialogue with the object to determine whether you can meet its conditions.

If you don't want the object to accompany you, or if it says it won't come with you, leave it there. Ask the guardian whether there is anything else in this chamber that you should notice and dialogue with. Then, if the object you found is willing, bring it with you as you leave the chamber.

Go back down the hill with your guide and whomever or whatever you are bringing with you from the last two chambers. Sit quietly in the garden. Gradually become aware of a presence approaching from behind. It is your power animal. Slowly turn around and look into its eyes. Dialogue with it. Ask what message it has for you, why it has appeared to you, what it wants from you, and what you can do for it. State what you would like to receive from it. Ask how its energy relates to your new story. Then ask it whether it wants to come with you. If it says yes, but has conditions, dialogue with it to see whether you can meet its conditions. If you don't want the power animal to accompany you, or if it says no, leave it there. If the power animal is willing, bring it with you when you leave the garden. Before you leave the garden, ask the guardian, "Is there anything else I need to know?"

Thank the guardian for helping you. You are now ready to return the way you came. If your soul part, the gifts, and the power animal have decided to accompany you, you will bring them back with you as you return to ordinary reality. Go back into the flowing water and allow it to carry you to the cavern. Accompanied by the energies you have brought with you from the lower world, ascend through the rock and soil to the place in nature you started from. Then, return to your physical body and your ordinary consciousness.

After your journey, decide where in your energy field any soul part, gifts, and power animal that accompanied you would best reside. Use your hands to guide these energies to the appropriate places in your own energy field—for example, near your belly or heart, or by your throat. Then, close sacred space.

Think about how you can use the information and symbols you received to help you move forward into your new story. Make a record of your journey so you can remember it and contemplate it further, and be sure to incorporate what you learned into your everyday life.

Each time you take this particular journey, you may have different experiences. You can always come back to dialogue further with what you find in any particular chamber, or to write a new soul contract.

Here is an example of a journey to the lower world in which a man became aware of the place that fear has in his life:

My journey led me first to the chamber of wounds. I expected to find many hurts I had experienced over a lifetime. Instead, I found family and the presence of love and compassion. I was asked, "Why are you here?" and told, "There is nothing here for you except love and compassion." I understood that I could live separate from my wounding experiences.

My next encounter was in the chamber of contracts. I was confronted with an understanding that I live in a noncommittal way. My contract was, in essence, to make no contracts. I learned that fear underlay this reluctance and blocked my way to engaging a new story. Moving forward with a new story would require decisions and commitment. Trust, not fear, would need to be my companion.

I next visited the chamber of grace, where I was greeted by bright light and a sense of love, compassion, and my divine nature. I also sensed that fear was by my side. Fear has been a major obstacle to advancing my path in life. I asked the light to come back with me, and it responded that it would—but I must leave fear behind. I hesitated, unsure whether I could relinquish fear in exchange for pure trust. I asked the light to come with me, but it sensed I was not yet committed to leaving fear behind, so it remained in the chamber.

I moved to the chamber of gifts to find a symbol to take back with me. It was an acorn. It came with a message that I was in transformation. The acorn represented a seed before it transforms into a tree, just as I was metaphorically a seed destined to transform into a new way of being as I entered into a new story.

Lastly, the journey ended with a visit by a power animal. I was approached from behind. When I turned to look, a deer faced me and spoke. It said, "I am peace and serenity. I lie down in green pastures and bathe in the sun. I rest and play. Life feeds me. I am wary, and fear protects me, but it does not dominate me. It does not steal my peace." Then it said, "Come with me. Let peace and serenity dwell within you."

The power of the journey was my becoming aware of the place fear holds in my life. Now I can identify the work that needs to be done so a new story can be created in freedom and in harmony with Source and me.

This man found an absence of wounding in the chamber of wounds, and in the chamber of grace, he encountered no figures but did come across light and a feeling of fear. He didn't do the journey incorrectly; he simply had a different experience of these chambers than others often have. The man's journey was valuable in that it gave him information about how fear fit into his life and energy to fuel important changes—information that came to him in the form of the light and the deer. Remember that your experience of these chambers might be quite different from this man's.

During a woman's journey to the lower world, taken with the intent of coming to peace with the fact that she was aging, a female cobra showed itself to her as her power animal. The woman had the following conversation with her:

> The cobra said, "I have been waiting for you for a long time. I will protect you. I am fearless, and I shed my skin. As you shed your skin, I will guard you and help you to transform fearlessly." Then, I knew it was time to transform my relationships so they don't hold me back—others will still love me even as my roles change. I told the cobra of my fear that I would have to shed my skin of all that I know and of those important to me, and that even though she had told me to be unafraid, I was still frightened. And how could I know that she would protect me?
>
> She said that she was with me right now, and that she would continue to show herself to me. When I asked how it feels to shed your skin, she said that it was freeing, joyful, and fun.
>
> After the journey, I realized that the shawl I was wearing had the image of two snakes on it. Although I had not noticed this design before, I did start to use the shawl when I journeyed and meditated. It had been a gift to me several years ago when I was preparing for a vision quest. I have always felt a sense of being covered, protected, and guarded as I did my spirit work. Later, when I was describing my journey experience to another person, I noticed the skin of a snake hanging on the limb of the large tree I had sat under.
>
> I continue to do my spirit work with my shawl. I often feel the energy of the cobra rise within me, unbidden, at times when I am feeling fearful or in danger. I continue to dialogue with her whenever I feel the need. And I kept the snakeskin as a reminder of her presence and power, and her fearless commitment to transformation.

One woman found her contract in the chamber of contracts to be "I won't get close to people so I won't get hurt." She rewrote her contract to be "I'll be open to close relationships so I can know love." She realized that she would need to develop inner resources so she would be less vulnerable. A man's contract in the chamber of contracts was "I'll try to succeed and gain power so I'll be invulnerable to what others can do to me." His new contract was "I'll do what pleases me and Source, and enjoy the peace and relief that brings." Another woman's contract was "I'll be invisible so I can't be seen and hurt." Her new contract was "I'll learn to protect myself so I can be who I am."

To learn to protect ourselves emotionally—and sometimes, physically—requires developing inner strength as well as inner and outer allies. Source can help us do so. Of course, the transition to new contracts is not always easy, but when we realize the constriction we experience when living according to our old contracts, the promise of expansiveness and freedom provide strong motivation for us to write a new contract and live in accordance with it.

A woman found a cowgirl in the chamber of grace. Here was a part of her soul that was not being fully expressed. The cowgirl told the woman that she needed to take more risks and spend time outdoors. The woman had loved horseback riding as a young girl but had not ridden in years. She realized how much she missed that liberating feeling and decided to nurture the part of herself that was a cowgirl.

Another woman found a ballerina in the chamber of grace. She was struck by the dancer's flexibility and athleticism. After dialoguing, she was reminded that as a consequence of her drive to be successful in the business world, she had become "inflexible," and her athletic prowess had atrophied. As a young girl, she had loved to dance, but she had stopped dancing because she had such a busy life. She vowed to honor and create space for her "inner ballerina."

In the chamber of grace, a doctor saw a young boy sitting under a tree, fishing in a river. The doctor had a conversation with the boy and realized he needed to remember to find time to refresh himself, be patient, and simply be still. The young boy agreed to come back with him, and the doctor pledged to incorporate the lessons of stillness, patience, and being in nature into his busy life.

This experience of seeing your soul part doing something outside in nature is common when visiting the chamber of grace. We seem to yearn to reconnect with nature and those natural parts of ourselves that have been lost.

In the chamber of gifts, a man found a goblet that reminded him of his need to empty some things from his life and fill his life with other things. A woman found a staff, which she knew she could use for support and protection. When you discover an object in the chamber of gifts, try to find a similar object in your everyday world that you can keep near you to remind yourself of its usefulness in changing your story.

Journey to the Upper World

This journey takes you to the upper world, which is the realm of the future and possibility. There are various forms of journeys to the upper world. This particular one I adapted from a version I learned from Alberto Villoldo. By taking journeys to the upper world, also called "the world of our becoming," you are doing destiny work. You are visiting the realms of possibility, where you can discover and connect with a destiny that you find more desirable. Some of these possibilities might be unlikely to manifest in everyday reality unless you identify and energize them. Pondering the following questions might help you to set your intent for a journey to the upper world:

- Do you think you are in touch with your best destiny?
- What new destiny would pull you forward more effortlessly?

To start this journey, you will ascend through a tree and then along a golden thread of light to the guardian of the upper world, with whom you will dialogue to learn if you can continue the journey. If the answer is no, ask if there are conditions you need to meet before being allowed to continue. If the answer is still no, descend the way you came and come back to ordinary reality. If the answer is yes, you will continue to ascend the golden thread until you encounter your celestial parents, with whom you will converse. Then you will travel upward through the realms of stones, plants, and animals, and then through the realm of humans, dolphins, and whales. In each realm, you will observe what is there and how it feels to be in this place. When you reach the realm of humans, dolphins, and whales, you will ascend to the realm of your becoming, where you will receive five objects or symbols, each infused with energy and information that can help you write a new story. You will bring these energies back with you to help you change your story's chapters on your health, your relationships, your vocation, and being of service, as well as to experience your best destiny instead of being tossed around by the winds of fate. In future journeys to the realm of your becoming, you can choose to ask for other symbols or objects that will be helpful to you in birthing these and other chapters in your new story.

Note that each of these upper world realms contains the template for all that ever was, is now, and will be within them. Remember, you can return to these realms again the next time you journey to the upper world and dialogue further with the energies you find there. You can also dialogue with them when you are not journeying in order to garner any insights they might have for you.

Again, because this is a detailed journey, you may wish to record it to play back while you are journeying rather than rely on memorizing all the parts. Begin the journey by opening sacred space, cleansing your energy field, doing mindful breathing, and focusing your intention on visiting the upper world and on what you might learn there.

JOURNEY TO THE UPPER WORLD

When you are relaxed and ready to start, visualize going to a tree that is pleasing to you. This can be a tree you are familiar with in ordinary reality or an imaginal tree. Envision yourself becoming part of the tree's rootedness, sap, limbs, and leaves. Exit through the top of the tree, ascending a luminous thread, and go up and up until you encounter the guardian of the upper world. Ask the guardian if it is a good day for you to journey. If the answer is no, ask if there are conditions you could meet that would allow you to continue. If the answer is still no, remain for a while if you like before returning to ordinary reality the same way you came.

If you are continuing your journey, set your intention to meet your celestial parents—the mother and father energies who have been and will always be with you. If they appear, greet and speak with them. Experience their unconditional love for you, and engage them in conversation. You can share your deepest thoughts and ask them questions. When you are ready to continue on your journey, say good-bye to your celestial parents, and thank them for being part of you.

Continue upward along the luminous thread or cord that travels through the realms of the upper world until you reach the realm of stones. What is it like to experience the awareness and energy of the stones?

Next, ascend along the thread of light to the realm of plants. How is the energy and awareness of the plants different from, and similar to, that of the stones? How does it feel to experience this energy?

When you are ready, travel upward to the realm of the animals. Sense the differences and similarities of the energy and awareness of the animal realm as compared to the realms of the stones and plants.

Ascend to the realm of humans, dolphins, and whales. Feel how this realm is similar to and different from the realms of the stones, plants, and animals. While you are here, take some time, if you wish, to talk with loved ones who have died. Notice a ladder leading upward. Climb it high enough to look out over the horizon and see the realm of your becoming, the realm of possibilities from which everything you experience originates.

Ask the energies of this realm to provide you with a symbol that would help you deal with your health at this time. Look for someone or something that brings you such a symbol or symbolic object. Ask these questions of the symbol or symbol bearer (whichever feels right to you):

- What message do you have for me?
- What do you want from me?
- What can I do for you?
- Will you give me _____ ? (Fill in your request.)

Next, ask for something that would be useful in your relationships. Ask these questions of the symbol or symbol bearer:

- What message do you have for me?
- What do you want from me?
- What can I do for you?
- Will you give me _____ ? (Fill in your request.)

Now, ask for something that will help you in your vocation—whatever it is you do in the world: your career, volunteer work, or homemaking activities. Ask these questions of the symbol or symbol bearer:

- What message do you have for me?
- What do you want from me?
- What can I do for you?
- Will you give me _____ ? (Fill in your request.)

Now, ask for something that would be of use to you in being of service to the world. Ask these questions of the symbol or symbol bearer:

- What message do you have for me?
- What do you want from me?
- What can I do for you?
- Will you give me _____ ? (Fill in your request.)

Now, ask for a symbol that can guide you to a destiny that would be more pleasing to you and to Source. Ask these questions of the symbol or symbol bearer:

- What message do you have for me?
- What do you want from me?

- What can I do for you?
- Will you give me _____ ? (Fill in your request.)

You now have five objects or symbols, each infused with energy. You will bring them back with you to help you change your story's chapters on health, relationships, vocation, and being of service to the world, and to help you achieve a more pleasing destiny for you and Source. Thank the energies that brought the symbols or objects.

Before leaving the upper world, ask it, "Is there anything else that I need to know?" Listen for the answer.

Return to ordinary consciousness the way you came: Descend the ladder to return to the realm of the humans, dolphins, and whales. Find the luminous thread and descend it, going through the realms of the animals, the plants, and the stones. Thank the guardian of the upper world for the journey, and say good-bye for now. Enter the top of the tree, go through the tree, and then separate from it. Come back to the world of everyday experience.

After the journey, use your hands to place the symbols or objects you received into your energy body. Then, close sacred space. Think about how you can use the information and symbols you received to help you move forward into your new story. Make a record of your journey. That way, you won't forget important aspects of it, and you will be able to refer to it later. Incorporate what you learned from this journey into your everyday life. Remember, you can dialogue further with any symbol or figure, using a working stone. Remember, too, that if you encounter a symbol or figure that exists in a transpersonal realm, you can undertake another journey to that realm to see if you can encounter it again and continue your dialogue with it.

Journeys to the upper world can yield many different insights. On a journey to the upper world, a man had the following experience:

I stood in the upper world. At first, it appeared like the Badlands, and then it morphed into a forest before becoming a lake. I stood at the shore looking out over the very large lake, which was surrounded by pine trees. I asked for a gift. Suddenly, it appeared: a kayak. I saw at once that it was strong and of good quality but felt a twinge of disappointment at its bland appearance. But while I gazed at it, the kayak began to darken and gradually become a beautiful red, a bit darker than fire-engine red. I was told it had come to me so that

I might travel swiftly and effortlessly. In return for carrying me to these lands, it told me, it wanted reverence. I wanted from it strength and the ability to go where I am meant to go.

As I stood before the kayak, the significance of the gift began to register, and I knew it was the perfect gift. I felt its presence in me and also began to imagine what it would be like to learn kayaking. When I asked it whether it would return with me, its response was human, emphatic, and full of profound enthusiasm, so intense that it was nearly impossible to put into words.

Symbols can have many interpretations. We bring to them our own understanding, which is influenced by our life experiences, even when they are universal. For this man, pushing past his resistance to explore what the kayak could provide for him allowed him to learn important lessons about traveling effortlessly through life instead of fighting against the currents.

Journey into the Absolute Darkness of Creation

You can use this journey, and the one that follows, to help you gain more experience in going to various transpersonal realms. With practice, your visits to such realms are likely to become more vivid and detailed, and you will be more likely to remember more of your journeys.

Prepare for a journey into the absolute darkness of creation by opening sacred space, cleansing your luminous energy field, and doing mindful breathing. When you are ready, you may begin.

JOURNEY INTO THE ABSOLUTE DARKNESS OF CREATION

Feel yourself falling down, down, down. As you fall, the light dwindles until it disappears. The darkness becomes thicker, and your fall begins to slow. Eventually, you reach a level where you are able to float with no effort. Allow your physical body to dissolve completely into the darkness. What remains of you? Do you find the absolute darkness to be serene or disturbing? Ask the darkness what message it has for you, what it wants from you, and what you can do for it. State what you want from it. Thank the darkness, re-form yourself, and return.

After taking the journey, close sacred space and later, journal about your experiences.

Journey into the Light of Creation

To take a journey into the light of creation, do the usual preparations: Open sacred space, cleanse your energy field, and do mindful breathing. When you are ready, you may begin.

JOURNEY INTO THE LIGHT OF CREATION

Feel yourself fall into a well of the light of creation. The light becomes brighter and more intense the farther you fall. When your fall stops, allow your physical body to dissolve completely into the light. How does that feel? Do you find the light of creation to be invigorating, or harsh and glaring? Ask the light of creation what message it has for you, what it wants from you, and what you can do for it. State what you want from it. Thank the light, allow your physical body to form again, and return.

After your journey, close sacred space. Then, reflect upon and write about your experiences. Compare the experiences of being in the dark and the light.

The journeys to the darkness and light of creation, as well as the other journeys described in this chapter, take you to energetic places that can inform and help manifest your new stories. Keep track of your experiences in these transpersonal realms, and bring them into your everyday life to help you make desired changes in the chapters of your new story.

Journeying will allow you to encounter a variety of energies. It can be helpful to understand some of the most common energies that you can work with, which you will learn about next.

CHAPTER EIGHT

Understanding the Energies
That Influence Your Story

In Chapter One, I alluded to the concept of momentum in perpetuating our life stories—and said that to release your current story and be available to your new story, you have to reduce the momentum of your life as you are now living it. You do this by letting go of the "weight" of your past, releasing the dense emotional energies that no longer serve you, and by slowing down the pace of your life so that you can experience stillness. In that stillness, it is easier to recognize the energies that have been affecting you and to hear the voice of Source guiding you.

The energy of motion that has been driving you forward along a certain trajectory can get converted into stored potential energy when you slow down and reduce the heavy burden of emotions such as anger, fear, disappointment, resentment, and regret. When you are rushing about, reacting to situations without much conscious thought, and feeling out of control, it's difficult to imagine what you might create and to begin writing a new story and bringing it to life. To transition from your current story to your desired new story, you need energy that will bring the new story to life, just as the seed requires a life force and other energies, such as nutrients in the soil, to sprout, become a seedling, and eventually, a flower.

If you don't access a powerful source of energy, it will be very difficult to manifest your new story. Willpower and intention are usually not strong enough to keep you from falling back into the old ways. To rechannel your energy more appropriately and gain fresh energy, you need to let go of situations and perhaps even people who drain you. You also need to relate in new ways to sources of energy outside yourself, such as the energies in nature and the cosmos, and seek healing energy through journeying to transpersonal realms.

There are many types of energy that you can work with. We all have a certain amount of vital energy, or life force, but we can increase the store of energy available to us or decrease it, depending on the choices we make during our lives. We dissipate and drain our energy when we engage in excessive exercise, ruminations, defensiveness, and obsessive behavior. We gain energy when we make healthful lifestyle choices, exercise appropriately, spend time in nature, and connect to the cosmos and to Source using techniques such as journeying. This chapter deals with the archetypes, or universal energies, that affect us.

Archetypal Energy

Humans encounter and experience archetypes within the collective unconscious we all share. They appear in human cultures around the world and across time and are often personified. The hero, the trickster, and the sage are examples. In using shamanic and Jungian practices, you will begin to consciously encounter these archetypal energies that organize how you think, act, and feel.

Archetypal energies are always affecting you, but you may not realize it. What is in your personal unconscious and the collective unconscious is hidden from the conscious mind. Dreams and Freudian slips, or strong feelings such as anger or shame that quickly and fiercely arise in a seemingly innocuous situation, can be signs that universal energies from your personal unconscious and the collective unconscious are active and influencing you. These hidden forces are often so powerful that the conscious mind is very limited in its ability to control them.

Archetypes call forth certain patterns that may be similar to patterns enacted by other humans but are unique to you. You might experience the archetype of the fool as a playful clown, encouraging you to take life less seriously. The same archetype might be experienced by someone else as a cunning and sophisticated court jester who dances on the edge of danger by revealing truth through humor. Your story and your everyday experiences influence how you perceive and are affected by any particular archetypal energy, and vice versa.

Although archetypes influence you, do not overly identify with them, even when you see their effects as positive. If you feel like the sage, recognize that you are not this wise figure all the time, nor should you be. You are meant to experience the many facets of yourself and express a range of universal energies, rather than trying to hold on to an illusion of being the ultimate mother or the perfect hero. The task is to dance consciously with archetypes, leading and following where appropriate.

When circumstances change or we are in a new stage of our lives, we ought to be open to allowing new archetypal energies to influence our stories.

Archetypal energies are in some ways similar to giant ocean waves. The waves are large and powerful enough to crush and drown us. Those who are skillful can learn to ride the waves for a distance and then rest ashore until they are ready to ride again. The wave is impersonal, but it can provide a grand ride if we know how to work with it.

WAVES

The lake's waves roiled
blue and mud-brown intermingled
inexorably moving into shore
and then again, again, again.
Where does the water really come from,
and whence does it return?
Does it learn from each visitation to the shore,
or does it flow mindlessly?

The lake smiles at the question.
"Look at me," she says,
"I repeat my dance of life with exquisite variation.
The sun, the moon, stars, wind, and earth are my partners,
subtly moving with me,
changing and being changed."

The conductor enjoys the dance and orchestration,
never knowing for sure the actual composition.
The birds and other animals move to the music, being fed and feeding.
Humans find their place by dancing
or are swept away by the music of life and submerged.

Fish know how to be in the water.

If we don't work with archetypal energies, our current stories will continue to conform to the old themes that served as organizing principles, such as futility or betrayal. The archetypal energies influencing us will continue to dictate what we will experience in ways that leave us dissatisfied.

Archetypal energies often appear in journeys and in dreams as beings—the representation of the fool or trickster might be a clown, for example. They can also appear as symbolic objects, such as a jack-in-the-box, or as animals. Animals have certain characteristics that, when looked at metaphorically, help us to better understand the many nuances of their archetypal energy. The attributes of jaguar, for example, include not only its peerless hunting abilities but also its scavenging nature—it eats jungle organisms that have died, cleansing the environment and clearing space so that new life can emerge. We can call on the jaguar archetype to aid us in discovering and transforming heavier energies we no longer want to influence our stories.

Whenever you encounter symbols or figures during a journey or in a dream, dialogue with them to learn more about them and how they are influencing you. By being open to the archetypal energies surrounding you, you can become filled with the fuel you need to make new choices that are in accordance with your new story.

The Role of Archetypal Energies in Your Soul's Journey

Earlier, you explored your story and looked at it from many angles. Now, knowing about archetypal energies, you have a new lens through which to view it: as a mythic soul's journey.

Your mythic soul's journey reflects the universal, archetypal energies that have been influencing you, although you may have been unaware of them. These energies can show up in your life again and again, forming patterns or themes. Have you been a *puer aeturnus,* the eternal child who has never grown up? Have you been like Hephaestus, who works long hours and seldom has fun, or Artemis, who is self-sufficient and loves nature, or perhaps Hestia, who cherishes mystery and solitude? If so, you may find that the movies, books, and stories you most relate to, and wrote about in Chapters Three and Four, are modern retellings of mythic tales that illustrate the influence particular archetypal energies have on you. Look closely at any popular fictional character, or narrative about a celebrity, and you will most likely be able to identify a story that matches up with archetypal energies and universal myths. Some of those may have been unconsciously driving your life, making you overly identify with such characters.

By consciously noting which archetypes have been living through you, you can choose to reduce their influence and bring in new archetypal energies that better serve you. Perhaps you long to live the story of Artemis, to be less dependent on others and to feel at home in the outdoors and in your body instead of being cerebral and anxious about what others will think of you. The energy of Artemis or any other archetype can infuse your story and influence its themes if you are willing to invite that energy in and let go of the energies that bind you to your old story.

You can also reduce the influence of certain archetypal energies, or alter how you experience them. There is more than one way to express any particular energy. Perhaps the clown within you would serve you better if its humor were less biting and cynical. Perhaps there is a new way for you to be an eternal youth, or to express the energy of perseverance without it being a Sisyphean perseverance that locks you into futile efforts.

There are many archetypal energies, some of which have been touched upon in this book already, but now you will learn about three major archetypes that are vital for helping you write a new story. They are personas, shadows, and contrasexual energies (the anima, a man's inner feminine energy, and the animus, a woman's inner masculine energy). Archetypal energies such as these can fuel what is known as a complex: a story with themes that is held in the unconscious and triggered by everyday experiences, causing automatic strong, emotional responses that are usually overreactions.[8]

Personas

Carl Jung talked about the masks, or personas (from the Latin word for "mask"), that we all wear from time to time. He considered personas to be archetypal energies.

All of us have many roles we are required to play in our lives. If we are conscious of what we are doing, we can see that it is adaptive to wear different masks in different situations. Our roles as fathers, mothers, sons, daughters, bosses, employees, students, teachers, friends, and lovers might be appropriate for some circumstances but not others.

Sometimes our roles seem to trap us, and we lose sight of who we are apart from the roles with which we identify. In the office in which I do healing work, I have a wooden raven with a mask on its head that I received as a gift. The raven is called "Earth Dancer." According to the story that accompanied the carving, when Earth Dancer first came to Earth, it could use its mask when needed in various situations. Eventually, the mask grew heavy and fused to Earth Dancer. The raven was unable to remove it, and Earth Dancer forgot its true identity. Sometimes, like Earth Dancer, we become too attached to our masks and are weighed down by them. When that happens, we find ourselves unable to take them off to reveal who we truly are. The powerful archetypal energy that formed the mask infuses it, trapping us in the mask and the role it represents. We look in the mirror and see only the persona, not the core self underneath. When this happens, we can turn to techniques that help us loosen or remove our masks, freeing ourselves from the domineering influence of the archetypal energy. Then we can see other possibilities for ourselves.

As you reflect on your story and engage in the practices described in this book, become aware of what roles have become attached to you—and you to them. Question whether they are still serving you and whether you would be better served by assuming new roles that permit greater flexibility. Remember that it is not necessary to actually disengage from all of your roles, only those you overly identify with and allow to dominate you so that you forget who you really are underneath.

You must learn to discern which roles no longer serve you and which of them you unconsciously identify with. By doing this, you ensure that you don't go through life robotically, without awareness. You always have the choice to take on new roles and discard old ones when a mask becomes weighty and unbearable.

Take time now to list all of your roles. Then, answer the following questions:

• Which roles do you adopt most frequently?
• Which of your roles no longer serve you?
• Which of your roles weigh you down?
• Can you relinquish some of your roles? Which ones? How will you do this?

Remember, all roles serve us in some way. If you are discarding a persona, find a way to honor its positive influences on you before you relinquish it. Later, when you have learned about rituals and ceremonies and working with nature, you may decide to use these techniques to honor, then release, the archetypal energy of a persona that is no longer serving you.

After you have reflected on the personas you would like to be liberated from, reflect on any new roles you would like to have in your life. What are they? How would they serve you?

The Shadow

Another archetypal energy is the shadow. The shadow refers to the unconscious parts of ourselves, positive and negative, that we don't consciously acknowledge. Although these shadowy characteristics are hidden from our awareness, shadow energy is very powerful. We expend enormous energy repressing the shadow's qualities, yet they show up in how we think, act, and feel. When this happens, we don't make use of the potentially positive energies these qualities contain.

We are mostly unconscious of our shadow elements because it can be painful to bring them into the light and admit they are part of who we are. Often, we end up projecting our shadow qualities onto others, which distorts our interpersonal relationships. Projection of shadow elements involves seeing in others positive and negative qualities that reside in us but which we disown, whether because we are ashamed of our inner elements or because we don't feel worthy to claim them. For example, we may see ourselves as generous but be unconscious of our withholding nature. We will then be particularly critical of those we see as withholding because that quality resonates with the withholding part of ourselves we deny.

It takes tremendous energy to hold the shadow element in the darkness of our unconscious. By letting it emerge into the light of our awareness, we can work with it and gain its energy for changing our story. For example, if a woman does not accept that she has a competitive aspect, she will struggle to prevent herself from being unduly influenced by this energy. She is likely to be competitive with others in an unbalanced or unhealthy way, and too assertive or not assertive enough. Consequently, she will become enmeshed with people who also have not accepted their own competitiveness and who manifest qualities that complement or mirror her own. She may feel that life always seems to be a battle, and that she always has to best others to get ahead, but will be unable to recognize why this is so.

Any shadow energy has qualities that can be used effectively for our life journeys. At times, we all need to be competitive to achieve what is important, and at other times, we need to be collaborative rather than competitive. Our shadow qualities can influence our new story in positive ways when we stop projecting them or repressing them. For example, you could become competitive in a friendly, playful way instead of fearing your competitive nature or unwittingly expressing it through sabotaging others you see as rivals. You could honor your hardworking nature without it causing you to be a workaholic, or a harsh taskmaster and perfectionist who exhausts other people and is always dissatisfied with your results.

When you gain insight into your shadow, you can make peace with the fact that you have shadow qualities. Once you become conscious of them and begin to work with them, their influence on you will be reduced. If someone implies that you don't take life seriously enough, you can decide whether you are comfortable being flippant in a particular situation. Then, you can make a deliberate choice to draw upon a different energy or continue as you are. You will replace your old habit of denying your behavior, or trying to repress your inclinations so as to please others and feel less shame, with a new, healthier habit of making your decisions thoughtfully and without embarrassment.

To discover and learn more about your shadow qualities, dialogue with any unfamiliar same-sex figures that show up in your dreams and your shamanic journeys. In Jungian psychology, an unknown figure of the same sex is likely to represent a shadow quality of yours (although it's also possible that a familiar figure will represent that quality). Remember, however, that dialoguing with figures that represent living people is not acceptable in shamanic work, although you can dialogue with, for example, a symbol representing your former marriage or the self you were when you were married.

Here is a dialogue a woman who sees herself as confident and strong might have with an unknown female figure she has encountered through shamanic work—a shadow figure who is timid and unsure:

> **WOMAN:** Why did you appear to me? Do you have a message for me?
> **SHADOW WOMAN:** I appeared so I could remind you that even though you say you are sure of yourself, you have doubts.
> **WOMAN:** What kind of doubts?

SHADOW WOMAN: Doubts about whether or not you are competent. You try to appear that way, but you work particularly hard to cover up your feelings of inadequacy.

WOMAN: Maybe that's true, but what can I do about it?

SHADOW WOMAN: Be honest with yourself about what you know and don't know. You will have much more energy if you stop pretending to know everything. People will still appreciate the competent woman that you are, and you'll become more tolerant of the seeming uncertainty of others.

WOMAN: Thank you. I am going to hold on to that insight and think about it. Can I come back and dialogue with you again sometime?

SHADOW WOMAN: Any time you wish, I will be here to dialogue with you.

Notice that in this woman's dialogue, she asked why the shadow woman had appeared—in other words, she asked for a message from her. Then she probed for more details, including advice on what she might do in her everyday life to address her shadow qualities. Finally, she thanked this inner figure, and acknowledged that she might need to come back and dialogue further once she has pondered the insights and begun to make changes in her life. We are not always emotionally ready to hear all that we need to know about our shadow qualities, so it is important to be open to having more than one dialogue with them. Each time, we should ask for insights and practical advice and, before ending the dialogue, thank the figure for helping us.

Dialoguing is an effective way to discover what characteristics and energies are hidden in your shadow. Another way is to have utter honesty and compassion for yourself as you identify some situations in which you thought, acted, and felt differently from how you see yourself. When have you been cowardly, untrustworthy, or foolish? When have you been uncaring, cold, or lazy? Next, list qualities you dislike in others. Which bother you the most? Again, with utter honesty, identify situations in your life when you have exhibited such qualities.

Remember that shadow qualities can be negative or positive. If you are attracted to people who have qualities you wish you had but feel you don't possess, those characteristics may be shadowy for you. List qualities you like in others but don't recognize in yourself. Where do you, in fact, show such qualities? Why is it difficult for you to acknowledge them?

Reflect on how you can become increasingly aware of who you really are and what qualities you have habitually hidden from yourself. Think about what specific steps you can take in your everyday life to recognize and work with your shadow elements, so that you can access their positive aspects and change your story to accommodate your authentic self.

Archetypes can be shadowy as well. You can access the warrior energy so as to stand up for yourself, but you want to express it in ways that are protective of yourself and others rather than controlling, bullying, and predatory. The lover energy can help you to be sensual and seductive in a positive way or in an exploitative way. By remaining aware of the shadowy aspects of the archetypes, you can be alert to those qualities in yourself and be cautious about how you express them or experience them.[9]

Inner Feminine (Anima) and Inner Masculine (Animus)

Every man and every woman has a contrasexual opposite within. Whether or not they are aware of this figure, it influences them. For a man, this contrasexual opposite is his anima: his archetypal inner feminine energy. For a woman, it is her animus: her inner masculine energy. In the same way that we can consciously choose to integrate the shadow aspects of ourselves into everyday life, men can integrate their inner feminine nature and women can integrate their inner masculine nature. This will improve the quality of a person's interactions with members of the opposite sex.

If you are male and you encounter an unknown female figure in your dream or on a journey, it may well be your contrasexual opposite, representing your inner feminine. A woman's inner masculine archetypal energy is likely to show up in her dreams or journeys as an unknown male figure. Sometimes, your contrasexual energy will show up as an opposite sex figure who is familiar, such as an old friend, a sibling, or a teacher.

These inner contrasexual energies don't just appear in dreams or transpersonal realms, however. They also serve as organizing principles for our relationships with the opposite sex in our everyday lives, so their qualities are often reflected in our romantic relationships as well as our friendships and family relationships. If your opposite-sex relationships are problematic, consider the possibility that the qualities of your contrasexual opposite inside of you, and your relationship to your contrasexual opposite, are causing difficulties for you. If you're a man and your inner feminine is pouty and moody, you may find that in your everyday life, a woman whose inner masculine is judgmental and argumentative can be difficult for you to deal with. She is likely to trigger your moodiness while you are likely to trigger her defensiveness and belligerence. All of this happens unconsciously for both of you.

Your lover's characteristics, which initially spark your attraction, can become the very qualities you dislike or resent if you have not done work with your contrasexual opposite. For example, let's say you are a woman who is attracted to a man you see as solid and dependable, the qualities of your contrasexual opposite, while your partner is attracted to you because he sees you as vivacious and lighthearted, qualities of his contrasexual opposite. The unconscious drives the initial attraction you both experience. But when your conscious attitude begins to dominate your perceptions, you may start to wonder, "What did I see in him? He is boring and no fun." And as his conscious attitude takes over his perceptions, he will see your qualities in a negative light and may think you are shallow and flighty.

Your conscious mind, which thinks it likes a particular type of person, needs to be reconciled with your unconscious mind, which may be driving you to choose a different type of person. This reconciliation can be fostered by becoming more aware of, and working with, your contrasexual opposite. Then, you can discover your contrasexual opposite's qualities in yourself and develop them. You will not feel the need to look to others to provide those qualities and complete you. So, for example, if you are looking for a vivacious, lighthearted person, you can develop those qualities in yourself and feel less of a need for a partner who can bring those qualities into your life.

You can have a different relationship to this inner figure—the contrasexual opposite—so that it transforms or has less of a negative effect on your relationships with the opposite sex. To begin changing your relationship to this archetypal energy, you can dialogue with an inner figure that represents your contrasexual opposite. For example, in a dream or on a shamanic journey, a man might encounter a judgmental, critical woman and recognize that his wife, mother, or female friends have these qualities as well. He might have the following dialogue with his inner feminine archetypal energy:

MAN: Why are you so critical of me?

INNER WOMAN: You want me to be. You have never grown up and want me to "keep you in line."

MAN: I really don't want that. I don't want to be the kind of person who has to be constantly criticized in order to find the motivation to change.

INNER WOMAN: I have no investment in criticizing you, but if I don't, you'll have to be your own critic, and make changes on your own. Can you do that?

MAN: I don't know, but I am willing to try. My relationship with you has not been working so well for me. Can you help me grow up and be less sensitive to criticism?

INNER WOMAN: You'll have to do that yourself, but as you grow up, you'll find me less critical.

MAN: If I try to change, will you still be with me and be willing to dialogue further with me? And are you willing to affect me differently?

INNER WOMAN: I will be with you, available for conversation, and I will change—*how* will depend on what comes out of our continuing conversations and your willingness to make actual changes in yourself, our relationship, and your relationships.

MAN: Thank you for the conversation. I look forward to talking to you again.

Notice that the man did not argue with his inner woman, or try to persuade her to have a different opinion. Instead, he listened to what she had to say about his hidden qualities and was open to insights, and he asked her about how he could change himself and his relationship with her.

The qualities of your inner masculine or feminine can vary depending on your experiences: your interactions with the opposite sex (particularly during your formative years), your culture's expectations of men and women, and your family's expectations. Your natural temperament can affect the qualities of your contrasexual opposite as well. For example, if you tend to be anxious, your contrasexual opposite might have a calm quality or an anxious quality, but it is likely to have been affected by your anxious nature. Acknowledging the inner feminine or masculine, and dialoguing with it, can help you learn about this force's influence on you and how you might better relate to your anima or animus in your new story.

If you are a man, describe what aspects of women you like and dislike. Consider the possibility that your inner woman might have aspects of the feminine that you like or dislike. If so, how do you think that has affected you? If you are a woman, describe what aspects of men you like and dislike. Consider the possibility that your inner man might have aspects of the masculine that you like or dislike. If so, how do you think that has affected your perspective, your choices, and your feelings?

If you are a woman, reflect on what "masculine" means to you, and which of those masculine qualities you have. If you are a man, reflect on what "feminine" means to you, and which of those feminine qualities you have. How can you work with the qualities of your contrasexual opposite to write a better story? As you better relate to these energies internally, you will better relate to them externally: Your relationships with people of the opposite sex will improve. You will have a chance to find your beloved and see the essence from which your beloved comes. Even then, you will have to work out your relationship in the crucible of everyday life.

JUST A GUY AND A GAL

Not across a crowded room
but against the backdrop of infinity
their eyes met
They recognized a soul mate

The yearning for completion
infused with the ambrosia
of oneness and dreams realized
Then slowly the hourglass
emptied the illusion, the projections
until all that was left
was another who
snored, annoyed, and
did not meet expectations
Not a toad or a frog but
certainly not a prince or princess
just a guy and a gal

Complexes

Complexes, a concept from Jungian psychology, are stories with themes and characters that live within the unconscious. These complexes are hidden from the conscious mind but nevertheless are charged with energy and ready to flare up like a fire that has had a sudden influx of oxygen. When someone "pushes your buttons," that person is triggering a complex. Your emotional reaction is intense because it is fueled by archetypal energies.

Complexes form as a result of life experiences, usually ones that occurred in childhood. These experiences often involve trauma. For example, if a child is raised by a parent who is neglectful, or is treated abusively by the community for being different in some way, that child may develop a complex. A complex involves stories about what transpired between us and the other people involved in the past events. Our memories of these events, and our conscious awareness of the stories we have wrapped around them, may be limited. We hold on to emotions about what happened in the past—emotions that remain energized within us in part because there is an archetypal quality to the story (or complex).

The theme of a particular story might be "an authoritarian, cruel father mistreats a vulnerable, impotent child." The story includes two characters, the father and child, and perhaps even a third—a rescuer. The archetypal energies of the tyrannical father and helpless child cause the complex to be powerfully triggered whenever we come across a situation that bears any resemblance to the story etched in our unconscious. A brusque, inconsiderate bureaucrat might infuriate one person and make her feel like a disrespected child, unable to fight back against the injustice of the authority figure, while the same bureaucrat might have very little emotional effect on someone else who has no complex about authority figures.

In exploring your story, you will begin to identify themes that may be interwoven with archetypal energies, forming complexes. Jungians say that one way to reduce the effect of your complexes—so that your unconscious, highly charged, emotional responses are much reduced and happen less frequently—is to undergo analysis. In analysis, you experience "transference"—that is, you transfer to the therapist your feelings about your problematic inner figures and are able to work out your conflicts with them through your interactions with the therapist. You also learn more about the complexes and how they get triggered, which gives you more control over them.

Another way to reduce the influence of your complexes may be to dialogue with personas, your shadow self, or inner figures, which you encounter in dreams or when journeying. The dialoguing process helps you to change the energy of your experiences because you are able to more deeply understand them and tolerate your discomfort in uncovering unpleasant, hidden truths about yourself and your past. Whether you use therapy or dialoguing, or both, the goal is to train your conscious mind to recognize situations that are triggering a complex and be able to make a conscious choice about how to respond rather than automatically reacting with strong emotions.

Until you begin taming your complexes, reducing their power over you, they will continue to affect you. You will feel a strong emotional charge, as well as a strong attraction or repulsion, whenever you come across a person or situation that activates one of your complexes. You might even attract such situations unwittingly. In therapy, this is called the repetition compulsion—we find we do the same thing over and over again. It's possible that we veer toward these complex-activating people and situations out of an unconscious desire to experience them differently from how we did in the past. Other people may be attracted to us for a similar reason. However the attraction works, we all find ourselves wondering at times why it seems the same types of people and situations keep showing up in our lives—and why we can't seem to make the situations work out differently no matter how hard we try. By working with complexes, we can start to free ourselves of the repetition compulsion. If we no longer find ourselves in the same old situations having the same old automatic emotional reactions, we will be less frustrated.

The next time you are in the grip of a complex, ask yourself, "What's happening here? What is the back story?" You may not be able to do this right away because of your strong emotional response, but you can ask yourself these questions after your strong emotions, triggered by the complex, have passed. As you do the exercises in this book, you will begin to see connections and themes that you hadn't realized were there. With patience, you will be better able to anticipate particular situations that will trigger a complex you have. Then, when one is triggered, you may be better able to talk to yourself and abate the intensity and duration of the complex because you have a better understanding of it. Good intentions and resolve to no longer overreact to situations that set off a strong, negative reaction are not enough. The practices in this book will help you become more aware of your unconscious dynamics and gain more conscious control over your complexes. Ask yourself:

- What kinds of situations are your triggers?
- What types of people "set you off" or "push your buttons"?
- What frustrating and upsetting situations seem to come up again and again in your life?

Through using shamanic and Jungian techniques, you will come to better understand and work with many archetypal energies that are affecting your story, whether through complexes that keep getting triggered, personas you can't seem to shake, or something else. After you begin doing shamanic and Jungian work, it's important to encounter and dialogue with two archetypal energies in particular: the energies of death and initiation. Both play a profound role in bringing about change. Although you may resist these concepts at first because of negative associations you might have with the words "death" and "initiation," I encourage you to read the next chapter with an open mind and discover why letting go of any fear about encountering these energies is important for transformation.

CHAPTER NINE

Working with the Archetypal Energies of Death and Initiation

S hamans recognize that life involves beginnings, endings, and major transformations. Rather than avoiding changes and clinging to what is familiar and seemingly under our control, we can use shamanic and Jungian techniques to work with the archetypal energies of death and initiation. These energies can help us manage our fears, be more flexible, and write better stories for ourselves. The archetypal energy of death assists us in letting go of that which is no longer serving us. The archetypal energy of initiation helps us to fully embrace our new stories and bring them to life, letting go of any ambivalence about the transformation and any unconscious resistance.

The Archetypal Energy of Death

All endings represent a form of death. The past gives way to the present, leaving behind memories and marking us with energetic imprints. Every loss is a reminder of time passing and the moment of physical death coming nearer. In part, we hold on to relationships, situations, emotions, habits, and belief systems to deny our mortality. In part, we do it out of a fear that we will not have enough time to bring a new story into manifestation. We also do it because we are afraid of the unknown. The old circumstances or behaviors might not be working for us, but what if the new ones turn out to be even less satisfactory? When we work with the death principle, we can rid ourselves of the fear of change and experience transformation as positive and pregnant with possibilities.

One of the reasons I became interested in shamanism was to die a good death. A good death involves taking care of as much unfinished business as possible before dying, and learning to live with death as an ally while we are still alive. Taking care of unfinished business not only includes preparing a will and determining the disposition of possessions but also bringing about emotional closure to situations and choosing to live the way in which we would like to be remembered.

All we have in life is lent to us and must be let go of at our death. The legend of Alexander the Great's deathbed scene tells how this young man who accomplished so much nevertheless was willing to leave it behind at death. According to the legend, Alexander the Great made three last requests of his generals. The first request was for his physicians to carry his coffin. The second was for riches from his treasury, including silver and gold, to be spread over the route to his grave. The third was for his hands to be left hanging over the sides of his coffin. He made these requests to demonstrate that physicians can't stop death, that accumulated wealth can't be taken with us, and that people come into the world with empty hands and leave the same way.

Living with death is an essential shamanic lesson. If you truly believe that you come from Source, and that you will return to Source after the death of your physical body, you reduce your need for material wealth and become less attached to your expectations. You learn to see death as a process, not a final ending. You can accept that while life is never completely under your control and will constantly change, you can still experience fulfillment and joy. You can affect your story rather than feeling trapped by it.

You might think of death as the force that kills off what is no longer useful to you, freeing energy for something new to grow or arise. Death energy works like the process of pruning: When you prune a plant, you guide the energy, or growth, in a particular direction. Cutting away excess growth on a rose bush reduces the competition for nutrition among the various parts of the plant, resulting in more blooms. Cutting away activities, relationships, ideas, and emotional patterns that are in competition for vital energy makes it easier to manifest your new story.

During a workshop, I led participants on a shamanic journey to interact with the death principle. One woman asked death for help in ending a long-standing pattern in her life, but I called the participants back to the here and now before she had finished her conversation with death. At first she was annoyed, but she suddenly realized that what she needed to do did not require further conversation. She just needed to follow through on what she knew she had to do. To avoid taking action we find difficult, we can let ourselves get caught up in analyzing a situation or talking about it past the point where the conversation is productive.

We need to be aware of and honor the process of death, whether it is literal or metaphorical, rather than avoid the discomfort of endings, because life and death will always be intertwined. We need to acknowledge the loss or death of relationships and situations and not rush into something new to avoid processing our grief. Otherwise, we might miss the insights and lessons that often come to us when we have done the difficult work of remaining conscious of the transitional pain of a breakup.

Death energy can be a powerful force, but like any energy, it can be weak, too. Once, when I was journeying, I encountered a lethargic death energy. I understood that it had value for me, and I had the fleeting thought that I should take it to a coffee shop to help it perk up! A problematic relationship or other situation that needs to change can drain us of energy, making us feel tired and depressed, if we don't bring to it the strong energy of death when it is needed. It is this energy that allows us to let go of what needs to be let go.

If we are not vegetarians or vegans, we should be aware that we routinely kill, or have others kill for us, animals that will provide us with meat so that we can be nourished. It behooves us to be conscious of those who kill for us—or who end situations or relationships for us. We must not abdicate our responsibility in these matters. As potential agents of death, we need to learn to bring about endings consciously, without malice or carelessness. This is true whether we kill animals, plants, ideas, relationships, or anything else. We have great power, and with it, a responsibility to exercise discernment and compassion.

MAKING ENDINGS

The jaguar drinks, reproduces, nurtures,
and kills
and eats others less strong.
We don't know for sure what it thinks and feels
when it is a bringer of death.

Do we know what we think and feel
when we kill others, ideas, relationships?
Is it vengeance, punishment, nourishment, freedom?
If for a greater cause
is the goal worthy of the death price?

Some killings are random, accidental, unconscious;
some premeditated.
Do we know what we are doing?

We need to learn when to let things die and when to help keep alive those things that have not yet fully expressed themselves. We should give to a situation or relationship what it deserves before we leave it or end it abruptly. We might want to end something if it has changed, if it bothers us, if it no longer feels good, or if it does not meet our needs and expectations. However, it is usually best to keep things alive until we have learned what we need to from the situation. Wisdom suggests that all things change and go through seasons. If we give up on life too soon in the winter, we miss the spring. If we end situations because we are feeling uncomfortable or resentful that they are not providing us with sustenance, we miss out on the potential fruits that we may harvest from them in the future.[10]

Journey to Meet Death

Before our birth, during our lives, and even after we die, death is our constant companion. The energy of death reveals itself to us in our thoughts and feelings toward it. We can attempt to relate to death by tricking it, denying it, conquering it, appeasing it, or submitting to it. We have the capacity to adopt any of these stances. By dialoguing with death, we may be able to establish a new relationship with it that works better for us. For example, perhaps we can relate to death as an equal and live in harmony with it. Maybe we can recognize its contribution to our lives without letting it be so powerful that we end situations prematurely—or the situations end themselves before we want them to. We can also dialogue with Source to learn more about death, because ultimately, Source is the final arbiter of whether something should die or end.

You can take a shamanic journey to meet the energy of death. But before you do, think about these questions, and consider them when setting your intention for the journey:

- What things in your life need to die? What needs to be born?
- What sorts of things do you kill, or end? How do you bring about these endings?
- Do you "kill" things consciously or unconsciously?
- What have you killed prematurely? Why did you kill them when you did?

To begin the journey to the energy of death, open sacred space, cleanse your energy field, do mindful breathing, and relax as you focus your intention on taking this particular journey and gaining any information from death that would be useful for you in changing your story.

JOURNEY TO MEET DEATH

Picture yourself walking down a long corridor toward a closed door. As you proceed down the corridor, notice your surroundings. When you get to the door, open it and step into a room where you will encounter death.

When you have entered the room, notice what your surroundings look like. What form does death take? Does it look like you expected it to look? Ask death what message it has for you right now at this point in your life. Ask, "What in my life is not serving me, and needs to be pruned away for me to flourish?" Then ask it what it wants from you. Ask death what you can do for it, and request from it that which you desire.

When you are finished with the dialogue, thank the energy of death for the conversation, and return the way you came. Come back to ordinary consciousness.

Close sacred space. Then, be sure to write down your experiences and reflect on them. Decide how you will incorporate them into your life.

Many people who have journeyed to meet death have changed their ideas about what death entails. One person said:

My relationship to death has dramatically changed, although prior to the journey I did not think specifically about having such a relationship. My initial thoughts were that death would be a dark and very sad place. During a journey to meet death, however, I realized that death is an aspect of Source and that it is a very brightly illuminated, inviting space. By the end of the journey, I felt that death and life are the same.

Here is another man's description of his journey to meet death:

I approached a corridor. It had a square stone entrance on the outside. Past the entrance, stones arched over the walkway, giving the corridor a cloistered feel. As I walked down it, I noticed there was natural light, perhaps from the rocks themselves, which had a slightly golden hue. When I reached the door, I saw it was made of wood planks with a black iron circular pull on the right. The door was round at the top.

I entered, expecting to see a grim-reaper-like figure. I did not. First, I noticed that the stone and light in the chamber were similar to those in the corridor. The size and the increased height of the ceiling gave it a character similar to a crypt chapel in a good-sized cathedral. Next, I noted the room was semicircular and sloped downward toward a stage area. Seeing no grim reaper, I initially assumed the room was empty except for me. Then, center stage, I spotted a beautiful, magnificently large cobra standing upright. It was full of strength, and seemed more than reptilian, somehow possessing along with an imposing, even seductive physicality, a deep wisdom, and a sharp intellect.

After a time, I approached the cobra, not quite timidly, and asked what message it had for me. The exchange between us was wordless, as if we telepathically understood each other's thoughts. The cobra said firmly that it desired for me to go and live life fully and courageously, so that when we are joined in eternity, I might be a worthy mate for it. There was a sexual dimension to this union, but much more. Interestingly, the cobra's gender was fluid throughout this journey, initially male, but then female, and male and female. Its response to me resonated deeply, for I knew that a union with the cobra was what I wanted, too.

I also want a long life, and I asked how many more skins I would shed before we were joined. The cobra responded, "Thirty to thirty-three." I had a sense that in order to live fully and courageously, I would need to mate often with the snake in this life. This was confirmed by the serpent.

When it was time to leave, I kissed its lips, and it kissed mine. I realized I had forgotten to ask what in me needs to die, but I now see that I already knew the answer.

The same man found himself to be in a very different setting while on another journey to encounter death. He said:

The corridor I entered was a hallway in an older building several stories in height. The hallway had the feel of the 1930s or 1940s, with high ceilings, transoms above the doors, no air conditioning, and linoleum tile floors. It felt like a school building, but also a bit like an office building. I was walking down a hallway to the right, or eastward.

I came to a door and entered a classroom where I knew death would be. It was a bit stuffy, with the morning air of a day that would soon turn hot. The room was rectangular, and the desks and chairs that filled it were shoved together for summer break. The door through which I entered was at the back of the classroom, and I turned to my left to look toward the front of the room. I saw a small, nondescript man dressed in a rumpled grayish suit and wearing a hat. He looked as much the bland bureaucrat as a teacher.

I made my way to the front of the room and addressed him, explaining my presence and asking him what message he had for me. As I did, I encountered a man who exuded dullness. Everything about him, not just his suit and hat, seemed gray. But when he began to speak, he ceased to be a pallid old man and became quite animated and sharp. His energy was anything but gentlemanly or bureaucratic; instead, he was forceful and abrupt, embodying an unmistakable if abrasive wisdom. He was not pleased to see me, he said emphatically. He reminded me of what death looked like the last time I encountered it and said, "Imagine me as a vital life force connected with sexuality and danger, not as an old bureaucrat! You have great potential, but you must seek a relationship with death as a living, powerful force, as serpentine, cobra energy." Then, he abruptly ordered me from the room. I departed, chastened, but understanding that he was right.

After encountering and working with death, we may feel stronger and renewed. This is the gift of working with an energy that we might initially think of as frightening or repulsive. Death can be a positive force, and if we renew our relationship with it, it can help us craft a new story.

However, not all death experiences are sublime. Years ago, I was in a group that was using shamanic techniques to simulate death experiences. Afterward, several people reported they felt ethereal and at peace, and had not wanted to come back into their physical bodies. During my own journey, however, I smelled excrement! Just prior to my journey, I had inadvertently knelt in dog droppings, and the odor followed me into my simulated death experience. We carry into our encounters with death the excrement and detritus of this lifetime. If we clean up our messes in this lifetime, they are less likely to follow us into our afterlife or make our transitions from endings into new beginnings difficult. Then the excrement can become fertilizer and nourish whatever it is we would like to grow.

Death as an Ally

All transformations involve a process of death and rebirth, of letting go of the old and bringing in the new. You want to hold on to what works for you and separate it from what is not working. You want to bring in what is desirable rather than what is novel and interesting but that turns out not to serve you. For example, after ending a relationship, it is important to truly let go of what did not work but retain kindness and compassion for the other person. When seeking a new partner, you need insights into what qualities are important to you that you did not have in your previous relationship. This way, you will not simply look for someone new and as different as possible from your previous partner, only to discover that your new partner and relationship are very similar to what you left behind.

How can we honor and feed the energy of death so that it is our ally, not our adversary? We gain energy for life and strength for working with death and accepting endings when we are mindful of nature, our activities, and our food. To be fully alive requires conscious reflection—not ruminating or obsessing, but taking time to find meaning and value in our experiences. It requires that we consider making changes, or accepting transitions, and trust that the unknown can actually be more satisfying to us than the familiar.

When we experience vitality, the robotic, deadened parts of us may revive and even transform. We can get in touch with our verve more easily when in nature. There, we sense the sap moving in the quiet trees and the presence of seeds underground that will open up to grow into seedlings. We are able to connect with this gestating energy. Then it becomes easier to slow down and be reflective, processing events and emotions and beginning to imagine what we might generate. Another way to become enlivened is to work with the energy of *puer aeturnus,* the eternal youth, bringing playfulness and curiosity into situations.

Reflection will help you overcome fear about shedding the old ways. Here are some questions that can help you in your reflection:

- In what areas of your life are you not being reflective? In what areas are you robotic or deadened, going through the motions in unconscious, habitual ways?
- In what areas are you split off from life and yourself, allowing aspects of yourself and your life to become stagnant or die?
- If you had a half hour to live, what would you do? What if you had one day? one month? one year?
- How can you use your answers to these questions to help you create your new story?

It's said that when asked what he would do if he had one hour to live, St. Francis replied, "If I were working in my garden, I would keep working in my garden." The Japanese poet Bashō, when asked at the end of his life if he had written a death poem, is said to have explained that he really hadn't needed to do that, because all of his life was his death poem. The Lakota Sioux visionary Black Elk stated that Lakota warriors going into battle would say, "Today is a good day to die."[11] Every day is a good day to die if we live it fully. By honoring this idea, we honor death and honor life.

The length of a journey, or of a life, is not as important as the attention we give each part of it. If we are not fully engaged and present with our journey, it will be wasted. When we multitask, we devote only part of our awareness to our current task and can lose the essence of particular experiences. At some level, our life journey is a hologram, with every segment containing the whole. If we savor each increment, even each minute, death can't cheat us of our journey. Every moment is all there is and is complete in itself.

The following three exercises will help you to become less fearful of death and change your relationship to it.

Writing Your Own Obituary

Write your own obituary, focusing on your accomplishments, associations, and relationships. Consider whether you would like to make changes in your life so that you could write a different obituary. Then imagine what your obituary would contain if it were written by others. Think about whether you would like their versions of your obituary to be different, and how you might change your life to make them so. You might also write a very short version of your obituary. What would you want it to say if it were only a few lines long?

Writing Your Own Eulogy

Write your own eulogy: an oration to honor and praise yourself after your death that summarizes the type of person you were. Consider what you might need to change in your life to make the praise in your eulogy honest, more pleasing to you, and well earned. Now imagine what your eulogy would contain if it were written by others. Think about whether you would like their versions of your eulogy to be different, and how you might change your life to make them so.

Experiencing Your Deathbed

In your imagination, assemble those you would like to talk to in your last moments, or those you simply want to be present at your deathbed. Use this occasion as an opportunity to forgive and to ask for forgiveness from others. It is also a time to give and receive blessings and love, and say things to others that you feel need to be said, even if they are painful. This is a time to speak your truth about your experiences. When you are finished, say your good-byes.

Write down what you would say, and what you imagine others would say. Ask yourself, "Would I be better served by saying these things now—or should I say them when I am on my deathbed?" By saying them now, you might find yourself freer to live more fully today in your new story.

A man reported that his imagined death experience healed his feelings toward his deceased mother. He said:

This ceremony gave me the opportunity to open up to anyone I wanted to speak with on my deathbed, and the words I shared with my mother released the weight I had carried for many years. Just to be able to apologize and get what I needed to off my chest enabled me to let go of negative feelings of guilt regarding her.

Removing the Fear of Physical Death

With wisdom, we see how we weave life and death and beginnings and endings into all that we do. Working with the energy of death can minimize our fear of physical death. Ultimately, everyone will die: Death is a nondiscriminatory service provider! When it comes time to end our connections with our bodies and to die physically, our awareness merges with the eternal, infinite, cosmic consciousness. However, if we can contact and interact with this consciousness in this lifetime, we can actually experience our eternal nature and minimize or remove our primal fear of physical death. We will no longer hold on to the false notion that death is a final ending and will have recognized that even the most frightening manifestation of death energy—actual physical death—simply leads to another way of existing. We become reborn into our spiritual selves because we now recognize our primary nature as eternal.

DEATH

Does the awareness before and after this existence
reckon this death
and that life?

All things have an eternal, living essence. When the form that the essence inhabits dies, the living essence goes back to the life pool and is transformed into something new. At the death of the physical body, individual life is subsumed by all life—just as a droplet of water is subsumed by the ocean. Perhaps the ocean knows the story of each droplet, but does the droplet itself remember its story after it has merged with the ocean?

AFTER DEATH

What does it mean to die?
When does it start, what ceases?
What dreams, what incomplete business,
what unfinished legacy?

The dream of immortality in this body
must be surrendered
the familiar, good and bad
traded
for an unknown surcease from struggle.

What might await me
in the Quiet?
Will I lose my individuality
or retain it
as I, with my individual essence
am recycled?

The road of life we all go down has death at the end of it. How quickly death comes to meet us on the road depends on many things, including our relationship with death, as well as the ayni we create at all of the levels of our being. Death is part of the interconnectedness of all things. When we recognize that death is an inevitable part of life, we write better stories and inhabit them more easily. As we age, we learn to appreciate the preciousness of every moment.

AGING

Skin sags, joints ache, vision fades
yearning dulls, joy still flows
hourglass trickling empty.
Organs falter, elimination troubles
less energy, more losses: What's it all about?
As the husk deteriorates, a choice:
intensifying despair,
or joy at lessons learned
contributions made,
bonds with the beloved, friends, family.

As the hourglass readies to turn
the cracking husk opens
to the light of eternity
and a joyful song reunites us

with the eternal presence:
never missing
but not always consciously experienced.

Now, the clamor of "stuff" quiets enough to
hear the voice of God
in the wind, the stars,
the grass, and all of Heaven and Earth.

The husk is cracking
but the joy of the journey still beckons
no matter the length of the path
or its unpredictability.
We can make good memories from here onward
despite—or is that in collusion with?—
vicissitudes each day may bring.

The Archetypal Energy of Initiation

Traditionally, shamans worked with initiatory energy to help others to be born into their spiritual nature. Initiations allow us to remember that we are expressions of divine energy—that we came from Source and will return to Source. Every initiation opens us to the possibility of feeling that we are inseparable from Source, a feeling that lets us realize we are eternal spiritual beings and not merely beings living an individual existence, confined to one particular time and physical body. Initiatory experiences enable us to feel our connection to the divine, giving us a new awareness that we bring into our everyday lives.

In shamanism, initiations often involve a ritualistic enactment of death to help the initiate overcome fear of actual death, and may incorporate physical or psychological pain, or both, for this purpose. Although the practices described in this chapter don't explicitly involve suffering, they could cause emotional pain as something dies, making way for the new. Often, change is uncomfortable yet ultimately beneficial.

If we are initiated into an awareness of our infinite spiritual nature, we realize that everything is a manifestation of Source expressing itself in an infinite number of ways. We are never separate and isolated from Source, even though we may feel that way. Once we recognize this, we become more comfortable using shamanic and Jungian techniques to feel our connection to Source and its various aspects. It becomes easier to let go of any resistance to the concept of transpersonal realms.

Whenever we let go of the old and enter a new state of being, a new mindset, or a new situation, our experience is not truly unique, although it has unique aspects. In a sense, whenever we take on a new role or embrace a new organizing principle, we are joining a community of people from the past, present, and future who have something in common with us. One example of this is when we become a parent and are thereby initiated into the community of parents. This change in role is accompanied by an initiatory energy that alters or marks that individual's personal energy field. The graduate will forever more be one who has completed training, and the person who overcomes an illness or trauma will be a survivor. There is no turning back or reclaiming the past. Then too, once we are initiated into our spiritual nature, we will never forget the experience. We will always be aware that we are connected to all expressions of Source. This awareness helps us find the courage to step onto a new and unfamiliar path.

Life transitions can be like initiations. If we see them in this way, we recognize how they change us energetically and connect us with other humans who have undergone similar experiences. We feel less alone, and perceive that we can draw upon the wisdom and energy of that larger group to inform, sustain, and inspire us. This is a great gift provided by initiatory energy.

One type of initiation that is not very common in American culture is that of undergoing an initiation into a lineage, such as initiation to the priesthood or an ancient tradition. When this happens, energy is transferred from a lineage holder to an initiate. This transfer allows the initiate to carry that lineage's vibration forward and to use it as needed.

It is possible to work with the energy of initiation on your own. You might ask Source to initiate you into a new group, such as a group of cancer survivors or parents who have raised children who are now grown, so that you can begin living according to a new story. It can be difficult to accept new roles in life—they are unfamiliar, and you may begin to doubt yourself. By focusing your intention on bringing in initiatory energy, you can release any ambivalence about the transformation you are experiencing.

Rituals marking initiation, such as confirmation, graduation, and marriage ceremonies, use traditional symbolism to help people fully shift into their new roles. Often, they involve symbols that serve as reminders of the transformation: a piece of jewelry with a religious symbol, a diploma, or a wedding ring, for example. Although initiatory rituals such as weddings and confirmations can be life changing, that is not always the case. In fact, these ceremonies can feel hollow if you don't fully embrace the transformation. Working with the initiation principle allows you to stop lingering and make the plunge into a new identity. It helps you release the energies that are holding you back from fully committing to the changes you want to make in your life.

The following is a journey that can help you bring in initiatory energy and dialogue with it. You may also wish to use some of the rituals in Chapter Ten to initiate yourself, or to undergo a group initiation. To begin the journey, open sacred space, cleanse your energy field, and do mindful breathing. Relax as you focus your intention on taking this particular journey.

JOURNEY OF INITIATION

In your mind, take yourself to a comfortable spot on a mountain. Invite in the archetype of initiation.

When you feel the initiatory energy arrive, notice whether it takes a particular form. What does it look like? What does it feel like?

Allow yourself to experience the energy of initiation and ask that energy what message it has for you today, what it wants from you, and what you can do for it. Then ask for what you want from it. What does it want to initiate you into? You may ask it to give you a symbol that you can dialogue with. (You can visualize this symbol when you dialogue with it, or use the working stone as described earlier in the book.)

Afterward, thank the archetype of initiation for its work with you today. Then, return to the time and place from which you started your journey.

Close sacred space after you have completed the journey. Then, think about how you can apply the lessons from this initiatory experience to your everyday life and to your new story, and journal about your insights.

The first time you take this journey, you may ask to be initiated into your spiritual nature. You may choose other intentions before entering into subsequent journeys; for example, you might ask to be able to fully accept that you are now a survivor of trauma. Alternately, you might simply ask Source to bring in initiatory energy for whatever transformation Source believes you should undergo.

INITIATION

Initiation transforms a nascent state
into a becoming.
Can suffering and fear
or their absence
pierce a miasma?
Does clarity reveal destiny

or is it the collective destiny of the initiators?
A forensic autopsy may help decide
or a sampling of postmortem poetry.

The Changes We Experience After Initiation

If we allow initiatory energy to influence us, our energy field changes and we soon see that the world reflects the changes we've experienced internally. We actually perceive and relate to the world differently, having been brought into the community of spiritual beings, trauma survivors, parents, warriors, teachers, healers, and so on. We see, attract, and become resonant to people and situations that we did not observe or feel drawn to previously. For example, a person who has become a parent may never again be able to watch news footage or movie images of children who are suffering without feeling strong emotions, such as an overwhelming sense of empathy or anger. Someone who has been initiated into his spiritual nature begins to feel a sense of connection to others who have been initiated into their spiritual nature. A person who has overcome an addiction never forgets what that experience is like but is no longer defined by it, for he identifies with a community of people in recovery from addiction. Perhaps he can easily spot the person in the crowd who is an addict or recovering addict, as he always has, but no longer feels compelled to connect with this person and use drugs with her. Perhaps he still attracts addicts who unconsciously recognize that he understands them and has the energy of one who has overcome addiction, which they desire. Whether he responds to their desire to make a connection with him is now his conscious choice, not an automatic and unconscious one.

If initiatory energy is not present or is weak when we are undergoing a life change, we may not feel that we have fully made the transformation. The newly single adult, the individual whose cancer has gone into remission, and the person who has come out of the closet as a homosexual may find it helpful to use shamanic and Jungian practices to usher in initiatory energy to release any ambivalence, resistance, or discomfort.

To further work with death and initiation energies that will support you in changing your story, you may wish to perform a ritual or ceremony. You will learn how to do this shortly, but first, it's important to know how you can work with dreams and nature to deepen your insights and bring in new energies that can support you in transforming your story.

CHAPTER TEN

Working with Dreams and Nature to Manifest Your New Story

Shamans and Jungians believe in the power of dreams to reveal the influence of archetypal energies and your unconscious on your current story. Additionally, dreams can yield wisdom from transpersonal places that give glimpses of what will happen in the future, or insights that will help you make decisions.

Working with Dreams

If you dream often, write down all your dreams and choose to work with the one you feel most intrigued or moved by. Later, you can come back to the others and work with them. If you rarely dream, or can only remember a few images or snippets of a dream, work with whatever you recall of the dream because it may contain valuable information for you.

There is no one right way to work with dreams, but I have found that following the 10 suggestions below, in order, can be very helpful.

1. *Go to sleep intending to remember your dreams.* In this way, you cue your mind not to switch to conscious thoughts about the upcoming day before you have had a chance to recall and record your dreams.
2. *Record your dreams in writing or on an audio device as soon as you awaken.* Don't try to analyze them as you record them because you might forget details that seem insignificant but later turn out to be important. A dream that simply seems odd or mundane and that doesn't evoke strong emotions might, nevertheless, contain very helpful information.
3. *Retell your dream aloud at least twice, and then write it down at least twice.* Recalling your dream aloud more than once, or writing about it a second or third time, is helpful because the changes you make in the retelling or rewriting can be revealing. For example, you might realize that as you are going over the dream

again, you are experiencing an unexpected emotion. Maybe you will notice that you are flatly reciting the details of the dream despite the fact that the events in the dream are, on second glance, disturbing. Perhaps you have inadvertently made omissions or additions to the dream; you can explore why that is.

4. *Choose some dream images to contemplate.* Notice what comes to mind instantly when you ponder some of the images you saw in your dream. What associations do you have to the images you recall? Don't consult a dream dictionary or think too much about all the many possible interpretations of the symbols and events in your dreams. Your personal experiences may determine which symbols appear in your dreams and what they mean, so don't be quick to interpret them in a general way. Try to identify anything in your waking life, perhaps even in your past, that might be related to or associated with the events that unfolded in your dream. For example, if you dreamed of being in your grandmother's kitchen while she was cooking, one interpretation could be that your dream was about nurturing or, more literally, your grandmother's nurturing of you. However, perhaps your strongest memory of being next to her as she cooked was the day your father had a heart attack and died, and that's what comes to your mind when you recall the part of the dream that took place in her kitchen. Perhaps the dream is about being blissfully unaware of impending danger, or about your lack of vigilance, or about being in a state of innocence prior to your world shattering. Exploring the common meanings of symbols that appeared in your dream should be left for later, after you have pondered your personal associations to the dream's images and dialogued with the symbols or emotions that were part of the dream. You do not have to ponder every image or every dream. You might wish to focus on the ones that are the most vivid or emotionally charged for you.

5. *Retell the dream again.* This time as you retell the dream, include any associations you have with particular images. Write down this new, expanded version of your dream that includes some of the associations you have discovered.

6. *Dialogue with dream images, symbols, or emotions that you feel would give you useful information.* Use your working stone if you find that helpful.

7. *Identify what your emotional state was in the dream and dialogue with that feeling.* Was there a situation in your dream that in waking life would have scared you but that seemed perfectly normal, or even amusing? Was there a seemingly benign image that stirred feelings of fear, dread, regret, or anger? The emotions you experienced in your dream are as significant as the meaning of the symbols, and both can be dialogued with to gain information and understanding. For example, if you felt angry during the dream and don't know why, you could dialogue with the emotion of anger. You could ask it why it appeared when you

were picking through a bowl of fruit in your dream and what significance this anger has given what you are going through in your life right now. Then you could dialogue with the bowl of fruit and ask it what message it has for you.

8. *Reflect on where in your waking life you have felt or are feeling emotions similar to those in the dream—and where you experienced or are experiencing the dream's themes playing out.* When do you first recall experiencing the dream's emotions and themes?

9. *Consider the universal meanings of symbols in your dream.* Think about what else a dream image might symbolize. For example, a lake or a forest might represent the unconscious, while a kitchen might represent transformation. When you work with your dreams to discover the wisdom they hold for you, keep in mind that a particular dream's message can be taken literally, too. For example, if you were to dream of a Golden Retriever, it might mean that some aspect of yourself longs to retrieve something "golden" and valuable that you undervalued and overlooked, or it might simply mean you will be adopting a Golden Retriever as a pet. If you dialogue with the Golden Retriever or any other symbol, remember to engage the symbol respectfully and listen to what it has to tell you rather than arguing with it or trying to impose your ideas on it. Thank it for its insights, and end the dialogue.

10. *Apply what you have learned.* Think about how you can use the dream's information and energy to change your life and your story.

If you follow these 10 suggestions, your dreams can help you discover unresolved issues and problems as well as possible solutions. They can also tell you that you are ready to make a change, or you have made it on the inside and now need to begin changing your behaviors and habits in accordance with the shift you have experienced.

Below is the dream of one man, which yielded for him important information and affirmation regarding his new story. He had the dream after he had been working on his story for a long time. It highlighted for him the importance of becoming comfortable with who he really was, not the person his parents, friends, or neighbors thought he should be. It was a dream, he said, that could only have occurred after he had let go of fears and habits that had been holding him back.

> I was asked to be a host on the television show *Saturday Night Live*. It was an honor. I had to ad lib and be completely original. Then someone joined me for a skit, and the juxtaposition of styles showcased my humor. I was authentic and original, and that made the skits funny. I was asked to return to host the show again because I had been such a success.

In the dream, my challenge was to discover and uncover how to be completely that person. At one point, cast members seemed as if they had forgotten me, so I had to remind them who I was. They then showed me tremendous respect.

The dream then shifted to my going into a vitamin store and debating with other customers about how to take certain vitamins. I was giving them advice and was not nervous; I knew what I did and didn't know. I left and was late for hosting *Saturday Night Live.* My tardiness would be okay, but I noted that I had put other people's needs ahead of my own once again, and I didn't want to do that anymore. This would be the last time I engaged in that behavior.

The man worked with his dream in the ways suggested in this chapter and concluded that, at one level, the dream was an affirmation from his unconscious and his soul that he could be honored for being himself, and that his greatest challenge was to discover how to be completely himself. He is learning ways to do this, including speaking up for himself, being more trusting, accepting that it's okay that he knows only as much as he knows, and not being so quick to put others' needs ahead of his own. He has evolved to a place of self-acceptance that feels very liberating for him.

You can apply the energy and information you have accessed through dreamwork to your everyday life. Perhaps the next time you are in a challenging social situation, or you have to confront someone with whom you are in conflict, this new energy you have brought into your life will calm your emotional agitation and you will feel courageous. When you have a dream that makes you feel confident, strong, or transformed, don't ignore it. Trust that your mind and Source are telling you that you can experience the same feelings, thoughts, and emotions in your waking life.

The insights and courage we get when we do dreamwork can help us to confront important truths and make changes, as shown by the following dream a woman had, which later was reflected in experiences she had in her waking life. While she did not understand the dream or what it meant when she had it, she trusted in its significance until it became clear to her.

In the dream, I am hiking with my sons in steep mountains and verdant valleys. We are passing under a railroad bridge, and I notice that the center span is decaying. I think that someone should be notified that it is no longer safe for trains. The dream continues, and now I am in the engine of a train with another person, perhaps my husband. Suddenly, I realize we are coming to the damaged bridge over the deep valley and know that the center span can't hold the weight of the train. I shout "Stop!" and we stop the train. I observe a smaller train coming toward the bridge, headed for a collision.

A month after I dreamed this, my husband and I were traveling through the Appalachian Mountains. We took a detour off the main highway to hike at a state park in the mountains. While hiking, I had some insight about some physical symptoms that I was experiencing and the level of stress in my work. I was thinking about how I should consider the way I spend time (and with whom I spend it) and how my eating, exercising, and financial habits were causing me stress.

When I began to share these insights with my spouse, it evoked what felt to me like criticism. I was like a sea anemone closing up. His words sent me from an expansive place of insight to a primitive state of being shut down in a second. At this time, we were driving through a verdant valley that ran between steep mountains. It was a narrow, winding road, and I suddenly had déjà vu, as if I knew this place. It was the place of my dream. This caused me to consider the important opportunity that might be present if I would say, "Stop the train . . . this bridge can't hold the weight." So, I forced myself to open up and "stop the train" of my complicity. I risked the argument that would ensue if I spoke about my hurt feelings.

Over the course of the next several hours, my husband and I intermittently processed what had happened, and it was a good thing. It became an opportunity to expose maladaptive behaviors on both of our parts, struggle through them to gain understanding, and make different choices.

Symbols and metaphors often serve as a bridge to a new story, or between our unconscious, which is ready for change, and our conscious mind, which has the job of manifesting that change in waking life. We may not feel ready to have the conversation we dread until a dream reveals that indeed, the energy is there, inside us, to support our stepping into a new story.

Besides working with the symbols in your dreams, remember to pay attention to symbols that appear to you in your waking life as well. If a song lyric or snippet of poetry keeps coming back to you, or you keep seeing an unusual object or animal as you go about your everyday activities, or you come across a few words that resonate for you, pay attention. If a symbol from your dream starts appearing in your everyday life, pay attention as well. Explore the symbols' possible meanings through dialogue and contemplation.

Working with Nature

Spending time in nature opens you to energies and information associated with the elements (earth, air, fire, and water), living creatures, and plants. In addition, using shamanic and Jungian techniques while you are outdoors calls in these natural forces to support you in making the changes you desire and acquiring the insights that will guide you in bringing your new story to life.

Source created and infuses nature, which is a reflection of Source itself. The sounds of birds, squirrels, crashing waves, and rustling leaves all register in the sensory processing centers of our brains. They bring us a sense of calm and help us to reduce the chatter of our busy minds. When we are in nature, it is easier for us to reflect on our own cycles of growth, death, and rebirth, and to contemplate how we might incorporate qualities such as balance and diversity into our lives. We need to create space for moments of reflection in order to write better stories for ourselves and for the greater whole of humanity. Shamans have always known that nature supports us in this important process of reflecting and dreaming.

A woman who had been doing shamanic work and incorporating the insights she gained into a new story for herself described nature's influence on her in this way:

> How do I dance with all of the obligations in my life? How do I have fun when appropriate, and reign with dignity when I am called to lead? How do I help those who spend much of their time feeling the same hopelessness and desolation that I have experienced only briefly? How do I do all this while providing for my family and being a good mom? These are the questions I dance with. I could probably get to the answers faster if I could go on a spiritual retreat each month, but life calls me to constant day-to-day action as a mother of young children, a leader of a company that faces challenges, and a partner in a new relationship. I've been encouraged to spend whatever time I can in nature, and I have found this one piece of advice to be surprisingly powerful and good. I am much more aware now of the leaves on trees, the movement of the planets in the sky or the phase of the moon, the water on the lake . . . and these observations help connect me back to Spirit.

Years ago, I attended a conference about Jung and religion. For the most part, the discussions were rather cerebral. But during the course of their presentations, several of the presenters made reference to time they had spent in nature—in the woods, in a garden, or by water. In every case, after they shared their nature experiences, I felt that the tone of their presentations changed. Their demeanors changed as well—they became more relaxed, natural, and engaging. Being in nature can help get us out of our heads and into our hearts.

Shamans regularly communicate with nature and Source, which resides in all of creation, through using their techniques and rituals outdoors. When working indoors, they often bring elements of nature into their rituals—for example, using water, fire, flowers, wood, and so on.

Shamans believe that Source speaks to us through all aspects of nature. They know that animals have consciousness and intelligence. A shaman may find significance in encountering a specific creature in nature, or a particular land formation, tree, weather event, or other natural occurrence. You, too, can choose to work consciously with these occurrences or formations, letting your intuition guide you to understand why, for example, a baby fox has suddenly crossed your path, or why the light shining through the trees creates a pattern on the ground that seems to have a specific message for you. Spend time in nature and listen to and dialogue with its elements. You might dialogue with the waters of the oceans, lakes, rivers, and streams; the mountains; deserts; wildflowers; birds; fish; sand; the sun, moon, and stars; or any aspect of the natural world.

Although it can be difficult to think of all aspects of nature as having energy with which you can interact, remember that even something as seemingly solid and inert as a rock is buzzing with energy. Shamans say the frequency of rocks is lower than, say, the frequency of trees or animals. Even so, rocks contain vast amounts of energy. The quality of their energy may become clear to you as you work with them and dialogue with them. Befriend the rocks and all of nature. You may find you can begin to sense what nature has experienced and seen.

Once, when I was walking among ancient ruins in Peru, I could feel pain and sadness there. Yet, I also sensed the transcendence that was present as well. I was cognizant that the ancient stones had awareness and carried the energy of patience. I dialogued with them to learn more about what they could teach me. They told me that it is better to be judicious about how I use my energy, that I can use it to do a few things well rather than waste it trying to do more things in an incomplete and non-embodied way.

PATIENCE

Waiting for guidance
is patience
if the guidance comes from an inner voice.

Patience requires letting go
of the expectations that events in time
must unfold in a certain way
and accepting the dance between the currents of life we can influence
and those we can't.

Patience is just one of many qualities nature possesses. When you engage transpersonal realms, including nature, try to have a personal relationship with whatever you are engaging. Honor the encounter as you would time spent with a dear friend, and allow yourself to become aware of your emotional response to nature and your interactions with it.

Once, I was talking with a shaman friend about fire. He asked, "What does it represent to you?" and I answered that fire contains all four elements: fire, of course, but also air, because air allows the fire to burn and is present inside the burning wood. Also, water and earth that nurtured the tree is in the wood being consumed by fire. "Fire," I said, "encompasses, devours, liberates, transforms, and recycles just as the elements of earth, air, and water do." I asked him what fire represented to him. He said fire was his friend, that it comforted and protected him. It nurtured him and made him happy. We both felt truth in our answers, but his showed a personal relationship to fire, not just an intellectual understanding of what it can be said to represent.

A woman went outside to do a sand painting (a ritual you will learn about later in the book) and reported the following:

> I walked to a spot where there was a small patch of dry, cracked, barren earth surrounded by patchy weeds and grass, which lay in the shade created by a very large, old, beautiful tree. There was a place where a section of the ground had been cracked and lifted up and split asunder, creating a vision of a heart split open that also provided a glimpse of what is underneath, and a passageway within. I did not feel called to do my sand painting in this place, but I did decide to dialogue with this natural formation.
>
> WOMAN: How were you formed? How did this happen?
> ANSWER: All the elements worked on me—the earth, water, the fire or heat of the sun, and wind. It took all of them to make this happen in this exact way.
> WOMAN: What is your message for me?
> ANSWER: When you want to open up, let go, or transform, go outside and allow nature to work on you. You don't have to be serious, have clarity, or do some special ritual or perfect ceremony. Just do it. You can be changed over

and over and over again, just as a stone becomes weathered, its hard edges softened by the flow of water.

WOMAN: What can I do for you?

ANSWER: Soften up and drink more water. Allow yourself to become flexible and supple. Allow your "juicy parts" to show.

WOMAN: But this sounds like what I would be doing for me, not for you!

ANSWER: Well, aren't we one and the same?

WOMAN: But if I soften up, won't that prevent my cracking open, opening up to the energies I need to bring in?

ANSWER: You don't need more cracking right now. You are already open. You need more softness, joy, laughter, and ease. Your sweetness will attract what you desire. Relax and remain open. Don't become stiff, calcified, and dried up.

WOMAN: As I think about it, that sounds like aging gracefully. Is this what the message is? That this is how I can age gracefully?

ANSWER: That, and much more. Trust and wait and keep doing your good work—and going outside—and your sweetness will bring more light into you. The confusion will clear. Love with abandon. It's okay—really!

WOMAN: Thank you for dialoguing with me.

ANSWER: I am here to dialogue with you in the future as well.

Notice that the woman was willing to converse with the natural spot as if it were an old friend offering her wisdom.

Although you may find it helpful to go outdoors with the intention of communicating with nature, it is also valuable to spend time in nature and simply be present among the trees, grass, and sky, with no agenda. Then, if you do experience a synchronistic event in nature, or notice an animal, plant, or rock that you feel a connection to, dialogue with what you are encountering.

With the help of Source, you can awaken to the voice of the entire natural world around you and gain insights and energy for creating a new story.

MEANINGS

The butterfly fluttered and wondered
what she would next become.
She alit upon a snapdragon and forgot the question.
The flower bloomed and faded,
Never knowing she was to us a metaphor, a symbol.

Find ways to be in harmony with the natural world around you. Express your gratitude and appreciation for nature. Nature can sense your regard and will respond. You can learn to feel and sense that nature is observing you even as you are observing it. Try to experience nature emotionally and viscerally. You will know you are in ayni and living a life pleasing to yourself and Source when you enjoy nature and you can't imagine exploiting it or destroying it.

All of us are part of the natural world, inseparable from it. We can show it our respect by minimizing our environmental footprint on the planet, by protecting existing species of animals and plants and discovering new ones, and by being good stewards. If we respect nature and work with it consciously and with integrity, we will see shifts in our lives and in our relationship to the natural world. When we are outdoors, we will start to notice animals and plants we have not noticed before. We will experience synchronistic events in which a happening in nature will seem to reflect what is happening in our inner journeys. This is what happened when a smoldering fire I had been working with suddenly flared up just as I silently committed more deeply to my shamanic path.

To reinforce your connection to the natural world, you can use objects from the outdoors in rituals. Leaves, stones, water, and natural objects can serve as symbolic representations of emotions, problems, energetic influences, and so on.

You can also use images from nature to inspire you. A man who was working with teams of people seeking to achieve accreditation of an educational institution shared this story:

> The work I do can be tedious and boring for me and those working with me. Having had exposure to totems and power animals, I felt inspired to use the mouse and owl to describe our work together. First, the team works like mice, hunting around and getting into all of the small hidden places to find data to use in the report. Then, the team moves to acting like owls, hunting the data mice, and digesting them. As owls, the team develops a broad view of which details are important. Then, the owl team members produce a pellet containing all of the "bones," or essential pieces, that can be put back together again when the pellet is dissected, forming a skeleton of information that makes sense. This way of explaining the process was entertaining and communicated exactly what the tasks were. It elicited the incredible talents of the people who worked together as a team to produce the "pellet."

You may find yourself drawn to use rituals and ceremonies to work with archetypal energies. Feel free to incorporate symbols and images from nature that have meaning for you. Next, you will learn about some traditional rituals and ceremonies you can use alone or in a group, and how to use symbols and objects to make them more powerful.

CHAPTER ELEVEN

Using Ritual and Ceremony to Manifest Your New Story

We can use ritual and ceremony to release our current story and make room for our new story to come into being. Both give us an opportunity to honor and express gratitude to Source and take us to a sacred time and place, where all is at the beginning, before creation, and the past no longer has a claim on us.[12] Everything is possible in this time and place, which offers energy and information that we can access and interact with. The inner changes we make may be invisible to others, but in time, they are revealed as we step into a new story for ourselves.

Ritual connects us to archetypal stories. It brings alive myths and themes that originate and reside in Source and appear across cultures throughout human history. These stories are expressed in many different ways, but their universal qualities are always present. We perform rituals to mark birth, death, marriage, hunting, planting, and many other activities. The ritual itself helps us to feel that we are not alone in our experiences, that we share with others certain universal experiences. Even a city dweller who has not experienced an actual harvest in the fields can use ritual to access the energy of harvesting and use it to breathe life into a new story for herself.

For a long time, I thought rituals and ceremonies required much effort and preparation. I've since realized that to achieve their benefits, being present and focused is all that is necessary. No formality or specific props are required. Ritual and ceremonies performed with intent, energy, devotion, respect, and gratitude to honor and communicate with Source are powerful—even if they involve just you, alone, shifting your awareness.

If you are part of a spiritual lineage, that is, a succession of teachers and students in a particular wisdom tradition, you can follow the prescribed rituals or ceremonies that are part of that tradition. But if you follow those rituals blindly, and experience them without emotion or a sense of connection to something larger than yourself, they will lack meaning, and you will not usher in new energies and new insights. You will simply be going through the motions.

Working with Rituals and Ceremonies

A ritual or ceremony can be used for expressing gratitude and respect, achieving closure or balance, shedding unwanted energies, and drawing specific types of energy into your life, such as initiation, death, and so on. You can also perform ceremonies and rituals to bring healing to the injured, unhappy parts of yourself. Your intention might be to become less moody, less critical of others, less dependent on comfort foods, or more focused on the positive aspects of your job. You might also wish to perform a ritual or ceremony to usher in a new chapter of your life, to acknowledge an ending and a beginning.

It can take more than one ritual to minimize the impact of a particular energy and draw in another to influence your story. You might start with one ritual and later, perform others to help you continue to shift out of the old habits and let go of the energies that have been influencing you. All energies derive from Source and are available to you.

Ritual and ceremony connect you to the energy of Source. Once you sense or feel this connection, you can use many effective ways to communicate with Source and to ask for help. Just as you do when journeying, you must become still, quiet, and open to be able to hear the voice of Source. Thus, the preparation techniques of opening sacred space, cleansing your energy field, and shifting your consciousness via mindful breathing are vital. Note that when you are working outside and opening sacred space, you should invite the spirits of the land to participate in your ceremony. These spirits are the energies of nature, and some believe they also include the spirits of people who once lived in a particular area. By inviting these spirits to work with you, you honor them and can aid in their healing.

The messages you receive from Source are expressed in a variety of ways. They may come to you as words but also as color, music, scent, visual images, and sensations that serve as metaphors. When you communicate with Source, you can use any of these languages to send your message, too. For example, when opening sacred space, as you turn and face each one of the four directions, your movements signal that you acknowledge the force associated with that direction. You can use words in your invocation and imagine colors or visual images that help you to connect with particular energies, such as envisioning a jaguar as you turn to face west and a hummingbird as you turn to face north, or whatever you associate with that particular direction. Then, when you acknowledge the forces above and below, you can imagine seeing images that represent or embody those powers.

The rituals and ceremonies I recommend can be performed alone or in groups. If they are done in groups, it can be interesting to compare experiences with other participants afterward. Sometimes, several people will experience the same images and sensations while participating in a ritual together. You might contemplate why these same messages came to more than one person.

The first ritual you will learn about, sand painting, is used in traditional indigenous communities and is similar to the sand tray practice in the Jungian tradition. Later in the chapter, you will be shown how you can create your own rituals and ceremonies to access energies and insights that will help you in writing, revising, and bringing into being a new story.

Sand Painting

A sand painting is a symbolic energetic representation of yourself and aspects of your life, which you work with to gain insights and new energies. It is difficult for the conscious mind to figure out the complex relationships among the various events and situations in our lives and how they influence us. By working with your unconscious mind through symbols in a sand painting, you can gain valuable insights and bring in new energies that will help you change your story.

One way to create a sand painting outdoors is to use a stick to draw a circle on the ground, and then fill that circle with natural objects such as stones, wood, and flowers, that represent specific areas of your life or emotional issues and behaviors you wish to address. You can also work indoors and create your sand painting with paper and pencil and symbols you draw. The key to doing a sand painting is to use your unconscious mind and intuit where to place the objects in the circle, sensing where they belong rather than using your conscious mind to figure out the most logical way to arrange them. Let's say you would like to address the fear that is holding you back from reaching your goals and making the changes you would like to make. You can find a natural object that you want to work with that will represent your fear—perhaps a stick, stone, or leaf whose shape catches your eye. Hold this object and, with intention, exhale into it while imagining that you are transferring your fear into it. Then place it in your sand painting wherever you sense it belongs. Next, consider the areas of your life where fear holds you back, and blow into various objects your specific fears, such as the fear of not being a good enough parent, or fear about being passed up for promotion at work. As you work with this sand painting, you may gain insight into your fears.

In creating a sand painting, you can choose to work with an emotional or behavioral theme, such as fear, ambivalence, or denial. You could also work with a chapter of your life, such as health or vocation. It can also be helpful to work with two aspects of your life that you suspect are affecting each other, such as health and mood.

When you have completed your sand painting, observe the patterns you have created and contemplate their meaning. For example, what objects did you choose to represent yourself and your feelings about relationships with others? What objects did you choose to represent your work, your hobbies, and your health? Where did you place them in the circle, and why? Once when I did a sand painting, I stepped back from it and realized I had made sure not to let any of the symbols of various aspects of my life touch each other. I became aware of how I had developed a habit of compartmentalizing, and that I did not carry into one area the wisdom I had acquired when dealing with another.

The first time you look at your sand painting, you might overlook something. If you come back to the sand painting several times, you are likely to catch things you missed and gain new insights. Dialogue with the objects and their energy to learn more.

The purpose of working with a sand painting is to gain the objectivity that might escape you if you worked on your issues internally by psychologically analyzing them or getting in touch with your emotions as you think about them. When your issues are represented by material objects you have chosen, it is easier not to identify with them because you have created an external representation you can see and manipulate. You can explore your emotions without becoming so caught up in them that you are blinded to what you need to learn and understand about yourself and your life.

Do not put representations of other people into your sand paintings—work only with representations of your feelings toward them. For example, you might choose an object to represent your feelings about your former partner, or to represent "parenting" rather than your child, so as not to affect the energy of an actual person without obtaining permission to do so.

Creating a sand painting in nature can be especially useful for bringing about transformation. By working outdoors, you invite in the energies of nature and the cosmos to help you heal and to bring into harmonious balance those aspects of yourself represented in the sand painting. You can call in the energy of the South, represented by the serpent or anaconda, to help you shed the pain of the past and walk softly on Mother Earth, for example. You might call in the energy of the West, of jaguar or puma, to help you find balance.

You might decide to leave a sand painting in place for several days, visiting it to see how it has changed or to make changes in it yourself. You might add more symbols, remove symbols, or change their locations within the circle as it feels appropriate. How a sand painting is arranged can give you information about processes occurring inside you. Is the sand painting crowded, unbalanced, divided, large, or small? Do you feel moved to rearrange it? Is there some aspect of yourself that doesn't seem to belong anywhere, that doesn't seem to fit in with the other parts of you? Has nature moved some object or brought a new one in? What meaning do you derive from that?

You can dialogue with the sand painting if you like, asking the four questions:

- What message do you have for me?
- What do you want from me?
- Will you give me _____? (Fill in your request.)
- What can I do for you?

When you sense you have learned what you needed to learn from your sand painting, use your arms to make gathering motions over the painting and use your hands to put its energies into your energy field wherever it feels appropriate to place them. Replace all the objects you used back into nature and erase all traces of the sand painting. Make the space pristine again, as if the sand painting had never existed, so that its energy does not continue to affect you. In this way, you can start anew and step into your new story. The energy of the sand painting will have been incorporated into you.

You interact with Source symbolically and energetically when you make and work with a sand painting, but as with all shamanic techniques, you have to apply what you have learned and allow the energy that has shifted within you to be expressed. You may need to do more journeying and dialoguing to discover why your unconscious mind might be resisting the transformation your conscious mind desires. Most of the time, change happens incrementally and cumulatively. The longing for a dramatic, life-altering experience that will forever alter your story and cure you of the old habits for good comes from the ego. Be amused by it, but don't expect to have that fantasy fulfilled by any ritual, regardless of how powerful it seems when you perform it.

After you have made, worked with, and disassembled a sand painting, answer the following questions in a journal, and come back to the pages later to see if you have any new insights.

- How did it feel to create a sand painting?
- Why did you choose the location you used?
- How did you choose the issues, concerns, and aspects of yourself and your life that you decided to represent in the sand painting?
- What objects did you choose to represent the aspects of your life that you wanted to work with? Why did you select those particular objects?
- What was it like to work with the sand painting after you initially created it? Did you come back to it more than once? What transpired when you came back to it?
- How did it feel to incorporate the sand painting's energies back into your energy field before you disassembled the sand painting?
- What changes or processes did you undergo or enter into as a result of working with your sand painting?

Fire Ceremonies

Fire ceremonies have existed in indigenous cultures around the world for millennia. They can help you to release old energies, open yourself up to new ones, and allow room for new possibilities to come into your life. Then you can live according to your new story rather than your current one. If you have recently made some energetic changes—perhaps due to journeying and dialoguing, or working with a sand painting—a fire ceremony can bring in more energy for transformation, and perhaps new insights as well.

Wood, or paper, is derived from the elements of fire (from the sun), water, air, and earth (via nutrients), so when you burn it you are releasing the energy of these elements. All are represented in and transformed by fire. In burning wood or paper, you are getting rid of something (the wood, the paper) but creating something new (ash, heat, light, smoke) as well. Something dies, and something is born.

Blow into a stick the energy of something you would like to release from yourself and your energy field. For example, if you wish to rid yourself of your sense of specialness that comes from ego, you can blow into a stick or piece of paper your desire to feel special. That stick or paper can be burned ritualistically. Then you can blow into a different stick or piece of paper your intention for something to be born—for example, greater humility—and burn that.

Blow into the first stick something you want to release. Blow into the second one something you want to gain. Burning the two sticks allows you to exchange one type of energy for another, such as the energy of egotistic need for the energy of humility. One woman blew into her first stick the energy of comparisons, dissatisfaction with what she had, and the desire for something more, and then blew into her second stick all that she wanted to exchange that for: appreciation for what she had, seeing the positive in her present situation, and enjoying and making the most of what she had. The smoke from the fire will carry away the old energy that no longer serves you, and shamans believe it will also carry your prayer for change up to the heavens. You can feel the energy of transformation, in the form of heat, infusing you. If you like, use your hands to bring the cleansing and energizing aspects of fire into your own energy field wherever it feels right to place them, such as near your belly, heart, and head. After you symbolically shed what needs to be shed and gain what needs to be gained, you can ask the fire to bring you harmony and balance.

Finally, to honor Pachamama, Mother Earth, thereby acknowledging your interconnectedness with Earth and its energies, blow into a stick your intention for the wellness of the planet and your feelings of gratitude. Then place the stick into the fire. As you reaffirm your desire to contribute to the good of all people and all creatures, you make it easier to feel your connections to the energies and entities outside of you. You recognize the fire's support for your transformation, as well as for the transformation of the collective. You may even experience taking in the energy of initiation, and feel yourself become a part of a community of people across time and across the globe who have felt what you have felt and experienced what you have experienced as you worked with fire. Watching a fire quietly can stir up memories you share with the collective unconscious of people sitting around fires to cook, share food, stay warm, talk, tell stories, sing, and perform rituals.

As with all symbols and energies you encounter, you can ask the fire what message it has for you and what it wants from you to help you to transform, better serve the greater whole, live more harmoniously, and breathe life into your new story. Listen to the answers that arise within you. Make your request of the fire: What would you like it to give you? Finally, ask what you can do for the fire.

You can perform a fire ceremony using a large outdoor fire or a fire in a fireplace, or you can simply use a candle flame and blow your intentions into scraps of paper rather than a stick, and then burn the papers. You can also cup your hands and blow your intentions into the air between your palms, then release your hands, allowing your intention to travel to the flame and be consumed and transformed.

When you perform a fire ceremony, you receive energetic, spiritual support for changes you desire. You then need to incorporate the lessons of the fire into your daily life to bring about change by making good choices and taking appropriate actions.

After doing a fire ceremony, take time to reflect on what you experienced and learned, and in a journal, record your answers to the following questions:

- Before doing the fire ceremony, what were your expectations of it? Were those expectations met? Were you able to let go of energies that no longer serve you, bring in new energies, and give energy for benefit of the collective good?
- How was your experience of the ceremony similar to and different from what you expected?
- How clearly were you able to "hear" the voice of the fire in response to your questions? Did you sense answers, or see them in your mind's eye?
- What lessons does fire have for you?
- How can what you experienced in your fire ceremony help you change your story?

Despachos

A *despacho,* from the Spanish word for "dispatch" or "send," is a ceremonial offering of gratitude to Mother Earth (Pachamama) and to Source. It originated in the Andes, and I encountered it in Peru. A despacho uses a folded paper packet containing within it symbolic objects that have been placed there during a ceremony. The prayer of gratitude is sent forth when the despacho is burned ceremoniously.

A despacho acknowledges and honors Mother Earth in all of her manifestations, as well as the unseen worlds to which we are connected: the past, present, and future; the lower world of our past lives, wounds, ancestral ties, and potentials; the middle world of our earthly existence; and the upper world of our becoming, which contains many possibilities for our destiny in this lifetime. It also pays tribute to the dance of the masculine and feminine energies and to the energies of harmonious thoughts, love, and actions.

You can do a despacho ceremony for these purposes but also to clear energies you no longer wish to have influence you, and to bring in energies for your new story, or to acknowledge and accept a significant change. For example, you might perform a despacho after committing to new health habits or moving to a new home.

Despachos can be done by one person, but they are often group ceremonies that involve harmonizing the energies of the participants. Let's say you wanted to bring harmony into your family after the sudden death of one of its members. A despacho would help everyone to begin to release the energy of grief and renew their commitment to the family, which now takes a new form. Shamans say that to bring in something new or expand upon something, work clockwise, and to shed unwanted things, work counterclockwise, the direction of banishment or removal. Thus, if you wish to bring harmony to a group of people, work clockwise, having each person place his or her offerings into the despacho.

To make a despacho, start with a square sheet of paper. The exact size is unimportant, but a piece of paper that is 18 by 18 inches works well. Fold the bottom third of the paper up and the top third of the paper down. Fold the right third of the paper across, followed by the left third. When you unfold the sheet, the creases will make nine squares—one in the center surrounded by eight around the edges.

The despacho ceremony can incorporate items found in your kitchen (such as bread and salt) or outdoors that serve as symbols that represent aspects of your life, Earth, Heaven, and the entire universe for which you are grateful and for which you seek to promote harmony. You can arrange the despacho's elements in many ways, according to various traditions or your own sense of how to do it as guided by Source. One method is to mindfully arrange the objects on the center square of the paper, intending each to represent a particular thing.

You might add to the center square any items you are using to represent that for which you are grateful. In doing so, you are offering to the heavens and to Mother Earth the energies of those items. You could, for example, sprinkle sugar to represent the sweetness of life, and cloves to represent life's spiciness. You might add items to represent fertility, renewal, joy, creativity, and the natural world: the oceans, mountains, rocks, plants, animals, and the sun, stars, and moon. You could add salt to represent life's savor or the healing release of salty tears. Paper money from a board game could represent gratitude for prosperity or a request for additional resources from the universe. Use seeds to symbolize new beginnings and creativity.

If it is a group ceremony, participants can sit or stand in a circle. When asked by the leader to do so, they can individually approach the place where these symbolically significant objects have been laid out, choose items that resonate for them, and then add those items to the despacho. They may wish to offer a prayer or blessing silently or aloud as they choose and add items—"This is for all the animals who have been abused," for example, or "This is for the nurses and aides who cared for Mother when we couldn't." It can be very powerful to hear what arises spontaneously from the hearts of those participating.

In traditional Andean ceremonies, coca leaves, stacked in threes, are used to represent the three worlds; you can substitute bay leaves. These stacks of three leaves are sent around the circle while the rest of the despacho is being assembled by the leader of the ceremony. As each stack is passed, each participant blows into it a prayer, blessing, or statement of gratitude or intention, and then continues to pass it along, each stack being infused with the energy of the individuals in the group. After each stack makes its way around the circle and back to the leader of the group, the leader then puts one red then one white flower petal on each stack (red representing feminine energies and white representing masculine energies). The leader offers his or her own prayers while adding each stack to the despacho.

When all items have been added to the despacho, you might sprinkle it with both red and white wine as another representation of the balance of feminine and masculine. If you are outdoors, pour a few drops of both red and white wine onto the ground as an offering to honor Pachamama. Then, simultaneously, everyone can silently ask of the despacho:

- What message do you have for me?
- What do you want from me?
- Will you give me _____? (Fill in your request.)
- What can I do for you?

To finish creating the despacho, fold the bottom of the paper up along the crease you made earlier, and then fold the top down, the right side in, and the left side in, forming a square packet. Use string or red or white yarn to wrap the packet and tie it closed. The leader of the group should now use the despacho to cleanse the energy bodies of the ceremony participants, moving it counterclockwise over each person's head, heart, and belly, then from top to bottom over the front, sides, and back of the participant. (If you are doing the ceremony alone, use the despacho to cleanse your own field.) Afterward, the despacho should be burned or buried, and everyone who participated in the ceremony should then incorporate into their lives the lessons learned.

When the ceremony is completed, you—and anyone else who participated—might reflect on the experience and answer the following questions:

- How did it feel to create a despacho? If you did a group despacho, how did it feel to hear the prayers of the individuals in the group?
- What did you choose to express gratitude for?
- How did it feel to incorporate prayers for help, if any, into the despacho ritual?
- How did you feel after burning or burying the despacho?
- How has doing a despacho ceremony affected your story?
- How can you incorporate into your everyday life the insights you have gained by performing the despacho ritual?

Doing a despacho ritual with a group was a powerful experience for one man, who described his experience:

> The communal ritual was moving to me because it was a concrete symbol for self and collective, unity with nature, and an appreciation for life and the energy that permeates the cosmos. I was surprised at how much I enjoyed engaging in ritual, something I would normally think is silly and would be resistant to because it reminds me of organized religion. But to my surprise, it seemed genuine and meaningful, and emotionally moving for me to the point that I cried. Multiple symbolic meanings and ideals merged together in that process, including the personal relationship I had with my mother, here expressed as a kind and nurturing life force.
>
> Later that night, we had ferocious thunderstorms and the tornado sirens blared throughout the nearby community. The next morning, some suggested that Mother Nature heard our prayers and was fertilizing and cleansing Earth. I felt these were projected fantasies, but something interesting happened.
>
> I was explaining to the group how moved I was by the creation of the despacho, and how I feel a need to create more rituals in my life. I also expressed my surprise because my mind is full of negativity and my Western intellect judges and criticizes everything that comes across its path. The morning was dark and gray, but just as I said this, the sun appeared in full force and

a ray of sunlight streamed through the stained glass window where there was a crucifix designed into the glass.

As this man discovered, in working with each other and nature, unexpected synchronicities can remind us of our interconnectedness and the power of working with the energies that surround us.

Creating Your Own Ritual

You can create your own ritual to let go of particular energies and bring others in. A ritual can help you embrace the new, and to feel comfortable with the internal changes you have made. The ritual can be as simple or as complicated as you like. Use your imagination and intuition in designing it. Incorporate any objects or symbols you desire. For example, if you feel drawn to work with water, you can work in nature near the ocean or a lake, pond, creek, or river. You can even work indoors, using a bowl of water. You can also work with a feather or smudge stick of dried sage to represent the air, or with manufactured objects that serve as symbols, such as items of jewelry.

Just as you did when working with metaphors and archetypes, recognize that a particular symbol can have a personal meaning as well as a universal one. For one woman, "moss" represented not the moss that grows when we are stagnant but a soft, giving, and humble plant that is rich with fertile scent. She remembered her father teaching her about moss when they spent time together in nature back when she was a child, so for her, it had a very personal meaning when she used it in ritual.

Your intent and attitude are important in any ritual. If you feel awkward, explore that. Is it the ritual itself you are resisting, or the change that it is meant to bring about? When performing the rituals and ceremonies in this chapter, be sure to open sacred space, cleanse your energy field, do mindful breathing, honor the spirits you invoke to assist you, and close sacred space, then reflect on what you have learned. Here are some questions you might answer as you ponder the ritual or ceremony after it has been performed:

- What was it like to create your own ritual?
- Was the process entirely intuitive, or did you research other rituals before devising your own?
- Is the ritual one that you are likely to do again? Might you do it on a regular basis? Why or why not?
- How can this ritual help you to change your story? How can you apply to your everyday life the insights you have just gained?

Use your creativity in finding symbols that will speak to you or, if you are working with others, to the whole group. A woman used the following ritual to enrich her work as an educator:

> I recently worked with rocks to deepen the experience of colleagues preparing to start the school year with a new group of students. We gathered in a circle and began to bless each other by simply naming the person on our left, and we passed a rock with the heft and feel of a human heart, from one person to the next, from one heart to the next. Each person held the rock in silence for 30 seconds to receive the blessings offered silently by others. Then, as we prepared to leave the circle, I handed to each person an ordinary-looking rock that had something unique about it, such as crystals, layers, or a fossil. The invitation was to see each student that passed through that teacher's door as unique, made in the image of God, with a beautiful soul. The calling of a teacher is to notice and seek out the beauty of each child, bringing it out into the open.

Group ritual can be a powerful way to bring people together and to cement a common commitment. Now more than ever, Earth calls to us to acknowledge our interconnectedness with each other and the planet. As we honor ourselves, the larger whole of humanity, and Pachamama herself, we bring healing to all.

CHAPTER TWELVE

Writing New Stories for Society

At the energetic level, we are connected to each other as well as to our society and the planet. Just as each of us needs to review our stories, and sometimes choose new ones, so too does the society in which we live. As individuals and as members of families, ethnic groups, and nations, we have myths or stories that we develop as circumstances change. Likewise, cultures and societies continually invent new myths and stories that are appropriate for a particular time and place, and their members develop rituals to honor those new narratives. For example, the story that we are all connected in caring about the losses strangers suffer has given rise to rituals of laying flowers, candles, notes, stuffed animals, and balloons where people have died or near their homes.

Now more than ever, we require some new societal stories, and rituals and practices to bring those new stories to life. We need myths that serve and enhance life in all of its forms so that we can become compassionate stewards of Earth and her inhabitants and navigate by a moral compass. Together and individually, we can write new myths and a new story for humanity. Each new individual story affects the larger, shared story.

What Needs to Change?

It is not difficult to come up with a list of ills besetting society that new stories could address. We are facing the consequences of many people adhering to religions that don't feed their souls. Many believe we must have economic progress at any cost, and we promote the interests of some people and groups as if they were inherently more worthy or deserving than others. For a long time, many of us have followed the lure of free-market capitalism: a dream of ever-increasing productivity, accumulation, and economic growth. Some regions of the world have prospered, but the gaps between the haves and have-nots is widening. Despite the emphasis on material wealth and high GDP as indicators of a country's overall health, many of those who have flourished materially don't seem happy. We know that we must write a new economic story.

In addition, we ravage and exploit nature and the planet—behavior that is not sustainable. Lacking adequate oversight and vision, we are running out of nonrenewable natural resources, such as fossil fuels, that we rely on for our ways of life. We are mismanaging renewable resources, such as fresh water, timber, and ocean fisheries. We, and the generations after us, face the consequences of global climate change and environmental degradation. At the same time, we continually develop and proliferate weapons of mass destruction that threaten the well-being of Earth and her inhabitants.

With the advent of an increasingly global community that is more connected than ever by travel and information technologies, the spread of good or bad happens far more quickly than ever before in human history. Disease and financial problems spread across the world almost instantaneously, causing disorder and panic to erupt in a matter of hours. We have not fully adjusted to this fundamental change in the human experience.

Many of us live in perpetual "fast forward" mode. To keep up our frenzied pace, we depend on technological gadgets to aid productivity. Unfortunately, these same devices also continually distract and divert us while making us feel that we must do more and not take time to be reflective. Popular entertainments can provide occasional, much needed escape from the constant pressure of having to process phenomenal amounts of information and societal changes. However, too often, they serve only as more unnecessary stimulation for us. We have allowed an overall dumbing down of public and private discourse to occur, and we have let many public school systems flounder. We worry about the condition of the world we will leave to our children, while our children worry about how they will clean up the messes we will leave behind. Changing our large, complex systems can feel like a monumental task, yet we sense it must be done.

As we deal with the demands of a continuously changing world, we often find the nature of the changes to be distressing, as shown by high rates of depression, anxiety, mental illness, and spiritual malaise. We are in a time of great transformation, and it is profoundly unsettling. Increasingly, people all over the globe are coming to the conclusion that we must make radical changes in many of our institutions and customs, and that to do so requires creativity and vision. In short, what we need is a new story to bring into manifestation.

Writing a New Story for Society

How do we begin to write a new story for the human species? Each of us as an individual can envision what concrete changes we would like to see made in society's story, then ask Source and its various emanations for help in achieving them. As we do so, it is helpful to consider the following questions:

- What changes would you like to see brought about in health care, education, economics, and the environment?
- How are you of service in the world? How would you like to be of service in the world? What is stopping you from being of service, or from serving in a way that is satisfying to you?
- How do you feel individuals can affect society most effectively? How can they draw strength from society rather than feeling overwhelmed by global ills?
- What new story would you like to see society give birth to? What can you do to help make that happen?

There is no question that the world in which we live has problems. Rather than be daunted by their magnitude and complexity, however, we can choose to maintain our sense of connection to Source, make incremental changes in accord with the dictum "Pray globally and act locally," and attempt to bring about societal changes through changing our own stories. Remember that Source is within us and we reside in Source. Every individual has the capacity to access the spark of Source and find the wisdom, opportunities, and energy to bring about the seemingly impossible and affect the larger story. As the Japanese proverb says, "Who will do the hard thing? Those who can. And who will do the impossible? Those who care." One caring person can make a tremendous difference in the world.

We can provide a model for society by changing our own stories. If we can learn to successfully interact with the transpersonal realms discussed in this book, we can make desired changes in our health, relationships, jobs, psychologies, relationship to Source, and ways of being of service. We can also make changes in other chapters of our stories, including how we treat Earth and each other. As we learn to recognize our negative shadow parts and become more conscious of our complexes, we will be less likely to have our complexes triggered or be bothered by negative qualities in other people. Then, we will be better able to stop ourselves before we become disrespectful or aggressive toward others.

Every one of us has the ability to vibrate with the frequency of love. We can put love into the matrix by letting it flourish in ourselves and by fostering love between ourselves and others. If enough of us do that, many positive changes will occur around the globe. As we change, so does the matrix, because everything is interconnected.

We can be of service—even if we do not do something revolutionary or that has a big impact on a large number of people. Our service may seem small and humble but may be of great significance to ourselves and to those we serve. One woman discovered that to be of service, she could assist others in expressing themselves:

> My idea of service has been evolving as a result of the shamanic work I've done. I am not sure yet what it is evolving into. I have learned that I can be of service by really listening to people. That is something I sort of knew, but my perception has changed a bit. I also received a strong message that creativity was a way to be of service. I do seasonal rituals, which seem to be a way of combining creativity with service. I helped a person write a play about her experience dealing with bipolar disorder. And I am currently helping a person edit a book based upon her journals.

As part of being of service, we can connect to the transpersonal realms on behalf of others. For example, we can use journeying, ceremony, and ritual for the benefit of all. Scientists in every field can journey to the places I describe in this book to get information about yet-unanswered questions. Physicians and biologists can journey and ask questions to better understand diseases and cures at the molecular level. Quantum physicists and cosmologists can journey and ask questions to better understand the relationship of the micro and macro universes, the origin and essence of dark matter and dark energy, and the place of our universe in a cosmos that potentially contains countless other universes. Psychologists, educators, and parents can take personal journeys or use group rituals and journeys to bring back new ideas and energy to fuel new stories about how we deal with mental illness, teach our young people, and parent effectively.

Ritual can connect us to eternal stories and bring alive myths and themes that already exist in potential in the Quiet. To heal both ourselves and our society, we need new myths to counter destructive myths playing out today. These new myths or archetypal stories can help us to develop a new, reciprocal way of interacting with nature and Source, allowing us to live sustainably on a planet inhabited by seven billion people. The myths can also help us write a new story of collaboration and cooperation, one in which people with differences live together in peace and share resources—and gross inequities cease to exist. As individuals, as well as collectively, we need to change our stories using ceremony and ritual, infused by love.

Individuals can journey on behalf of their societies to the lower world and find the places of wounds and resources. Negative energies can be cleansed and extracted. People can journey to the upper world to envision and energize more fulfilling collective destinies. The secret is that we can all do these things for ourselves, our neighborhoods, our communities, our countries, and the whole world.

In a workshop I led, the participants split into groups of a dozen or so people. Each group created a ceremony to energetically bring about change regarding an issue or cause that the group felt strongly about. For example, one group created a ceremony to bring change to our health care system, and another group created a ceremony to reduce violence in society.

In each group, participants journeyed to the Quiet, death, the lower world, and the upper world to gain insight and energy for support in transforming their chosen issue. They first asked for the Quiet's wisdom and help. They asked death for its aid in identifying what needs to die for change to occur. In their lower world journey, they asked what wounds and contracts were maintaining the status quo in the issue they journeyed for, and how the wounds might be healed and the contracts rewritten. They also accessed energies in the chamber of grace and the chamber of gifts that could be used to facilitate change. Then, each found a power animal that carried energy and information for transformation. Next, they went on an upper world journey to receive a symbol that could help actualize a different destiny or outcome than the current one for the issue they were journeying on behalf of. Finally, each participant dialogued with the various energies they encountered.

Each of them shared their experiences with the group. They were surprised to learn that many of their fellow group members' experiences were similar. They discussed together what themes emerged from their journeys and dialogues, what factors needed to change to interrupt the continuation of that which they wished to amend, and the solutions that were suggested to them during their individual work. They then wove their individual experiences into a summary that reflected the group's work. From this, they created a ceremony to present to all of the workshop participants.

The ceremonies that the groups created were beautiful and moving. I believe that the energetic vibrations that they gave back to the Quiet and the matrix created ripple effects and set in motion positive change for the issues each group worked on. The changes may come in unexpected ways and in an unpredictable time frame, but I believe their work will make a difference. The ceremonies created by each group did not contain a 10-step action list—they contained more subtle, abstract ideas and energies that would first influence the Quiet and the matrix and ultimately, people's hearts, souls, and attitudes. It can be difficult for those raised in the West, where much emphasis is placed on analyzing and planning using the rational mind, to embrace the idea of making changes at an energetic level before bringing the conscious mind in to make sense of it all. However, this process is effective for change.

You may find that the energies you work with on your journeys—often in the forms of symbols and inner figures—will influence not only you but those around you. During a journey, a woman encountered an inner figure of a magnificent, regal, tall woman who embodied kindness and compassion. This inner figure told the woman over and over again, "Reign with dignity." The woman asked the inner figure what she meant and was told not to be afraid of her own power and to be compassionate. The inner figure said that she would continue to be involved with the woman and together, they would figure out what needed to happen in her life. The next day, the woman was at work and found herself discussing with a coworker a potentially troubling situation. She decided to quietly call on the energy of the regal woman she had encountered in her journey. The coworker suddenly said, "However we handle this, we must have dignity for everyone involved." The woman was struck by the fact that her coworker used the word "dignity," and wondered if the coworker had been unknowingly influenced by the woman's own commitment to work with the regal, female inner figure and bring dignity to the situation.

Fueling a New Collective Story

Most of us want a world where the essence is love and joy rather than fear, violence, and negativity. But at an energetic level, there is a battle between those who want to sow and harvest crops of negativity and those who wish to sow and harvest positivity.

Instead of becoming caught in negativity, we can choose to work with more positive energies. We can give and receive love, and learn to forgive ourselves and others. By forgiving, we release the negative energies we direct toward others; resentments and grudges can dissolve. Holding on to negative feelings does not serve us, others, or Source. Those feelings can make us physically ill and psychologically distressed. They can also derail our life plans. When we are in ayni, right relationship with ourselves and the world around us, we are much better able to set in motion changes that will benefit our communities and society.

Source loves us so much that it gives us free choice. It lets us choose to live in ways that are harmful to ourselves and out of harmony with the essence of Source, which is love. Many of us know which choices best serve us and which honor Source, yet we continue to make other ones. We choose to consume food and drink that damage our bodies. We destroy relationships and give in to anger and bitterness. We devalue a relationship with Source and the role of service in our lives. Yet we always have the option of making different choices and changing our stories.

People who approach the world as being a fundamentally good place will generally have their expectations of the world met, even though bad things will happen to them and others at times. Conversely, people who believe the world to be a bad, dangerous place will generally have their expectations met, even though good things happen to them and others from time to time. There is an old Cherokee story about a grandparent teaching a grandchild about life. The grandparent says that everyone has two wolves inside of them: one that is kind and loving, and one that is angry and full of spite. The grandchild asks which wolf is stronger, and the grandparent replies, "The one that you feed."

We feed the wolf who is kind and loving—and help it flourish—when we make a practice of expressing gratitude daily, performing acts of compassion, and entertaining loving thoughts. These actions in turn cause our feelings, thoughts, and behaviors to change and to achieve a higher vibration. Conversely, if we give in to anger, pessimistic thoughts, and selfish and uncaring behaviors, we lower our vibration and feed the wolf that is angry and full of spite.

One time, a shaman and I made a sand painting together. As I divided the sand painting into quadrants, the shaman commented on the precision with which I made the divisions. I said, "Well, after all, I am an engineer." He laughed. Letting his intuition guide him, he drew a dove in the sand painting, and I, also guided by intuition, drew a dragon. We wondered how the dove and dragon could coexist. Would the dragon devour the dove?

Many of us have consciously and unconsciously created dragons that have eaten the dove of peace. We have not always acknowledged how we have treated others or how we have fanned the flames of conflict. Change will not occur until we realize the consequences of all of our thoughts, words, feelings, and actions, and then, as best as we can, consciously choose new ways of operating that promote peace, love, and harmony instead of conflict, hate, and destruction. Making the choice sets up what we will create and feed on.

DECISIONS

What to eat and drink
to exercise or not
to play or work
to be with whom?
What decides,
who decides
how we spend our time?
Who cares?
What difference
does it make?

Many people feel ensnared in uncaring bureaucracies, perhaps at work or in the health care system, or they are in family situations in which they feel discounted. When we feel our needs are unmet, we tend to reject new ideas and become more cynical, fearful, and angry and less likely to help society. We are more likely to want to help society when we find new ways to have our needs met.

When we discover how wrong some of our actions have been and how we have contributed to the problems, we might find the impetus to make meaningful changes in how we think and behave. Such changes must be heartfelt, however, or we risk falling back into our old habits of thinking and acting. We need to fuel our new stories with positive, never negative, energy.

BATTLE

In the battle
some die fighting for glory, nation, or their God.
The survivors depart, glad for their lives,
yet expecting new orders for frenzied combat
designed to advance an ephemeral agenda.
Others, knowing some battles to be eternal,
soberly pick their times to fight.

Meanwhile, they care for their cause
and when their guardianship is sufficient,
the frequency and duration of battles decrease.

We can't be truly spiritual until we attend to injustice and inequality in our day-to-day lives. Even with the best intent and spiritual evolvement, it can be difficult in the moment to move beyond the primitivism and violence that lies within each of us.

However, it is not enough to take a stand against the negative energies that surround us. We need also to affirmatively promote the good. For example, we need to protest against violence, unjust economic inequality, and environmental degradation. We also need to take active steps to create a world where violence is not an acceptable answer, and where those who have much share with those who have little. We need to restore our environment to ensure that it is cleaner and more sustainable. We need to focus not just on problems but also on solutions, and on spreading information that can help others. Social media and the Internet can be used for this positive purpose.

A shamanic worldview and new stories, written and brought to life as a result of using the techniques in this book, will cause changes in the larger, collective story. Remember that we must be careful not to use shamanic techniques only as tools for better knowing ourselves. We have an obligation to take what we acquire as a result of journeying, doing ritual, and the like and bring it out into the world instead of simply enjoying the experiences as individuals. We have to act in ways that benefit the larger whole.

Working with Perceptual Levels to Address Societal Issues

We can address societal issues from the four perceptual levels (which were described in Chapter Two). For example, consider the issue of reparations for past injustices. I was watching a news program about a church service that had been interrupted by a protest. The theme of the service was to commemorate the end of the transport of Africans across the Atlantic Ocean for slavery more than 200 years ago, and the protesters demanded an apology for the events of the past. The service had been organized by the Church of England, which at one time had owned thousands of enslaved people on Caribbean plantations. The newscasters discussed the pros and cons of governmental reparations to the descendants of slaves.

Each level of perception—the body (the literal), the mind (the mental and emotional), the soul (the mythic), and Spirit (pure energy)—offers a possible solution. At the literal level of perception, solutions might include apologies and financial reparations to individuals. At the level of mind, a solution might be to help descendants of slaves move beyond their negative legacy by providing them with better education and opportunities. At the levels of soul and Spirit, a more encompassing and enduring solution might be creating a world in which conditions for the possibility of exploiting others have been eliminated and no one is ever enslaved, literally or figuratively—a world in which freedom is not just a slogan but an organizing principle. Solutions to society's problems at the levels of the soul and spirit are the most effective and long lasting.

If the problems with health and medicine were addressed using all four levels of perception, we could make much progress. Inflammatory processes that lead to disease could be addressed not only by consuming anti-inflammatory foods and food supplements but also by supporting ourselves and others in better managing the inflammatory emotion of anger and the thoughts that exacerbate it. At the level of the soul, or the mythic, the energetic healings mediated by shamans could promote harmony and calmness that serve as an antidote for inflammation.

A shamanic worldview of healing and holism could lead to individuals making better, more healthful choices about eating, exercising, and managing stress. Medical care could become holistic, too, emphasizing prevention and fostering wellness at the levels of mind, body, and soul. Interventions at all of these levels would help people to avoid acute illnesses as well as chronic diseases. This multilevel approach to health would be far more effective than our current way of addressing the issue: reacting to physical ailments when they appear and treating them in a purely physical way with scalpels and medications.

Catalyzing Individual and Societal Change

It's not just health that we need to look at holistically; all major positive transformations can be most easily brought about using interventions at more than one level. For example, to halt the environmental despoliation of Earth, we need to alter not only rules and laws but also people's attitudes and behaviors. We need to appeal to both the mind and the soul by offering practical solutions as well as a new story. An example of how a new story can evolve can be found in the 2002 movie *Whale Rider*. The leader of a Maori group in New Zealand is enmeshed in an old story, and he vehemently resists the nontraditional concept of a female successor. However, he eventually comes to realize that his people need a new story and that his granddaughter is the one best suited to succeed him. He relinquishes his rigid worldview and adapts his people's traditions to meet the needs of a changing world.

One of the stories commonly embraced in America that needs changing is the myth that if we only had a smaller government and people exercised more responsibility, all our problems would be solved. An efficient government and more personal responsibility are both desirable. However, a new and better story would be that government, the private sector, and individuals all work together as partners, in balance and with respect for each other, acknowledging the rights and responsibilities of all people in society. The information and ideas that would help us write that story might come from looking at our history and seeing what we have done in the past that we should do again, such as having better cooperation between government and business. At the same time, we should look at what did not work in the past and embrace the positive changes we have made. Otherwise, we may lose sight of their importance—for example, ensuring that opportunities are equal for men and women as well as for people of all races, religions, and sexual orientations. We can look at other societies to see what ideas and approaches we might borrow from them. Insights can also come through journeying and dialoguing, and the sharing of thoughts and feelings using modern technology as well as traditional communication sources, such as articles, books, and community meetings.

How do we energize these new stories for society? I believe that lasting motivation to act comes when people are touched at the imagistic, mythic level, which leads to deeply rooted soul changes. We stir people at the levels of soul and spirit through music, art, images, metaphor, myth, color, poetry, ceremony, and ritual. To bring in a new story, we can use these tools.

When we see a movie, we might not know why a particular scene touches us, but it does. It's not necessarily predictable, or rational, but there are certain kinds of themes that some people are deeply moved by—classic themes such as the underdog facing great odds, or the boy and girl from opposite sides of the tracks finding love, or the suffering of good and decent people serving as a catalyst for someone to find her voice and her power. Classic movie images include Sally Field in *Norma Rae* standing on a table in the midst of a loud nonunion factory and holding up a handwritten sign saying "Union," or Tony singing to Maria from across a room, plaintively revealing his love for her, in *West Side Story*. These images speak to us at a soul level, as can "viral" videos and photographs, songs, or other works of art. All can help us tap into the energy needed to propel us forward into a new story with new themes.

What are the themes that would motivate people to make the changes discussed in this chapter? Some are doubtless universal, such as making the world better for our children and grandchildren, but many vary among cultures and from person to person. Nevertheless, each of us has a responsibility to find and live from themes that can serve and change society. We can choose to tell a story about giving to others in ways that don't diminish or deplete us. Themes of mutual benefit and humble sacrifice for the good of the larger whole, including ourselves, can be a part of our new, better stories for our communities, countries, and species.

Collaborating and Cooperating

Humanity shares an abundance of abilities. Although we each have gifts, we also have areas in which we are not very competent. To balance the strengths and weaknesses we all have, we need to both give and receive through collaboration and cooperation. Those who are accomplished in one domain can help those whose skills or talents differ.

To collaborate with others, we must communicate in their language and appreciate different points of view. If we hope to soften their resistance to finding common ground with us, we must listen.

It can be challenging to acknowledge and honor what others bring to the table, but if we do so, we can bring about a much better story for all. In America, conservatives would benefit from thinking and perceiving more expansively and examining the rules and boundaries they have set. Liberals would benefit from limiting government expenditures that may place unnecessary and unfair burdens on individuals and society. Libertarians would benefit from seeing the interconnectedness of all people, while socialists would benefit from recognizing that particular talents and personal qualities are not evenly distributed, and seeing that there is value in rewarding individual efforts.

Our communities are stronger when many voices and perceptions come together. One woman heard grumbling in her town when new members were elected to the village board and started to split opinions 3–2. Those who enjoyed how easy it was when all votes were unanimous were not able to appreciate that having diversity on the board might be an asset. Then again, if in the future that particular board splits on every opinion according to rigid ideologies, it will experience the stagnation that we currently see at the national level in the United States.

Similarly, in our families, workplaces, and social and spiritual groups, we need to think about how we come together and create harmony and movement with those who have differing opinions. Being obstinate and waiting for those we disagree with to "see the light" and change their minds is not the way to collaborate.

None of us are individuals in isolation. Everything and everyone in the universe is in relationship to everything and everyone else. When we live in ayni and contribute to others' well-being, and gratefully accept others' contributions to us, we affirm and enhance our connectedness. I believe Source guarantees that the more we give, the more we get of love and compassion. These energies pick up momentum after we send them out into the matrix, and return to us with greater force.

Another way that we as individuals can influence society is by working with organizations. We might feel moved to donate to or volunteer for ones we find worthwhile. When we interact with the world in ways to promote positive change, it's a wonderful feeling—a feeling of rightness and being in the flow. Unfortunately, such feelings can dissipate if we give back without feeling or focused intention.

When working with others, the challenge is to always keep in mind the ultimate goal of helping to serve the larger whole and have the organization be a means to achieving that goal, and not a goal in itself.

ON SERVING SOURCE

The rocks are patient, very patient.
They are aware of almost everything.
Since the beginning,
they noted the frenetic, ephemeral activities of humans.
When asked if it hurts to be carved,
they answer, "No.
We are what we are, our essence unchanging."
The rocks are very quiet and bring love.

The plants love to dance in the wind,
aware that they help Source with creation.
They are happy to play, give beauty,
and offer themselves up for nourishment to all creatures.
They shine love.

The animals know they represent wondrous diversity
Jaguar, antelope, bee, zebra, snail,
cricket, starfish, mongoose, eel—
all so separate but alike.
They are great teachers for those open to learn
and in their way, they teach love.

The human beings, the awakened ones,
are here to serve Source,
to help bring into being what does not yet exist
except in the Quiet.
They contain the energy and essence of the rocks,
the plants, and the animals.
Their diversity is infinite, and in constant interplay,
searching for ayni, right relationship.
When humans, too, can truly love
then hallelujah, hallelujah.

God, Source, consciousness, life indwells
but is only experienced, never completely known.
She, he, we are to be celebrated and honored
and we need to serve others and life
with love and intent.

Be Present

To better serve others, we need to learn to become fully present in each moment. When our personal energy is in a diffuse, unfocused state, we can't connect with others. Although shamanism involves experiencing altered perceptual states and traveling to non-ordinary realities, it requires being focused and present in these realms so that we can bring about powerful, beneficial changes in the world of everyday experience. To change the world of the here and now, we must be present in it and work with practices that awaken us and keep us mindful.

Look for the Good in People and Situations

Some of us can perceive flaws in individuals, organizations, and society quite easily. It's much harder, though, to see the potential for good in certain people or institutions that we have judged as inadequate or inferior in some way. Many things are possible, even if they are not probable. It behooves each of us to attempt to see the possible good in people and situations. This helps us to see the potential for solutions and make those possibilities for good become more probable. Then, we become part of an interconnected energetic network of positive change. In the process, we change, too, as we begin to see a wider range of possibilities for ourselves.

Understand and Respect Others Who Are on Different Journeys

We are all on a mythic journey. Individually, as groups, and as nations, we need to respect and be tolerant of the journeys of others, to not impede or be impeded by them. Some may be moving more slowly than we are, while others may be moving more quickly. Impatience and jealousy can distract us from our own journeys. It's best to focus on dreaming our own dreams and writing our own stories.

To be better able to serve others and work with them more effectively, we need to try to understand their frame of reference and life view. Then, we can give them what they need and not what we think they need.

Our particular life filters determine our perceptions. Temperament, upbringing, and cultural norms create these filters. Because human cultures are diverse, many people become polarized when it comes to such topics as politics, race, religion, and economic systems. If we have a spiritual bent, our filters might become more universal and our perceptual lens may grow wider. Even so, we can underestimate how limited our viewpoint is. The practices in this book can help us to move beyond our filters and "see" in a new, more objective way. By being open to information from transpersonal places such as the Quiet and the matrix, we give ourselves a chance to develop new attitudes and ideas.

Enlisting Source's Aid in Addressing Societal Problems

Shamans throughout history have called on their connection with Source by making symbolic representations of natural phenomena, such as a flood, fire, or hurricane. By working with the representation, the shamans prevent or influence events in the everyday world. We, too, can make symbolic or imagined representations and use them to work respectfully, playfully, and intently with Source and bring about change.

On a trip to Alberta, Canada, I was working with a shaman friend who is a Blackfoot elder. We were energetically reactivating ancient Native American sacred sites in Canada. We worked with images in our minds to connect these sacred sites to ones in

South America and to the love aspect of the Quiet and the matrix. We then linked this network of connections to places where decisions are made that affect the world, with the hope that the decisions can become more in keeping with the love aspect of Source. Shamans believe that energy follows intent. Bringing an amplified form of the agape energy of the Quiet to places where important decisions are made is a way to help tip decisions away from ones that favor the self-interest of leaders and policy makers and toward the best interests of all the people.

All of us can do similar work on behalf of all people. We can connect with energetic power places, infuse them with the energy of love, and imagine lines of energy stretching from those places to locations where decisions are made, creating an intention that the decisions made there reflect the loving nature of the Quiet.

All of us can serve as conduits of energy for Source and help bring about transformation—as long as we remain open to Source's ideas about how change occurs. Witnessing and participating in ritual and ceremony can help us change the energies affecting our world. If we respectfully record ritual and ceremony on video and share the video with others, the depictions may inspire people to take action. For example, a video of medicine women doing healing ceremonies on behalf of Mother Earth would allow viewers to vicariously participate and, perhaps, be moved to do healing work on behalf of others. As more people perform such ceremonies and share them with others, we can arrive at a tipping point in society in which the vibrations of our collective field rise to a new, higher level.

Reconnecting to Mother Earth

The shamanic reverence for Mother Earth is an essential attitude for these times. Otherwise, we will be killing the goose that laid the golden egg—and killing each other as well. We need to live sustainably on the planet and clean up and more thoughtfully manage our renewable resources, such as fresh water and trees. We need to conserve and find new alternatives for those resources that are exhaustible. We need to celebrate and express gratitude for the life we live and attempt to make the world a less polluted, safer, more just, and more loving place for our children.

According to the shamanic lore of the Andes, the Pampamesayoks are caretakers of Earth, the Altomesayoks are caretakers and stewards of culture and the stories of humankind, and the Curak Akullek are seers of future possibilities. In a sense, all of us are part of these lineages, whether we have been formally initiated into them or not. The archetypes of the caretaker, storyteller, and seer live within us and can be activated by our intent. We have a responsibility to act for the betterment of others, our culture, and our planet. We need to act and not simply ponder, intellectualize, and ruminate.

Earth and all her inhabitants are encompassed by the feminine energy of the Great Goddess. When we don't honor her and the feminine in all her aspects, civilization suffers. If we improve our treatment of women, children, and the unprotected, we will begin to foster attitudes that lead to the protection of our waters, soils, mineral resources, air, forests, and all nonhuman life. We must put a halt to violence and acts of aggression and exploitation, and become more aware of the effects of our choices on others. For example, when we act in ways that contribute to global warming and the flooding of small, poor coastal villages, or pollute the land, water, and soil, we are not being protective of Pachamama, our Earth Mother, and her inhabitants. We need to see Earth as a living being to be honored and revered. When we do, we will awaken to the importance of treating Earth's inhabitants with deep respect, too.

When people reconnect to Mother Earth, the reconnection motivates them to make changes at other levels of their lives. This happens because they feel their responsibility to those with whom they are connected and to our planet, and they yearn to strengthen those connections. Consider how people are increasingly turning to forms of spirituality that have commonalities with Native American and indigenous spiritual practices, including strong elements of connection to and honoring of the natural world. I suspect that as people immerse themselves in these more Earth-based forms of spirituality, they will feel and become more connected to those around them. This is likely to lead to their making wiser ecological choices, even if that requires some sacrifices and changes of habit. It will probably also cause them to feel a greater desire to give back through service to others.

When we have a shamanic perspective, we recognize the interconnectedness of all things, and we understand that all of our thoughts, emotions, and actions have consequences. Therefore, we might choose to be less careless about what we do, what thoughts we entertain, and how we manage our emotions.

When we acknowledge and honor the vitality of all things, including our planet, we seek to keep our environment clean and free of toxins. We also see the connections between our bodies and health, our thoughts and emotions, our life choices and journeys, and our relationship to a creative Source that surrounds and inhabits us.

Each of us might find it healing and transformative to spend more time in nature— in woods, deserts, mountains, prairies, and gardens, and by water. As explained earlier, when we are in nature, we can ask it what it wants of us, what message it has for us, and what we can do for it. We can also make a request of nature. As we spend time outdoors being contemplative, we might develop a reverence for all of nature's grandeur that can inform and re-inform our attitudes in all areas of our lives and cause us to learn new ways of serving Earth as well as our fellow human beings.

How can the powerful ideas embedded in shamanic—and Jungian—techniques be of use to more people, and to society, in replacing their stories? Shamans and Jungians believe that all problems have a spiritual cause and, therefore, a spiritual solution. That solution is changing or replacing those energies that are fed by negativity. When we believe in ayni and in using ritual and ceremony to express gratitude to the heavens and Earth for the opportunities this life gives us, we want to help those less fortunate. We become eager to experience peace and maintain our environment, and we develop a deep respect for the complex interrelationships in nature. Our stories enlarge to incorporate how we become more open, kind, and responsible. As we make changes in ourselves and our stories, the changes ripple out and affect those around us. As more people become better able to hear and heed the voice of Source within and to consciously choose to live their best destiny, it becomes easier to transform society on a large scale.

To change the larger collective story requires more than a few journeys and dialogues that lead to changes in our individual stories. It requires a lifelong commitment to the process of discovery and renewal in our own lives that will contribute to discovery and renewal in the lives of all.

CHAPTER THIRTEEN

Living According to
Your New Story

In this book, as you have worked with your story, you have come to know yourself better. You have connected to a greater power and observed its various aspects, and gained new insights about how you can be of more service in the world. You have learned a variety of ways to discover your existing story and its themes and to write and begin to live according to a new, more satisfying story. You now know shamanic and Jungian practices you can use to help you inform and energize your new story, and you know that for your story to become manifest, you have to take action. You also know that no practice or ritual will instantly change your life, because transformation is a process.

Making Good Individual Choices

I hope that in addition to being inspired to change your individual story, you will start to see yourself as being part of a larger community that is interconnected energetically and shares wisdom and energies. I hope you will feel a desire to change the larger, societal story for the better. You can do this by bringing new insights and energies into your own life, because your well-being affects the well-being of all.

The myriad interconnections we all have to energies, forces, peoples, and things that surround us can be sustaining, informative, and supportive. When you can recognize these interconnections, you gain perspective and feel a greater sense of equanimity, because you know that you are not alone in experiencing universal emotions or in being affected by archetypal themes and stories. Instead of feeling powerless and caught up in existential angst, you can contemplate the organizing principles influencing the events of your life. You can see your life from fresh perspectives and realize that you have more freedom to live differently and make new choices than you once thought you had.

As you become more aware of this freedom, you also become more aware of your responsibilities. In the words of the old gospel song, "You've got to walk the lonesome valley/ You've got to walk it by yourself/ There's no one here can walk it for you/ You've got to walk it by yourself." You have to make choices, steer your own course, and not look to others to constantly coach or encourage you to do what you know you have to do. It is important not to look to a teacher, counselor, or healer to tell you what decisions and changes to make. They can provide you with wisdom, perhaps, but you must make your own choices.

Once, while I was journeying, I encountered energies that were enveloping and oppressive. I tried my usual ways to dispel them—calling on helpful energies I had worked with before and even calling on Source for help—but unlike in the past, nothing I tried drove them away. I somehow knew that it was completely up to me to figure out what to do, and as soon as I recognized that was the case and made a conscious decision not to allow the oppression, the distressing energies and the fearful aspects of the encounter lifted. I decided to dialogue with the experience. I gained insight as to how in more than one area of my life, I had been unconsciously dependent on others to fix things. The experience helped me to grow up and take responsibility for myself in new ways. I realized that while others may help us discover wisdom, ultimately, we are the storytellers of our lives, and we are responsible for our choices.

CHOICE

After endless analysis,
the pain of never finding
the good mother, the good father, the good. . .
requires a choice to move on
or to remain immobile and bitter about what can never be.

But those who choose to move have more freedom,
a larger space, within the bounds of their existence.

Whatever our choices,
Earth Mother and Sky Father envelop and sustain us.
I wonder what entities embrace and support them
as they move within their larger bounds?

From time to time, revisit the questions you asked yourself when describing your current story. In addition, review your new story. Are you living according to it? Or are you living according to the old story? If so, why is that? Do you need to rethink your new story, or bring in new energies and insights using shamanic and Jungian techniques?

Even if you have difficulty changing your story, you can learn to change your attitude. You can do this by harnessing your will and calling upon the help of Source. You can loosen and let go of your expectations and judgments of yourself and others, and learn to be patient and allow things to evolve as they need to. Self-compassion can help you accept yourself as you are—even as you continue to change your story, yourself, and your life. You can learn to be grateful and appreciative for the chance to live in and learn from this lifetime. You can even learn to become aware that your world is observing you, just as you are observing it.

Whatever you are having difficulty with, you can dialogue with it, whether it's a behavior of yours, an issue that is plaguing you, a physical symptom that's bothering you, and so on. For example, if you are struggling with your moods, dialogue with them. Let them inform you. As you change your attitude toward them, they will change. Take your moods to the Quiet and the matrix, and let them be informed and transformed by those energies. You can learn to embody love, kindness, and beauty. You can learn to experience the joy of being fully alive.

It's All Okay: Accepting and Learning from Your Resistance

The techniques in this book may at first seem hard to use and very foreign. You may feel you're not getting the hang of it or doing it right. Yet, if you are persistent, you will have moments of grace when Source provides you with exactly the experiences you need to begin living according to a new and better story. When you have patience and are willing to continue to face uncomfortable truths, despite some feelings of resistance, you will be rewarded. I believe that everyone who continues to use the practices in this book will eventually experience a powerful transpersonal connection.

What should you do if you are not able to journey at all, or if you don't have the experiences that I am describing or that you are expecting to have? For example, on a journey to the lower world, suppose you enter a chamber that is empty. Remember that you can dialogue with and gain information from anything, so you can dialogue with the energy of not being able to journey, or with the empty chamber. What it tells you can be useful. You can ask the empty chamber what its message is for you. During a journey, you can dialogue with a physical sensation, your sense of not journeying correctly, your sense of frustration, or anything else you experience. Whatever you are dialoguing with, ask it what message it has for you, what it wants from you, and what you can do for it, and state what you want from it.

When you are in a transpersonal realm, you might see images that you think are banal and irrelevant, or symbols that you have seen many times before in journeys or dreams. Your first thought may be to dismiss them as unimportant, but there is always a purpose for what you receive and experience during a particular journey. It is important to work with the images to discover what they have to tell you right now in your life, even if you think you've figured them out before. They would not have appeared unless they contained information that is valuable for you. It is up to you to decipher why they came up for you again. Honor what you receive during work with transpersonal realms because, in an uncanny way, you receive exactly what you need from Source.

Be aware that there may be parts of you that don't want to change. Respect the part of yourself that is resistant or reluctant and honor it. Dialogue with it and learn from it.

Patiently Waiting in a State of Possibility

Often, when working to integrate new insights, there is no alternative other than to bear the tension of being "betwixt and between" your current story and your new story. This liminal space is filled with ambiguities and paradoxes, but it is necessary to be there, fully present, for gestation to occur.

New energies will come to you from your unconscious and the collective unconscious when it is the right time for you to experience them. At some point, you may receive a message from Source in the form of a symbol, or an inner knowing, that you are ready to receive and work with a new energy that will serve as an organizing principle for your new story. You can't force these energies to show up when you want them to, but you can invite them to come in.

When the new energy arrives, your experiences and memories may live within you differently. So, for example, a person could continue to experience fatigue, which is unwanted in the new story, but the experience of fatigue changes due to new attitudes, thoughts, feelings, and beliefs organized by a different archetypal energy. Perhaps by accessing the energy of the sage, the person accepts that fatigue is a reminder of the need to rest and ponder rather than always be engaged in action.

As we wait in patience, things that we never anticipated can happen. Sometimes, pondering others' stories, fictional or otherwise, can help us put our stories and those of others in better perspective. For example, I have always liked the flying bull story: A man is captured during a battle and brought before the king to be executed. He tells the king, "Let me live one year and I will teach your prized bull how to fly." The king is intrigued by this offer and agrees to spare the prisoner for one year. As they are leaving the audience with the king, one of the prisoner's captors asks, "How could you make such an offer? You know bulls can't fly." The prisoner says, "Who knows what will happen during the next year? I could die, the king could die, the bull could die—or I might even teach the bull to fly!" Being patient means being open to possibilities and not worrying about time frames.

SEEKING THE RIGHT TIME

Waiting or acting,
Where acting bleeds off anxiety from inner turmoil
Eating, drinking, drugs, and sex
placate anxiety for a while—
but then it's back.

Tolerating anxiety
'til the sweetness and joy of the fruits of unhastened time
reward the waiting.
Proper closure before moving on:
unripened fruit is hard and bitter
if too ripe, soft and spoiled.
The right time announces itself.

Sometimes waiting contains action that can unravel
and mend inner turmoil
even if the action is to merely observe.
Some actions contain waiting
'til the adamantine clarity of the right time.
Some actions assuage anxiety better than others
if the action connects us to universal energies—
the sun, moon, stars, nature.

Do we choose synchronistic moments
when inner and outer align,
or do they choose us?
We can get closer to choosing if we learn stillness
and simultaneously see the inner and outer.

Integrating Your Experiences into Your Life

As you become more experienced and proficient in navigating and exploring transpersonal realms, you might be tempted to do nothing with the energy and information you bring back because you are simply enamored of your shamanic and Jungian experiences. You might love to tell others about them, thinking them quite mysterious and fascinating, but make absolutely no use of what you learned. If you want these experiences to be transformative and lead you to changing your life, you must be vigilant about integrating the wisdom and energy gained into your new story.

Remember that although it is important to listen to the voice from your unconscious or from transpersonal realms, you never are obligated to do as it says. You are always the one in control. Once you make a change in your life, you can see how it feels and, if you decide you don't like it, you can make another choice. You may decide that your original choice was a mistake, but don't let this close you off to receiving information in transpersonal realms at another time. Doing so does a huge disservice to you as well as to Source.

Your feelings and how you perceive and interpret the events of your life matter, but it is also vital to discover your soul's calling and the organizing principles you wish to work with and have influence your experiences. By engaging with transpersonal realms, you can become more in tune with your soul's desires. This will positively affect your story. Your choices will be more consistent with your soul's desire for this lifetime.

After encountering and working with various energies, it will be up to you to choose to manifest your story by changing your emotional, behavioral, and cognitive patterns. Even the strongest energy for positive change can dissipate if you resist working with it.

Ongoing Practices for Manifesting a New Personal Story

The more deeply and rigorously you engage in the practices in this book and learn from them, the more you will experience the paradoxically simple yet unfathomable nature of Source. Consider the principle underlying this exchange between a student and martial arts *sensei* (teacher):

> The student asked the sensei, "If I practice three days per week, how long will it take me to earn a black belt?"
> The sensei replied, "Six years."
> The student asked, "What if I practice four days per week? How long will it take?"
> The sensei responded, "Nine years."
> The student, confused, asked, "If I practice five days per week, how long will it take?"
> The sensei answered, "Twelve years."

After a student earns a black belt, some senseis start the student once again with the beginner *katas* (traditional patterns of movement). This time, though, the student is expected to experience and master the deeper truths of the seemingly simple practices.

The more deeply we engage in a practice, the more we come to realize the vastness of that which we are striving toward. We become humble as we learn to rethink our goals and to better appreciate the process of working toward them. Earning a black belt, for example, doesn't feel as important as mastering the teachings that come only with long devotion to the practice. This concept also holds true in our quest for personal transformation. We can learn to live more effortlessly and gracefully while we construct new stories for ourselves. We never stop writing new stories!

Periodically reflect on your current story, your desired new story, the information and energy you are receiving from your transpersonal work, and the changes that you have been able to make in your life—and the ones you have not been able to make. Take the time to create, implement, and review plans of actions or lists of specific goals in order to be clear on what you intend to do differently in each of the new chapters of your life. Clearly defined goals can help you bring your new story into being.

If using your will and intent is not sufficient for making changes, revisit those transpersonal places that your intuition tells you will be most helpful to you.

Create space in your life to use the shamanic and Jungian practices you've learned. It's important to be respectful to the energies involved, and to fully appreciate the insights and messages you receive.

I suggest you visit each of the transpersonal realms at least once a month, journeying once or twice a week, spending the 10–30 minutes it takes to travel to one of these realms and interact with the energies and information you find there. Let your intuition guide you as to the order in which you do the practices. If you have no preference, do the dissolution visualization in Chapter Five first. Then do the journeys to the Quiet and the matrix, the journey to meet death, the journey to the lower world, and the journey to the upper world. From time to time, do the journeys to Absolute Darkness and the Light of Creation to practice your journeying skills. Dialogue at any time with whatever comes up in your journeys or life: a symptom, a dream figure, or a feeling about which you'd like to gain information and develop a more conscious relationship. Work with your complexes and your personas, shadows, contrasexual opposites, and other archetypes as they come up in your work.

In addition to journeying, spend time in nature and working with your dreams. Engage the energies of death and initiation, and use fire ceremonies, despacho ceremonies, sand paintings, and your own rituals to help you release old energies and bring in new ones. If you did not finish the exercises in Chapters Three and Four, go back and do so to gain further insights and get a clearer idea of what you would like to bring into your life and how you would like to change it.

If you find yourself resisting certain transpersonal realms, it is probably a sign that you should make a point of journeying there. Challenging though it may be to face certain truths to be found in the Quiet or perhaps the lower world, you must not let fear or discomfort hold you back from engaging Source in these places.

Do not only be concerned about what you can gain from these transpersonal experiences—also consider what you can give back to them. Remember to prepare for shamanic practices by opening sacred space, clearing your energy field, and doing mindful breathing. It can be healing to simply open sacred space and be quiet within it, letting yourself experience the energy contained within the space. When you finish your work, close sacred space by thanking all of the energies you've invoked for their presence and help.

Whenever you do shamanic work, thank Source and recognize that you are unique but also a part of a larger, collective, creative force. Give thanks for the opportunity to be part of the magnificent unfolding of creation. Be who you are, no more and no less.

You may also find that the techniques in this book enhance and are enhanced by other practices that decrease mental chatter and bring you into communication with your body and spirit as well as with Source. For example, psychoanalysis, psycho-therapy, Western medicine, meditation, qigong, and traditional Chinese medicine can complement the practices you have learned about and make it easier to manifest your new story.

As powerful as your journeying experiences may be, do not look to one journey, dialogue, or ritual to rid you completely of an illness, a psychological problem, or long-standing behavioral pattern. In America particularly, we look for a quick fix or magic bullet. Shamanic and Jungian work for changing your story is something you do regularly, establishing a spiritual practice. At times, you will feel a profound shift inside you, while other times the effect of using these techniques will be less dramatic. The techniques are meant to be used for gradual change over time, not to instantly cure you of your ills.

A friend of mine was in Kyoto, Japan, gazing upon a Zen garden. As he was ponder-ing the simple beauty of the garden, a voice interrupted his reverie. A Zen monk at his shoulder said, "The garden is nothing, nothing. It's what you make of it." So, too, it is up to each of us to make meaning of our encounters with Source, to honor the experiences, and to bring what we have gained into our everyday activities, writing a new story with new organizing principles.

Our stories are affected by archetypal energies and universal themes, but we also are influenced by our religious, political, and economic views; our social class; our educa-tional and vocational experiences; our relationships with our parents, family, friends, neighbors, and coworkers; where we live; and our DNA. The challenge is to be free enough from their influences to make choices in the present moment that better serve Source and us.

To Be In the World But
Not Of the World

One of the themes of this book is that we each must find a way to bear the tension of being spiritual entities in physical bodies with an earthly existence. It is not enough to seek either spiritual experiences or worldly successes to the exclusion of the other. We need to find a way to connect to Source so that our earthly experiences are guided by that connection. When we fail to reflect on our experiences, our lives lack meaning and become shallow. Yet, we should not reflect so much that we fail to have experiences. Sometimes, we must simply be present in the moment.

REFLECTING OR BEING

A dolphin under, then on top.
Alpha and omega.

Reflecting or being—
what an exquisite dilemma.

To me, the hardest, most important part of the work of being human is to wrestle with the banal, confusing, and unsatisfactory aspects of our lives while never forgetting our relationship to the Quiet, the matrix, and the unconscious realms. To keep persevering is a great act of faith and power.

The more we use techniques for accessing transpersonal realms, the more open we are to non-ordinary reality and the realization that we are part of the matrix, always connected to Source. We can see our journeys or stories as mythic, with universal themes, and feel our connection to all human beings throughout history and across cultures. We can embrace the rhythms and cycles of life. It becomes easier to let go of our youth, because we recognize that while the period of youth has passed, the qualities we had in our youth can be retained. We see that we never have to let go of our youthful exuberance, or the energy of curiosity that infused us at a special time in our past, even as the wheel turns and we move forward into a new stage of life.

Some might interpret incorporating Source into all aspects of life as a mandate to "go with the flow." But rather than being passively swept along by life, bringing Source into our lives means understanding the nature of things and being in harmony with them—at times, actively, and at others, passively. For example, when caught in the turbulence of life, we can let ourselves be carried and tumbled around. Or, we can look for a current out of the turbulence that we can swim with and find a new direction that is more congenial to the dyad of us and Source, separate but one.

SEPARATE YET TOGETHER

The warrior trekked alone, serving an ideal,
Never clear whose it was—or if it mattered.
The lover swam in seas of emotion
And lost himself in the abyss, never to see the light.
The king surveyed his kingdom
And saw that it was good
But wished to be any one of his subjects.
The magician transmogrified himself and others
So they were unrecognizable.

Hmmm.

At the banquet, the lover prepared the meal,
The warrior cut it into portions,
The king served,
And the magician blessed the food.
The cockroaches and mice consumed the crumbs.
Who best serves the Tao?

Part of us will always be in the process of rewriting our stories and breathing life into them, but another part can rest comfortably knowing that striving for a better, new story is less important than living moment to moment, feeling our connection to Source. Maybe these two parts of us can come together in balance and allow us to experience the peace that surpasses all understanding.

Afterword

One day, I was riding my bike on a path in the countryside and decided to stop at a coffee shop that served as a gathering place for folk musicians. While there, I listened to a group of musicians improvising some bluegrass music. A beautiful young woman sang a haunting rendition of "Barbara Allen." It reminded me of times I spent in Kentucky as a boy. As I continued on my ride, I was inspired to improvise words to a song that went with a melody that popped into my head, and I sang it to myself, almost like a mantra, as I rode. The song was:

Sometimes I think that I'm going crazy
as I sit by the phone,
waiting for a voice to cheer me up,
but in my heart I know I'm alone
all alone as I think of the years I've wasted,
waiting for someone.
Someone who'll give my life more meaning
and bless the things I have done.
All alone as I think of the family I came from
and all the things I missed.
All alone as I think of the life I'm living
and yearning for some bliss.
But sometimes when I am very quiet
I glimpse an inner place,
that I know I can only get to
when I transcend time and space.
Right now I don't know how to do that,
I don't have the key,

so I guess I'll keep on waiting, waiting,
waiting for me.

The song that emerged reminded me of the futility of waiting for someone else to make my life worthwhile, of regretting things I missed in my upbringing, and of reflecting on existential angst but doing nothing about it. The new way forward was glimpsed to be an inner place that connected me to infinity. It was a place only accessible when I could be very quiet, still, and empty, thus allowing the grace of infinity to be seen and experienced. Once I tasted infinity, my life has never been the same, but I am reminded that accessing the inner place requires an ongoing practice of intention. For me, the song has been a powerful symbol in a sequence of symbols that have emerged from time to time to aid me on my journey.

The place that transcends time and space is the shaman's place of beyond the known. This experience was a step on the way to my goal of knowing myself, which in turn leads to allowing others to know me and living with a greater sense of wholeness and service.

In my remaining journey in this lifetime, I hope to co-create with Source a life of love, service, and meaning, and to have some fun and joy in the process. When I can remember that the essence of the Quiet, of life, is love, all else falls into perspective, and seemingly big issues become less so. Truly, love conquers all.

AFTERWORD

In the stillness
A cicada's song
cracked a soul
not ready to be seen.

Too late for reparations.
The hardened surface
dissolved in renewed awareness
releasing ancient truths.

The stillness now
a balm for wounds self-inflicted
the cicada's song
a call to face the dawn.

The fledgling stretched
to see forever
but a purple iris
blocked the view.

Near journey's end
The weary traveler listened in the stillness
as the cicada's song birthed a purple iris
the traveler smiled and saw forever.

My wish for you is that you can co-create with Source the life you want, and that your dance with the Quiet is loving, soulful, meaningful, and ultimately joyful, and that you can connect to the unconditional love in the Quiet and radiate its essence.

As I have learned to wait more quietly and patiently, I have met more of me. I hope this book will help you to develop more patience, better understand who you are, and write a new, more satisfying story.

Endnotes

PREFACE

1. Walsh, R. & Vaughan, F. "On transpersonal definitions." *Journal of Transpersonal Psychology*, 25 (2): 125-182, 1993.

CHAPTER TWO

2. Jungian active imagination: For more on active imagination, see August J. Cwik, "Active Imagination: Synthesis in Analysis," in *Jungian Analysis*. 2nd Edition. ed. Murray Stein. Peru, IL: Open Court Publishing Company, 1995.

3. Four levels of perception: Many wisdom traditions identify four (or five) energy bodies or levels of perception. For more on the four levels of perception, see Villoldo, Alberto, PhD. *The Four Insights: Wisdom, Power, and Grace of the Earthkeepers*. Carlsbad, CA: Hay House, 2007.

CHAPTER THREE

4. "A map is not the territory it represents." Korzybski, Alfred. *Science and Society: An Introduction to Non-Aristotelian Systems and General Semantics*. 3rd Edition. Lakeville, CT: The International Non-Aristotelian Library Publishing Co. 1949, p. 61.

CHAPTER FOUR

5. Jewish folktale about the sultan. Oberman, Sheldon. *Solomon and the Ant: And Other Jewish Folktales*. Honesdale, PA: Boyds Mill Press, 2006.

CHAPTER FIVE

6. Sacred space as a place of timelessness, infinite possibilities, and new beginnings. See Eliade, Mircea, Willard R. Trask, translator. *The Sacred and The Profane: The Nature of Religion*. Orlando, FL: Harcourt Brace Jovanovich, 1987.

CHAPTER SIX

7. Across from an empty chair. Using an empty chair in the process of dialoguing is similar to a technique from Gestalt therapy. For more about the empty chair

technique in Gestalt therapy, see, for example, Meier, Augustine, and Micheline Biovin. *Counseling and Therapy Techniques: Theory and Practice*, Chapter 4. Thousand Oaks, CA: SAGE Publishing, 2011.

CHAPTER EIGHT

8. Many archetypal energies. For more about archetypes, personas, shadows, contrasexual energies, and complexes, see Stein, Murray. *Jung's Map of the Soul: An Introduction*. Peru, IL: Open Court Publishing, 1998.

9. The shadowy aspects of archetypes, such as the lover and the warrior. See Moore, Robert, and Douglas Gillette. *King, Warrior, Magician, Lover: Rediscovering the Archetypes of the Mature Masculine*. New York: HarperOne, 1991. My poem *Separate Yet Together* in Chapter Thirteen was inspired by their work.

CHAPTER NINE

10. We should give a situation what it deserves before leaving. As stated in *Tarot and the Journey of the Hero,* "Only in the consciousness of fulfillment can we go on our way with dignity. If we haven't fulfilled what a situation requires of us our leaving is merely running away." Banzhaf, Hajo. *Tarot and the Journey of the Hero.* York Beach, ME: Samuel Weiser, Inc., 2000, p. 124.

11. "This is a good day to die." Neihardt, John G. *Black Elk Speaks: Being the Life Story of a Holy Man of the Oglala Sioux, The Premier Edition.* Albany, NY: Excelsior Editions, State University of New York, 2008, p. 11.

CHAPTER ELEVEN

12. Ritual and ceremony take us to a sacred time and place. In his book *The Sacred and the Profane*, Eliade wrote extensively about sacred time, or the eternal present, and its role in ritual and ceremony. See Eliade, Mircea, Willard R. Trask, translator. *The Sacred and The Profane: The Nature of Religion.* Orlando, FL: Harcourt Brace Jovanovich, 1987.

FINDHORN PRESS

Life-Changing Books

For a complete catalogue,
please contact:

Findhorn Press Ltd
117-121 High Street,
Forres IV36 1AB,
Scotland, UK

t +44 (0)1309 690582
f +44 (0)131 777 2711
e info@findhornpress.com

or consult our catalogue online
(with secure order facility) on
www.findhornpress.com

For information on the Findhorn Foundation:
www.findhorn.org

green press
INITIATIVE

MIX

**Paper from
responsible sources**

FSC
www.fsc.org

FSC® C013483